SELF-HELP IN URBAN AMERICA

Kennikat Press
National University Publications
Interdisciplinary Urban Series

General Editor
Raymond A. Mohl
Florida Atlantic University

SELF-HELP IN URBAN AMERICA

Patterns of Minority Business Enterprise

edited by
SCOTT CUMMINGS

National University Publications
KENNIKAT PRESS // 1980
Port Washington, N.Y. // London

Copyright © 1980 by Kennikat Press Corp. All rights reserved. No part of this publication may be reproduced, stored in a retrieval system, or transmitted, in any form or by any means, electronic, mechanical, photocopying, recording, or otherwise, without the prior written permission of the publisher.

Manufactured in the United States of America

Published by
Kennikat Press Corp.
Port Washington, N.Y. / London

Library of Congress Cataloging in Publication Data
Main entry under title:

Self-help in urban America.

(National university publications: Interdisciplinary urban series)
Includes bibliographies and index.
1. Minority business enterprises—United States—Case studies. 2. Minorities—United States—Economic conditions—Case studies. 3. Cooperation—United States—Case studies. 4. Collectivism—Case studies. I. Cummings, Scott, 1944–
HD2346.U5S44   338.6'42   79-20621
ISBN 0-8046-9251-3

CONTENTS

INTRODUCTION

1. COLLECTIVISM:
   The Unique Legacy of Immigrant Economic Development   5
   SCOTT CUMMINGS

**PART ONE: THE CULTURAL AND FAMILIAL ROOTS
OF COLLECTIVE ECONOMIC DEVELOPMENT**

2. ASIAN ENTERPRISE IN AMERICA:
   Chinese, Japanese, and Koreans in Small Business   33
   IVAN LIGHT
3. CLAN STRUCTURE AND ECONOMIC ACTIVITY:
   The Case of Greeks in Small Business Enterprise   58
   LAWRENCE A. LOVELL-TROY

**PART TWO: ORGANIZED RELIGION
AND COLLECTIVE ENTERPRISE**

4. MORMON RESISTANCE AND ACCOMMODATION:
   From Communitarian Socialism
   to Corporate Capitalism   89
   O. KENDALL WHITE, JR.
5. THE PROFITS OF NONPROFIT CAPITALISM:
   Polish Fraternalism and Beneficial Insurance   113
   in America
   FRANK RENKIEWICZ

6. A PLACE FOR EVERYONE:
   Slovak Fraternal-Benefit Societies 130
   M. MARK STOLARIK

PART THREE: THE POLITICAL AND IDEOLOGICAL BASES OF COLLECTIVISM

7. FINNISH-AMERICAN COOPERATIVISM:
   The Radical Years 1917–30 145
   MICHAEL KARNI
8. COLLECTIVE ECONOMIC ACTIVITY
   AMONG SERB, CROAT, AND SLOVENE
   IMMIGRANTS IN THE UNITED STATES 160
   JOSEPH STIPANOVICH
9. THE EXPANSION OF THE PUBLIC SECTOR
   AND IRISH ECONOMIC DEVELOPMENT 177
   DENNIS CLARK

PART FOUR: COLLECTIVISM AND ASSIMILATION: THE TRANSITION TO ORTHODOX CAPITALISM

10. JEWISH ENTERPRISE IN TRANSITION:
    From Collective Self-Help to Orthodox Capitalism 191
    MARK S. ROSENTRAUB AND DELBERT TAEBEL

    NOTES 215
    INDEX 232
    CONTRIBUTORS 235

INTRODUCTION

SCOTT CUMMINGS

COLLECTIVISM
The Unique Legacy of
Immigrant Economic Development

This collected volume comprises original essays examining patterns of economic development among immigrant minorities. The history of ethnic enterprise in the United States is a fascinating but largely unexplored field. While the volume of recent scholarship in the area of Black entrepreneurial and business development has been satisfactory, comparable research describing the commercial and economic activities of ethnic minorities has lagged. The revitalization of scholarly interest in ethnic minorities has partly rectified this widespread scholastic deficiency. Most of the recent works in the area of ethnic studies, however, have focused upon immigrant cultural institutions or described ethnic political attitudes and behavior. Relatively little has been written about the self-help institutions and mutual benefit societies created by immigrant groups. In this volume, the term "self-help institution" refers to the numerous organizations established by ethnic minorities to deliver urban social services, provide life insurance benefits and unemployment compensation, and make available not only jobs but also the capital necessary to purchase real estate and finance small businesses and related commercial ventures.

Most immigrant groups entered the urban and industrial arenas at a time when few public services were available. While the number of social welfare institutions increased dramatically during the 1880s and 1890s, few had developed sufficient expertise to deal with the numerous problems of urban life. Despite the limited success of settlement houses, most agencies lacked professional staff, had a limited understanding of complex urban problems, and failed to coordinate the delivery of services. Not only were public services scarce, but comparable amenities in the private sector were expensive.

During the period of labor-intensive industrial development, industrial and mining accidents were numerous, and working conditions within the factories and sweatshops were abysmal. Describing a typical sweatshop, Kelly wrote:

> Every tenement-house is ruinous to the health of the employees. Basement shops are damp, and entail rheumatism. They never afford proper accommodations for the pressers, the fumes of whose gasoline stoves and charcoal heaters mingle with the mouldy smell of the walls and the stuffiness always found where a number of the very poor are crowded together.[1]

Unemployment and disability insurance was largely unavailable. Death and burial benefits, life insurance, and adequate health care programs were typically outside the financial grasp of newly arriving, urban immigrant groups. Likewise, access to capital for purposes of purchasing real estate or financing small business development was extremely difficult to secure through the private sector. Yet many immigrant groups created institutions and organizations designed to deal with these problems. The numerous ways in which ethnic minorities responded to the absence of social services, welfare benefits, and access to capital is the subject of this volume.

It is this book's intention to illustrate the fact that many immigrant groups responded *collectively* to the conditions posed by urban and industrial life. The self-help institutions created by many ethnic minorities emphasized collective rather than individualistic modes of economic development. Even the unique forms of capital accumulation embodied collective goals and aspirations. In some cases particular groups adopted explicitly socialistic and communitarian modes of economic development. For the orthodox traditions of American economic thought, collectivism is an alien concept. While trade unionism is typically portrayed as a collective attempt to improve the life conditions of working men and women, other types of political and economic movements among immigrant minorities are not usually described as collective responses to urban America. The failure of many historians and social scientists to recognize the importance of collectivism in the economic arena is a uniquely politicized scholastic oversight.

History is not a neutral accumulation of recorded facts and events. The compilation and interpretation of historical data is partially a reflection of the values, attitudes, and ideological beliefs of those in a position to record and interpret. The ethos of rugged individualism is not only a cornerstone of American cultural folklore; it seems to have saturated the American intellectual and academic community as well.

The legacy of Weberian sociology has prompted many social scientists to conceptualize the social dynamics of mobility, employment, income distribution, and the distribution of wealth in individualistic terms. America's fascination with the ideological celebration of rugged individualism was partly legitimated for the intellectual community by Weber's analysis of the relationship between Protestantism and capitalist economic development.[2] Interestingly, Weber himself never doubted the preponderance of communitarian influences upon trade in the world context. Post-Weberian writers appear to have misinterpreted his original analysis. Within the context of American immigration history, the application of Weber's thesis to patterns of ethnic enterprise is biased in a curiously parochial direction. As Mills argued, many of the scholars contributing to the early literature dealing with urban and ethnic studies were reared in small town, Midwest, Protestant settings.[3] Interestingly, many of the immigrant groups which established collective economic institutions were either Jewish, Catholic, or Oriental in origin. And while I am not suggesting the presence of excessive nativism on the part of many early urban and ethnic scholars, it will become apparent that many of the essays appearing in this volume pose a serious challenge to orthodox ideas premised upon individualistic notions of economic development. Some of the essays invert the logic of the orthodox contention that a strong relationship exists between capital formation and personality traits rooted in excessive individualism. Indeed, some evidence presented suggests that the present status of prosperous immigrant groups rests upon a collective and communitarian economic base. The case studies of Jews and Mormons illustrate this contention.

A large body of sociological literature suggests a connection among family socialization experiences, personality traits, and socioeconomic position. While the classic functional theory of stratification is supposedly sociological rather than social psychological or cultural, it is essentially an attempt to explain income differences between individuals rather than groups. Despite the claim that sociology focuses upon the group rather than the individual, most social theories of economic development lack an explicit group or collective orientation.

Economists, like many historians and sociologists, have also failed to develop or recognize the collective themes appearing in American economic history. Human capital analysis and marginal productivity are the economists' analytical equivalents to achievement motivation, delayed gratification, fatalism, and functionalism in the field of sociology.[4] All of these concepts stress social psychological, motivational, and individualistic explanations of income distribution, capital accumulation, and employment. Explaining how many sociologists use these terms to explain poverty, Ryan argues "the stigma, the defect, the fatal difference—though derived from environmental forces—is still located *within* the [individual.]"[5] Gordon demonstrates how orthodox economists employ these concepts: "If some individuals have low productivities, they are primarily to blame for their disadvantages."[6]

The idea that distinct ethnic groups produce, distribute, and consume resources is largely alien to orthodox modes of economic thought. As is emphasized in a widely used economics text, "Economics is based upon facts concerning the activities of individuals and institutions in producing, exchanging, and consuming goods and services."[7] Here "institutions" refers to business and commercial establishments, as well as the banking and financial communities. The fact that immigrant groups created explicitly economic institutions for purposes of influencing the distribution of income and wealth and expanding employment opportunities has largely escaped the attention of most economists. In most economics texts one finds no mention of immigrant banks or credit unions, mutual benefit societies or fraternals, cooperatives or lodges, or collectively owned commercial and agricultural operations. While immigrant self-help institutions were integral features of American economic history, one finds little or no mention of them in standard economics texts.

ETHNIC STRATIFICATION: The Failure of Traditional Perspectives

Because traditional explanations of immigrant economic behavior have escaped critical examination, the history of ethnic enterprise has been partially obscured and widely misunderstood. Even in areas where individualistic biases appear to be absent, orthodox thinking is premised upon faulty analytical assumptions. The classic works of Park and Burgess contributed greatly to the understanding of intergroup conflict and competition and generally shaped the way many social scientists conceptualized the economic behavior of ethnic groups.[8] Their general discussions of ethnic stratification, however, are not only simplistic but largely inaccurate. Their *invasion and succession* theory, drawn largely from biological models, describes a mechanistic process whereby each newly arriving immigrant group enters the economy at its lowest occupational levels. As subsequent groups enter the economy, previous incumbents of low paying jobs are supposedly pushed upward occupationally and outward geographically. These traditional descriptions and explanations of immigrant occupational mobility and patterns of ecological settlement are inadequate for several reasons.

Historical Perspectives. First, data drawn from historical accounts simply do not support the idea that newly arriving immigrants entered the economy at the lowest occupational levels. Many groups not only entered the economy at differing points of industrial development but at varying levels of the occupational hierarchy. Second, there is no evidence supporting the notion that patterns of occupational mobility among one immigrant group are directly influenced by the arrival of another. In fact, considerable historical data support the idea that newly arriving immigrants were often used as strikebreakers, undercutting and undermining the economic position of established groups.[9] Many established workers "eyed the foreigner for what he was at the moment—a cheap competitor, whose presence undoubtedly held down wages and caused unemployment in temporary local situations."[10] At best, the relationship between the successful economic activities of one ethnic group and the arrival of another is specious.

A major contention of the essays in this volume is that the sources of immigrant social mobility and economic activity are to be found within the cultural and historical traditions of particular ethnic groups and embodied in the collective self-help institutions created by the group. Over and above the unique cultural and historical traditions possessed by ethnic minorities, however, it is essential to see the economy itself as the major impetus shaping the specific kinds of occupational and commercial activities pursued by immigrants. Groups adapted to the economic and political conditions confronting them at the time of arrival. Ethnic economic institutions were established in response to industrial conditions and as mechanisms furthering the systematic exploitation of employment opportunities. Cultural and historical traditions provided a base of nonmaterial resources shaping a collective economic response. Specifically, it is the contention of this volume that *collectivism*, and not *rugged individualism*, was a major force shaping ethnic economic development.

The American economy expanded and diversified greatly between 1850 and 1920. Growth in the industrial sector directly influenced patterns of European immigration. During the 1880s industrialists systematically recruited skilled craftsmen from Wales, England, Germany, and Sweden to work in the steel mills and serve as machinists, carpenters, miners, and textile workers. Throughout the period of labor-intensive industrial development unskilled workers were recruited from Southern and Eastern Europe. Supposedly more docile than their Northern counterparts, workers from Southern and Eastern Europe poured into the cities and the factories. Industrial growth and immigration were obviously related to urban patterns of settlement in the major manufacturing areas of the North and Midwest. Developing a clearer understanding of the relationship between industrial development, immigration, and patterns of neighborhood settlement, contemporary scholars are now able to explain more fully the processes that resulted in the presence of particular ethnic groups not only within distinct occupational categories but also within specific industrial sectors: "The Italian concentration in construction and the Polish in steel were related to the expansion of these industries as these groups arrived."[11] The concentration of Eastern European groups in the extraction, mining, and steel industries has been described by several scholars.[12] Jewish and Italian involvement in the garment and construction industries has also been discussed by numerous historians, as has Irish Catholic movement into the public sector.[13] The important theoretical point to stress, however, is that the propensity of groups to enter specific sectors of the economy was shaped largely by the simple expansion of opportunity for industrial and public employment. And the expansion of specific employment opportunities for ethnic groups was partly fortuitous, being related to the type of industrial development taking place at the group's time of arrival.

As groups pursued fairly specialized kinds of employment opportunities, they also created organizations and institutions designed to facilitate greater access to goods and services. Drawing from established cultural practices, some ethnic groups adapted their institutions to the immediate demands and conditions of urban and industrial life. While students of immigrant life and culture have begun to clarify and refine traditional notions surrounding ethnic occupational patterns, the specifics associated with how immigrant neighborhoods mobilized to respond to the global conditions of urban and industrial life are not well known. Knowledge that many Eastern European immigrants secured employment in the steel and extraction industries does not illuminate the unique ways in which these groups responded to the absence of social services and limited availability of housing opportunities. Likewise, Jewish concentration in the garment business or Italian involvement in construction or stonecutting does not clarify how members of these groups were able to establish cohesive urban neighborhoods, purchase real estate, or deliver social services to members of the community. It is important to see the totality of immigrant economic responses rather than focus solely on ethnic occupational characteristics.

Contemporary Perspectives. Contemporary data dealing with ethnic stratification often stand in isolation from a meaningful historical framework. In order to provide an appropriate link with the past, it is useful to describe the present socioeconomic characteristics of ethnic groups.

This description will help establish a contemporary framework through which to interpret and understand the historical data appearing in this volume. The contemporary data illustrate not only the level of occupational specialization characteristic of many ethnic minorities but also clarify the extent to which selected groups have achieved prosperity. Greeley has examined the varying levels of prosperity achieved by European immigrant groups.[14] By pooling the results of recent national surveys, he has described the occupational characteristics of ethnic groups. Additionally, his data analysis provides information dealing with income distribution, educational attainment, and rates of occupational mobility. Generally, he reports that Jews and Irish Catholics have achieved fairly high levels of prosperity. He also contends that Catholics have exhibited marked patterns of upward social mobility. His interpretation of these patterns, however, lacks historical depth. I will return to this point shortly.

In order to provide a more detailed description of the socioeconomic characteristics of ethnic groups and supplement available evidence, additional survey data were analyzed. These data were collected as part of the activities of the Advisory Commission on Civil Disorders.[15] During the late 1960s, over 2,500 white residents of Baltimore, Cincinnati, Chicago, Cleveland, Detroit, Gary, Milwaukee, Newark, Philadelphia, Pittsburgh, St. Louis, San Francisco, and Washington, D.C. were surveyed. Because Catholics and Jews are largely a Northern, urban population, this data set represents an ideal source of information to describe the contemporary socioeconomic characteristics of ethnic groups. Typically, most nationwide surveys do not include enough Catholics and Jews to allow for accurate analysis. In the fifteen-city survey, Jews and Catholics comprised a large proportion of the total sample.

Table 1.1 shows the distribution of religio-ethnic groups within various sectors of the U.S. economy.[16] Generally, the patterns revealed in the table are consistent with information drawn from American economic history. Overall, Catholics cluster in the manufacturing and industrial sectors of the economy:

From the 1890's on, a steadily increasing proportion of the American working class was Catholic. In the first thirty years after 1890, more than 16 million immigrants poured into the United States, mostly, from the predominantly Catholic countries of Eastern and Southern Europe. They poured into the cities, into the factories, and into the unions. Labor leadership was provided by the Irish and South German Catholics. The rank and file were the later immigrant Catholics: Italians, Slavs, Hungarians, Rumanians.[17]

TABLE 1.1 Distribution of Ethnic Groups within Various Sectors of the Economy (Percent)

Economic Sector	Catholic					Protestant					Jews	Other
	Other	French	German	Irish	Polish	Eastern European	Italian	Other	German	British	Irish	Scandinavian		
Agriculture and mining	.3	.0	.0	1.4	.6	1.8	.0	.0	.0	.5	.0	2.8	.0	.0
Construction	11.1	.0	11.3	8.2	6.2	5.5	10.4	6.0	8.6	5.8	12.6	5.6	2.9	4.5
Manufacturing of durable goods	6.9	4.3	13.0	7.3	16.1	10.9	8.8	9.0	8.2	6.9	11.5	1.0	2.1	6.5
Metal and steel	14.9	8.7	5.6	7.8	9.9	20.0	8.5	17.6	13.7	9.0	16.1	11.1	1.2	10.4
Transportation and automotive	9.4	8.7	5.6	1.8	16.1	9.1	4.4	6.0	5.2	5.3	9.2	5.6	.0	2.6
Food and tobacco	2.1	8.7	4.0	5.0	1.2	5.5	1.9	2.5	3.9	2.1	2.3	2.8	1.2	1.9
Textiles	2.1	4.3	.0	.0	1.2	.0	4.1	2.0	1.3	.5	.0	.0	7.4	1.3
Pulp and paper	.3	.0	1.1	.5	1.2	1.8	.9	.5	.9	.5	2.3	.0	.4	.0
Printing and publications	1.0	4.3	3.4	1.8	2.5	5.5	4.1	1.5	2.6	.0	.0	5.6	2.1	4.5
Chemicals	.7	.0	1.1	1.4	.6	1.8	1.6	2.0	1.7	2.6	3.4	.0	.8	1.9
Petroleum and coal	.7	.0	.0	1.4	.0	1.8	.0	1.5	.9	.0	3.4	2.8	.0	.0
Rubber and plastics	.7	.0	.0	.0	.0	.0	.9	.5	.9	1.6	.0	2.8	.4	.0
Leather	.0	.0	.0	.0	.0	.0	.3	.0	.0	1.6	.0	.0	1.2	.0
Manufacturing of nondurable goods	1.0	.0	1.1	1.8	.6	.0	.3	1.0	1.7	.5	.0	.0	.4	.6
Transportation, communications, utilities, sanitation	11.4	12.9	13.1	13.5	6.7	3.6	10.9	8.0	7.6	8.9	9.1	2.8	3.6	9.0

TABLE 1.1 (continued)

Economic Sector	Other	Catholic					Protestant					
		French	German	Irish	Polish	Eastern European	Italian	Other	German	British	Irish	Scandinavian	Jews	Other
Wholesale and retail trade	10.8	21.7	12.4	14.2	9.9	12.7	14.5	15.1	12.4	13.8	8.0	19.4	34.2	19.5
Finance, insurance, and real estate	4.9	13.0	1.1	4.6	2.5	5.5	3.8	4.0	6.0	6.9	5.7	5.6	5.8	4.5
Business and repair	3.1	.0	5.6	3.7	1.9	3.6	3.5	2.0	3.4	3.7	1.1	.0	5.3	4.5
Personal services	3.8	.0	1.1	.0	2.5	3.6	3.2	.5	1.3	2.6	.0	2.8	1.6	1.9
Entertainment and recreation	.0	.0	.0	.9	.0	.0	.9	.5	.0	.0	.0	2.8	.8	2.6
Professional and related services	5.2	8.7	9.6	9.1	8.1	1.8	5.7	10.6	8.2	16.4	5.7	13.9	15.2	13.6
Public administration and public sector	9.4	4.3	10.7	16.0	11.8	5.5	11.0	9.0	11.6	7.9	9.2	13.9	13.2	9.7
TOTAL	288	23	177	288	161	55	317	199	233	189	87	36	243	154

Source: *Racial Attitudes in Fifteen American Cities* (Ann Arbor, Michigan: Institute for Social Research, 1973); data compiled by the editor.

About 40 percent of Polish and Eastern European Catholics are involved in the manufacturing of durable goods, the metal and steel industries, or the production of automobiles and heavy equipment. These data corroborate numerous historical accounts describing the kinds of industrial opportunities pursued by Eastern European immigrants.[18] The contemporary data indicate that these groups are still extensively involved in the same industrial sectors in which employment was initially obtained. Italians, on the other hand, show a somewhat different pattern. Nearly 15 percent are involved in wholesale and retail trade. This corresponds to historical accounts depicting Italian movement into small business enterprise and the service sector.[19] Additionally, Italians are highly represented in construction, transportation and communications, utilities and sanitation, and public administration. These data also corroborate early historical accounts of Italian economic activities. In comparison to all ethnic groups, Irish Catholics have the highest proportional membership in the public administration category. In light of the historical data depicting Irish involvement in the public sector, these findings are not surprising.[20] The Irish are also extensively involved in wholesale and retail trade, transportation, utilities, communications, and sanitation.

The Germans, like other Catholic groups, are heavily represented in the manufacturing sector. Additionally, they have a fairly large contingency involved in wholesale and retail trade. More than any other Catholic group, however, the French appear to be extensively involved in wholesale and retail trade, 21.7 percent, and finance and real estate, 13 percent. Little systematic research has been directed toward developing a fuller understanding of the French Catholic entrepreneurial experience. Although the number of cases is very small, the data appearing in table 1.1 suggest the need for more knowledge about the economic activities of French immigrants. Overall, the patterns appearing in the *other* Catholic category do not appear to be significantly different from those exhibited by their ethnic counterparts.

Among Protestant groups, some interesting findings appear. Irish Protestants are heavily represented in the manufacturing sector. Nearly 50 percent are employed in construction, the manufacturing of durable goods, metal, and steel, and the automotive industry. Irish Protestants are disproportionately represented in working-class industrial sectors. Interestingly, almost 50 percent of the Irish Protestant respondents are first generation Southern migrants; undoubtedly, they came north in search of industrial employment. Irish Protestants appear to constitute a unique case of internal migration. Like their European predecessors, the economic incentives associated with their migration appear to be dominant. Knowledge about Irish Protestant economic behavior, however, is almost nonexistent. British Protestants are disproportionately involved in the professional and service sectors and wholesale and retail trade. These data are consistent with accounts describing this group's commercial and business activities.[21] Otherwise, British Protestants are distributed fairly evenly throughout the various categories of the manufacturing sector.

Similar to British Protestants, Scandinavian-Americans are heavily represented in wholesale and retail trade, professional services, as well as the public sector. Also, Scandinavians are represented in metal and steel. German Protestants are also involved fairly extensively in the steel industry. This latter finding is consistent with historical data depicting the extent to which American industrialists systematically recruited German and Scandinavian craftsmen during the early developmental phases of the metal and steel industries. Jews reveal the most distinctive degree of employment specialization. About 34 percent of Jews in the sample were employed in wholesale and retail trade. These findings are not surprising in light of historical data describing Jewish economic activities.[22] Additionally, about 15 percent of Jewish Americans are employed in professional service occupations, and another 13.2 percent are found in the public sector. Overall, then, over 60 percent of Jews sampled were employed in just three sectors of the economy.

Table 1.2 gives a clearer indication of the specific occupational categories occupied by the groups included in the survey. Occupational categories are collapsed according to traditional census groupings. As was clearly suggested by the data appearing in table 1.1, most Catholic groups cluster in blue collar occupations. In fact, all Catholic groups except the French have over 50 percent of their members employed in blue collar occupations. Italians have the highest degree of blue collar involvement, 65.8 percent, followed by the Poles, 65.2 percent and Eastern Europeans, 57 percent. The French have, by far, the highest membership in the professional and managerial categories, 34.6 percent.

Among Protestant groups, the Irish are heavily represented in working-class occupations, 67.5 percent. They are followed by German Protestants and the residual *other* Protestants, 55.7 percent. British and Scandinavian-Americans have the highest proportion appearing in the professional and managerial categories. In fact, Scandinavians have more respondents appearing in professional occupations, in comparison with all ethnic groups. Overall, however, Jews have the highest proportion appearing in white collar occupations, 76.7 percent, as opposed to 63.3 percent of Scandinavians. Generally, then, the occupational data appearing in Table 1.2 provide a more precise interpretation of the information

TABLE 1.2 Occupational Characteristics of Religio-Ethnic Groups (Percent)

Occupation	Catholic							Protestant						
	Other	French	German	Irish	Polish	Eastern European	Italian	Other	German	British	Irish	Scandinavian	Jews	Other
Professional and technical	11.5	19.2	15.4	10.3	11.2	6.9	7.1	10.0	12.7	16.6	9.1	26.3	21.8	18.8
Farmers and farm managers	.0	.0	.0	.0	.0	1.7	.0	.0	.0	.0	.0	.0	.0	.0
Managers, officials, and proprietors	11.1	15.4	8.5	10.3	3.9	13.8	9.5	9.5	10.7	10.7	8.0	7.9	28.4	17.6
Clerical and kindred	9.8	7.7	12.8	10.7	8.4	13.8	8.3	14.3	13.9	17.1	12.5	10.5	10.9	11.4
Sales	5.2	3.8	3.2	7.4	3.4	1.7	3.3	4.8	2.5	3.4	.0	18.4	15.6	3.4
Craftsmen and foremen	20.7	15.4	28.7	19.8	28.7	27.6	29.5	18.6	28.7	18.0	27.3	13.2	8.6	17.6
Operators and kindred	21.6	23.1	16.0	18.5	25.3	19.0	23.5	27.6	19.3	18.0	29.5	13.2	6.2	10.8
Private household	.3	.0	.0	.0	.0	.0	.0	.0	.4	.0	.0	.0	.4	.6
Service workers	8.2	.0	8.5	8.6	9.0	5.2	8.3	7.1	6.1	5.4	5.7	2.6	3.1	7.4
Laborers	5.9	3.8	1.6	4.1	2.2	5.2	4.5	2.4	1.2	2.4	5.7	2.6	.4	.6
Armed Forces	.3	.0	.0	.8	1.1	.0	.0	1.0	1.2	1.0	.0	.0	.0	.0
Student	1.6	7.7	1.6	2.1	.0	.0	.9	1.9	1.6	5.9	1.1	2.6	3.1	8.0
Other	3.6	3.8	3.7	7.4	6.7	5.2	5.1	2.9	1.6	1.5	1.1	2.6	1.6	4.0
TOTAL	305	26	188	243	178	58	336	210	244	205	88	38	257	176

Source: *Racial Attitudes in Fifteen American Cities* (Ann Arbor, Michigan: Institute for Social Research, 1973); data compiled by the editor.

presented in the first table. And like the historical information provided, the survey data detail a profile of ethnic specialization, not only within specific industrial sectors, but also within distinct occupational categories. Data describing the distribution of income are presented in table 1.3. As might be expected, the income data fall pretty much in line with the information appearing in the previous two tables. Reflecting their occupational and industrial involvement, the French exhibit the highest levels of income among Catholic groups. The Poles, Eastern Europeans, and Italians manifest the lowest income levels. Among Protestant groups, the Irish revealed the lowest income levels; over 60 percent report annual family incomes below $8,000. British and Scandinavian-Americans report the highest income levels among Protestant groups. Jews report the highest annual family incomes in comparison with all ethnic groups.

Table 1.4 presents data dealing with years of school completed and includes two sets of figures. First, percentage distributions reflect educational attainment levels within four distinct categories. Second, mean scores reflecting the actual number of years completed are presented. As would be expected, French Catholics, British and Scandinavian Protestants, and Jews reveal the highest levels of educational attainment. Poles, Italians, and Irish Protestants reveal the lowest levels of educational attainment.

Table 1.5 completes the socioeconomic profile of ethnic groups. The table shows the distribution of home ownership among ethnic groups. Home ownership is generally considered a very poor indicator of the distribution of wealth in the American economy. Generally, corporate stock, business and professions, and other types of fixed assets are much more highly concentrated than is the distribution of home ownership. Among Catholics, the highest levels of home ownership appear among Poles and Eastern Europeans. Historical accounts suggest that immigrants from Poland and Eastern Europe viewed home ownership as a very desirable goal and invested any surpluses toward pursuit of that end. On the other hand, groups with uncertain attachments to specific geographic areas, like the Jews, did not invest savings in the accumulation of real estate. This perhaps explains why groups serving as urban merchants, such as French Catholics, Jews, and some British Protestants, appear to be apartment dwellers rather than homeowners. This generalization, however, does not hold for the Scandinavians, 60.5 percent of whom are homeowners.

Several observations can be drawn from these data. First, differing levels of prosperity have been achieved by immigrant minorities. Generally, there appears to be a slight connection between length of residence and prosperity, the older immigrant groups having achieved

TABLE 1.3 Annual Family Income by Religio-Ethnic Identification

Income	Catholic							Protestant						
	Other	French	German	Irish	Polish	Eastern European	Italian	Other	German	British	Irish	Scandinavian	Jews	Other
Less than $5,000	19.8	30.7	12.4	17.9	12.3	11.2	15.3	22.5	17.2	20.7	19.2	13.5	13.5	20.8
$5,000 to $7,999	30.3	19.2	31.0	28.3	32.5	31.5	31.4	29.6	24.2	26.3	42.2	32.4	16.6	25.5
$8,000 to $9,000	19.4	15.4	28.1	18.9	22.1	18.5	21.9	17.8	24.1	17.6	18.0	5.4	10.4	18.1
$10,000 to $13,999	19.4	15.3	18.6	22.9	24.5	25.9	22.8	15.8	22.4	19.1	13.2	24.3	26.1	22.1
Over $14,000	11.2	19.2	10.2	12.1	8.5	13.1	8.6	14.3	12.1	16.5	7.2	24.3	33.5	13.4
TOTAL	278	26	178	223	163	54	314	196	232	194	83	37	230	149

Source: *Racial Attitudes in Fifteen American Cities* (Ann Arbor, Michigan: Institute for Social Research, 1973); data compiled by the editor.

TABLE 1.4 Years of School Completed by Religio-Ethnic Identification (Percent)

Years of School	Catholic							Protestant					
	Other	French	German	Irish	Polish	Eastern European	Italian	Other	German	British	Irish	Scandinavian	Jews	Other
Some high school or less	47.0	34.5	48.2	37.5	51.6	36.2	50.9	50.8	42.3	32.2	58.8	21.1	23.3	33.0
High school graduate	31.0	26.9	32.8	35.9	35.4	43.1	38.6	29.1	35.2	28.8	26.7	31.6	33.9	28.4
Some college	10.9	15.4	11.2	16.9	7.9	18.9	5.8	10.3	11.8	18.8	4.4	21.1	21.7	21.1
College graduate	11.2	23.1	7.9	9.6	5.1	1.7	4.7	9.9	10.6	20.2	10.0	26.3	21.0	17.7
TOTAL	313	26	189	248	178	58	342	213	247	208	90	38	257	176
x̄ (mean)	11.2	12.3	11.3	11.7	10.6	11.3	10.5	10.8	11.5	12.4	10.8	13.1	12.7	12.1

Source: *Racial Attitudes in Fifteen American Cities* (Ann Arbor, Michigan: Institute for Social Research, 1973); data compiled by the editor.

TABLE 1.5 Distribution of Home Ownership by Religio-Ethnic Identification (Percent)

Home Ownership	Catholic						Protestant						
	Other	French	German	Irish	Polish	Eastern European	Italian	Other	German	British	Irish	Scandinavian	Jews	Other
Own or buying	55.6	38.5	61.9	55.6	65.7	63.8	58.4	53.3	49.2	40.9	42.2	60.5	50.2	50.6
Rent	44.1	57.7	38.1	44.4	34.3	36.2	40.8	45.8	49.6	56.7	57.8	39.5	49.0	48.9
Other	.3	3.8	.0	.0	.0	.0	.9	1.4	1.2	2.4	.0	.0	.8	.5
TOTAL	313	26	189	248	178	58	342	212	246	208	90	38	257	176

Source: *Racial Attitudes in Fifteen American Cities* (Ann Arbor, Michigan: Institute for Social Research, 1973); data compiled by the editor.

slightly higher occupational and income levels. Third, early patterns of occupational and industrial involvement have persisted. While it is reasonable to assume that early patterns have been considerably weakened and altered, they are nonetheless present in the contemporary work experiences of many ethnic groups.

In terms of the essays appearing in this volume, the survey data suggest the need for two observations. First, this volume is not to be construed as a success story, a uniquely collective version of the Horatio Alger mythology. While several groups, including Jews, Mormons, and Orientals, have apparently achieved a fairly high degree of success in American society, other groups clearly have not. While these other groups have not reached prosperity, they do appear to have achieved at least the trappings of working-class stability.

Second, while the survey data are extremely useful, some analytical categories are too general to provide a more precise profile of ethnic stratification. For example, the Scandinavian category does not reveal the varying economic experiences of Finnish, Swedish, and Norwegian immigrants. Also, the Eastern European category masks the different historical experiences of the numerous Slavic ethnic groups. Additionally, several groups, such as Greeks, Orientals, and the Spanish-speaking, are clustered too geographically or too few in number to appear in sufficient quantities in a sample survey. Consequently, data describing their socioeconomic experiences are incomplete.

Nonetheless, the data do reveal systematic patterns. Ethnic groups are not distributed randomly throughout the economy. There do appear to be unique historical circumstances associated with contemporary patterns of ethnic stratification. More importantly, however, is the contention that ethnic stratification is produced by forces more pervasive than fortuitous industrial events. A fuller appreciation of the distribution of ethnic groups in the American economy can only be gained by a detailed examination of their uniquely collective adaptations to urban and industrial life. And while I do not disagree with Greeley's recent contention that contemporary data dealing with ethnic stratification suggest a strong relationship between culture and achievement, he provides us with little or no explanation of the possible dynamics of that relationship. This book will attempt to rectify this deficiency.

CASE STUDIES OF IMMIGRANT ECONOMIC DEVELOPMENT

Like the survey data analysis, the historical saga represented by the essays in this volume is incomplete. The economic experiences and activities of thirteen immigrant groups are discussed: Japanese, Chinese, Korean, Greek, Mormon, Polish, Slovak, Irish, Finnish, Serbian, Croatian, Slovene, and Jewish. The groups selected for analysis provide a unique cross-section of collective approaches to economic development. The failure to include particular groups in no way suggests a judgment about the value of studying their economic and commercial activities. Practical considerations prevented more comprehensive coverage, and a more complete analysis must await further scholarship.

The essays here represent several research traditions in the social sciences and humanities. While most of them are case studies, the unifying theme is collective adaptation to urban and industrial life. Nearly all the essays make use of original historical documents, files, and records. Additionally, ethnographic and in-depth interview techniques, as well as the survey research approach are represented. For students in the social sciences and history, then, much can be learned about the creative application of research techniques. Unlike many primary research endeavors, the scholars preparing essays for this volume have tailored their methodological approaches to the specific requirements of the given problem. Their cultivation and analysis of existing files, records, and primary data sources is at times ingenious and represents the best traditions of intellectual craftsmanship.

The book itself is organized in four sections. The first two essays examine the cultural and familial sources of collective economic development. Summarizing earlier work dealing with Japanese and Chinese-American entrepreneurial activity,[23] Light presents new findings on the commercial activities of Korean immigrants. Similar to the institutions and practices characteristic of Japanese and Chinese business enterprise, Korean activities also manifest collective approaches to economic development. While not as strong as Japanese and Chinese patterns, Light argues that ethnic solidarity is an influential force shaping the Korean business system. Lovell-Troy has applied selected aspects of Light's analytical model to explain the business activities of Greek immigrants in Connecticut. He finds that nearly 60 percent of Greek immigrants in the urban areas of Connecticut are self-employed proprietors of pizza businesses. Further, he reports that approximately 40 percent of all pizza businesses in the state are owned by Greeks. Through detailed ethnographic interviews of two immigrant extended families, Lovell-Troy reveals the cultural and familial mechanisms by which entrance into the restaurant business is facilitated. Generally, Lovell-Troy presents evidence and argument showing how the norms of familial life influence economic activity among Greek immigrants. While not as collective in approach as Oriental merchants, Greek businessmen in no way approach the highly individualistic modes of capitalism described by Weber.

The book's second section contains three essays describing the religious roots of ethnic business enterprise and social service delivery. The most important theoretical finding derived from these essays is found in the inversion of the Weberian thesis. Generally, all three studies stress the idea that certain types of religious principles provide a collective basis for the accumulation of capital. White examines the gradual transition from communitarian to capitalist modes of economic development among Mormons. Today the Mormon Church boasts significant financial holdings in major corporations. The extent of wealth owned by the church, while unknown, is reputed to be substantial. White develops a convincing argument demonstrating that contemporary Mormon capitalism rests upon a collective and communitarian economic base.

Renkiewicz explores the nonprofit capitalism characteristic of Polish fraternals and mutual benefit societies. Several elements of Polish history and social organization provided the organizational impetus shaping the community development in Polish-American neighborhoods. He argues that ethnic solidarity and nationalism provided the collective spirit necessary to the successful establishment of Polish fraternals. More important to the success of the fraternals, though, was the organizational and administrative technology drawn from the Catholic Church.

Stolarik examines the creation of mutual benefit societies among Slovak immigrants. His data show how Slovaks were able to develop cohesive neighborhoods, deliver social services to residents, as well as provide social welfare benefits. Generally, most Slovak lodges and fraternals were rooted in religious institutions. The lodges typically distributed benefits and delivered services within Slovak neighborhoods on an egalitarian basis. While individual gain was possible, most lodges attempted to enhance the common good and pursue collective ends. He suggests that Catholicism provided the values that gave rise to Slovak collective enterprise.

The third part examines the political bases of collective economic development. Karni's analysis of Finnish cooperatives in Minnesota, Wisconsin, and Michigan documents a strong connection between political ideology and economic development. Extensively involved in the American socialist movement, Finnish immigrants implemented their ideological principles and beliefs by building communitarian economic institutions. Finnish cooperatives were not only efficient but so productive that they forced many privately owned businesses into bankruptcy. Karni traces the rise and fall of Finnish cooperatives through the first half of the twentieth century. Stipanovich compares the economic activities of Serbian, Croatian, and Slovenian immigrants. He argues that not every immigrant group organized their collective economy activities in the same fashion, despite similar historical and cultural experiences. In comparison to Serbian and Croatian economic institutions, evidence and argument are presented showing that Slovenes were more collective and communitarian in their approach to community and neighborhood development. Consequently, suggests Stipanovich, Slovenes were able to deliver more services and amenities to members of the community.

Clark examines the Irish Catholic blending of political and business activities. He shows how the public sector was used as a unique form of collective economic development in Irish neighborhoods. Through control of municipal government, the Irish were often able to expand the public sector, thereby providing municipal employment and urban social services to an ethnic constituency. Not only was public sector employment provided but public funds were used to stimulate private investment in Irish neighborhoods. His case study of contractors in Philadelphia illustrates the unique features of self-help in Irish neighborhoods. By using the public arena to stabilize the harshest edges of urban life, the Irish approach to neighborhood development can be seen as a unique forerunner of contemporary welfare state liberalism.

In the last section of the book, Rosentraub and Taebel explore Jewish economic development. Not unlike White, they argue that once a group has achieved prosperity, earlier forms of collective enterprise give way to more orthodox capitalist activities premised upon self-interest. Drawing from a sample survey of Jews residing in the Dallas-Fort Worth metropolitan area, Rosentraub and Taebel find little evidence of collectivism, ethnic economic solidarity, or patronage among prosperous Jews. Generalizing from their case study, they suggest that collective activities among contemporary Jews have shifted from the economic to the social arena and, further, that a large Jewish middle class has emerged, showing little interest in delivering services or aid to Jews still living in poverty. They suggest that Jewish enterprise has shifted from collective self-help to orthodox capitalism.

THE POLITICAL SIGNIFICANCE OF COLLECTIVE ECONOMIC INSTITUTIONS

There are dangers involved in drawing political inferences from the essays appearing in this volume. Nonetheless, several observations and generalizations do appear appropriate. Most importantly, the past economic experiences and activities of immigrant groups seem relevant to present attempts to stabilize and develop low income, urban neighborhoods. I am not talking only about the urban Black and Chicano populations but about all groups now experiencing economic deprivation in the city. Present urban policies seem to be formulated in isolation from historical events. The familiar dictum echoed by scholars is that public officials should learn from history. What, then, can be learned from the economic experiences of immigrant groups?

Few public officials disagree with the idea that creative and fiscally responsible programs are needed to revitalize low income urban neighborhoods. Additionally, most planners and students of urban life recognize that neighborhood deterioration is simply a manifestation of poverty, discrimination, unemployment, and limited access to social services and related urban amenities. Further, the lessons learned from the War on Poverty years suggest clearly that remedies to the complex problems of urban poverty are not only expensive but also cannot proceed in a piecemeal or fragmented fashion. Not only do reform programs deplete federal and municipal resources, they also unwittingly undermine the strength and autonomy of neighborhood culture and institutions. By relying upon outside financial assistance, many urban neighborhoods become dependent upon external political forces. This dependency relationship decreases community control over neighborhood resources and increases the likelihood that the neighborhood's fate will be shaped by extra-community agencies and political bodies. What is obviously needed, then, are programs to strengthen and develop neighborhood resources, encourage neighborhood autonomy, and generate sound business practices.

Contemporary strategies of community and neighborhood development often appear within the context of encouraging minority enterprise or reforming the welfare system. The problems associated with low income neighborhoods, however, extend to areas of health and sanitation, family relations, inadequate transportation, and limited access to cultural and recreational facilities. Housing stock also suffers considerably in low income neighborhoods. While the federal government has created several housing programs, including Section 8 rental and the 236 plan, the results have been less than satisfactory. More housing units have been abandoned since implementation of these programs. These abandoned units will continue to deteriorate, further destroying the physical integrity of many urban neighborhoods.

Evaluating the successes and failures of recent reform programs is difficult. Within the framework of immigrant economic development, however, it is fairly easy to understand and explain why certain programs have succeeded and others have failed. Clearly, immigrant economic activities illustrate the importance of collective and communitarian approaches to neighborhood development. Despite the failure of many students of urban life to acknowledge the role of collectivism in immigrant economic history, and although legislators seldom endorse collectivism as a legitimate approach to neighborhood development, both historical and contemporary data suggest it can be an effective way to mobilize and distribute resources.

Most urban areas experiencing neighborhood decline have initiated various programs designed to halt the downward spiral of community deterioration. One method recently developed in many cities appears similar in philosophy to the collective approaches developed by immigrant groups. I am referring to what many planners call a local or neighborhood development corporation (NDC).[24] The neighborhood development corporation is generally a service-oriented organization operated for the benefit of the community. The corporation implements programs and delivers services often not available in the public arena. Most NDCs, to date, have been involved primarily in housing development and rehabilitation. Food cooperatives, day care centers, and other services are among the new programs offered by existing local development corporations.

Several characteristics of the NDC make it an effective method to deal with the problems of neighborhood and community development. First, it typically operates on a nonprofit basis, so NDCs can function in areas where the private sector cannot perform effectively or efficiently. If profits are secured, they are usually reinvested in community and neighborhood enterprise. Like many immigrant economic institutions, then, NDCs have the potential to operate according to communitarian and egalitarian principles. Second, the NDC can often develop programs capable of addressing specific neighborhood problems. Since the NDC itself is usually controlled by neighborhood residents, local groups and individuals are capable of focusing the corporation's activities on important and immediate community issues. In this respect, the NDC is also similar to ethnic economic activities. Third, the NDC blends the revenue-generating capabilities of a corporation and the public service emphasis of municipal government. This feature also parallels immigrant economic institutions. This combination often avoids the bureaucratic restrictions associated with government programs and the public service constraints posed by the necessity of profit in the private sector. Last, the NDC requires the involvement of community residents. By contributing to the success of the corporation, the residents are also helping themselves. The NDC is a unique mechanism by which group action is converted into self-help and the common good is translated into self-interest, another feature similar to ethnic economic activities. Since citizens contribute to the activities of the NDC, community awareness is a logical by-product. In attempting to insure the NDC's success, the community's sense of political efficacy is bolstered and neighborhood autonomy often becomes a tangible goal. A goal of the NDC, then, is to create an environment of success in low income neighborhoods. A brief examination of other cities' experiences with NDCs will illustrate the variety of activities these organizations are capable of producing. The parallels with immigrant economic institutions are striking.

The Neighborhood Housing Services, Inc. (NHS) is a type of neighborhood development corporation pioneered in Pittsburgh in the late 1960s.[25] NHS organizations operate primarily as quasi-public corporations with strong ties to neighborhood groups and institutions. They are typically private, nonprofit corporations composed of representatives from the targeted neighborhoods and from the city's banking and commercial sectors. NHS's objective is to save urban neighborhoods from urban renewal programs by bringing existing housing stock up to code standards. The basic idea is to make loans available to potential homeowners in high risk neighborhoods. These high risk applicants receive loans at no or very low interest rates. The success of the Pittsburgh program has led to the establishment of other NHS groups throughout the country. Presently, the NHS idea is operating in fifty-two neighborhoods in forty-six cities around the nation.

Another NDC is the Union Sarah Economic Development Corporation (USEDC).[26] The USEDC is a private, profit-oriented NDC with its stock owned by a parent, nonprofit organization. The USEDC was founded in St. Louis in order to serve a low income, Black area of the city. USEDC's objective is to initiate economic redevelopment and neighborhood stabilization. The USEDC is involved in neighborhood manufacturing as well as small, locally owned business enterprises. Additionally, it has a revolving loan fund for minority contractors and recently has become involved in real estate development.

A third illustration is the Urban Development Corp. (UDC) of New York State.[27] Patterned after the Tennessee Valley Authority (TVA), this state-wide agency was created in 1968 as a response to the state's housing problems. The UDC included a policy-making board of directors and functioned in the manner of a private corporation. Initially it attempted to insure administrative decentralization and neighborhood autonomy. The UDC was also given the capacity to create subsidiary corporations for various local purposes. Each subsidiary was controlled differently by the parent UDC; the UDC was working fifty-four projects involving 43,000 housing units, as well as numerous other economic ventures.

The power of the UDC began to weaken in 1973, due to several external conflicts and pressures. UDC's bond ratings were lowered from class A. The executive director became accountable to the state governor rather than a local board of directors. Finally, the interest rates charged to the corporation were sharply increased. Eventually, conflict with private interest groups and numerous political obstacles posed by various interest groups undermined UDC's support base. Although UDC appeared capable of responding to numerous neighborhood problems, its effectiveness was neutralized by competing political interests, internal conflicts, and a scope of operation which was probably too large. In 1975 the Urban Development Corporation ceased to operate.

A final illustration is the City Wide Development Corporation of Dayton, Ohio.[28] Real estate development in high risk areas of the city is the major focus of this corporation. This program is largely controlled by the city, with twenty-two of a twenty-eight-member board of trustees being appointed by the city council. Remaining board members are appointed from each of six neighborhood planning councils established by the city. Dayton has divided the city into three types of neighborhoods: stable, strategic, and transitional. Most attention is given to the latter two. Working with lending institutions, City Wide has established a low interest loan program which enables individuals to restore and improve existing housing stock. Another federal housing program, Homesteading, allows City Wide to sell houses at 75 percent of appraised market value after the corporation has brought the target houses up to the city's code standard. Each buyer must agree to maintain and live in the house for at least five years. Several million dollars have been invested by City Wide over the past several years.

The New York experience notwithstanding, the growing popularity of neighborhood development corporations is illustrated by a survey of over 140 cities—all receiving Community Development grants—conducted in 1977.[29] Of the 115 cities responding to the survey, over 31 percent had established some type of NDC. These corporations were primarily involved in housing programs. Twenty-one percent had also established economic development corporations to assist the emergence of small businesses.

It would not be wise to claim wholesale success on the part of NDCs. Their failure, however, appears to be associated with a dilution of local autonomy and control, excessive concern with the maximization of profit, and inadequate marketing strategies.[30] Individualistic modes of neighborhood development do not appear effective. Encouraging individual minority enterprise or inducing the private sector through subsidies and tax incentives to serve low income neighborhoods benefits a small group of entrepreneurs or those who already control a disproportionate share of the wealth.

Clearly, the unique legacy of collectivism is more than just a passing interest among students of ethnic history. Collectivism has immediate relevance to U.S. urban policy. Specifically, failure to recognize the role of collectivism in community and neighborhood development on the part of many urban planners, and nearly all legislators, is indicative of an approach to urban policy rooted in an uninformed commitment to rugged individualism and orthodox capitalism. By defining collectivism as an alien or explicitly Marxist mode of economic development, many legislators reveal an unabashed ignorance of immigrant economic development in particular and American history in general. By ignoring the importance of collectivism in shaping minority economic development, many effective ways to accomplish neighborhood revitalization are overlooked. It is hoped that this volume can serve not only to rectify deficiencies in knowledge about self-help in urban America but also as a manual endorsing collective and communitarian approaches to neighborhood development.

PART ONE

THE CULTURAL AND FAMILIAL ROOTS OF COLLECTIVE ECONOMIC DEVELOPMENT

IVAN LIGHT

ASIAN ENTERPRISE IN AMERICA
Chinese, Japanese, and Koreans in Small Business

The foreign born have been persistently overrepresented in the U.S. business population in this century.[1] Explanations of the alien's proclivity for commerce reduce to two simple ones and a welter of complex variants. First, disadvantage theory has claimed that foreigners pile up in small business self-employment because they are disadvantaged in the general labor market by poor English, inferior educational credentials, unemployment, discrimination, and so on. Labor market disadvantages encourage foreigners to turn to business in greater proportion than do the native born. An alternative view is the cultural theory of entrepreneurship.[2] This theory has explained the overrepresentation of particular foreign groups in the business population on the basis of the group's cultural attributes. For example, the proverbial business acumen of Jews, Chinese, and Armenians may be taken to explain why these groups have contributed more firms to the business population in proportion to their number than have other Americans.

Both theories confront obvious objections. The disadvantage theory explains the overrepresentation of the foreign born in business but has trouble accounting for intergroup disparities. Why should some foreign groups have higher rates of business enterprise than others, and why should the foreign born in general have much higher rates of business

---

This article is based on preliminary analysis of data collected under grant SOC 76-12348 from the National Science Foundation. The author gratefully acknowledges NSF support. Professor Edna Bonacich is co-principal investigator. She has contributed many valuable comments and reviews to this manuscript. However, this portion of the preliminary analysis has been assigned by mutual agreement to Professor Light.

proprietorship than Mexicans and especially Blacks, the most disadvantaged of all? On the other hand, the cultural theory of entrepreneurship satisfactorily answers intergroup differences but cannot encompass situational pressures which mold alien groups. Of course, the cultural and disadvantage theories need not exclude one another; structural disadvantage may befall groups who do not possess unusual qualifications for commerce. Conversely, people who confront no structural disadvantages in the labor market may nonetheless possess special endowment for business enterprise. In this sense, white-skinned Quakers and Mormons have been heavily represented in American business, but structural disadvantage has made little contribution to their enterprise. In general, the foreign born have confronted barriers in the American labor market, and these barriers have encouraged them to attempt business self-employment for want of a wage-earning job. Thus, initial disadvantage has been a universal of foreign absorption in American labor markets although some groups have, admittedly, been more disadvantaged than others.

ORTHODOX AND REACTIVE VERSIONS

At present, the most lively sociological questions pertain to intergroup differences unexplained by disadvantage. One possibility is that the propensity to engage in business proprietorship ("entrepreneurship") is genuinely cultural. This is the orthodox meaning of the cultural theory of entrepreneurship. An analogy is the migration of Gypsy fortunetellers. Before debarkation Gypsy migrants already know how to tell fortunes, and their cultural baggage includes prophetic endowments (knowing how to use crystal balls, etc.) other groups simply lack. Another possibility is that alien status releases latent facilitators which promote entrepreneurship. In this second case, the facilitators emerge from the minority situation rather than the cultural baggage of a particular group. An example is enhanced social solidarity attendant upon minority status. Insofar as enhanced solidarity encourages entrepreneurship, a situation has brought out a collective response which is not cultural in the orthodox sense. For example, Maris and Somerset observe that "immigrants often ... consolidate a racially distinct commercial network since entrepreneurship is a characteristic response to minority status."[3] This entrepreneurial response is situational if immigrant groups in the same situation always produce it. On the other hand, what is situationally engendered is a collective propensity to respond rather than, as in the disadvantage theory, a set of obstacles that compel an uncoordinated but universal circumvention. This sort of individualistic circumvention arises, for example, when a rainburst induces people in a stadium to put up umbrellas. Here crowd action is in unison, but each individual has made a separate decision and acts independently of others. In contrast, a collective propensity endows a minority with ambitions, motivations, institutions, skills, and so on, which distinguish members from nonmembers. These constitute entrepreneurial "assets" in Barth's terminology, but the term "resources" is more general and does not lend itself to confusion with financial assets.[4] Mere disadvantage confers no collective resources. This is the reactive interpretation of the theory of cultural entrepreneurship and its point of divergence from disadvantage theory.

This distinction between reactive and orthodox interpretations of minority entrepreneurship is a new one necessitated by the rapidly accumulating literature on this topic. However, a conceptual distinction does not necessitate an empirical repugnance because both types of entrepreneurship may coexist in the same group. In fact, both versions have appeared. In one, orthodox and reactive cultural resources facilitate ethnic entrepreneurship; in the other only enhanced solidarity (reactive) matters. Light contrasted Chinese, Japanese, and Blacks in business proprietorship prior to World War 2.[5] The problem posed was why disadvantaged Asians should be overrepresented in business proprietorship whereas disadvantaged Blacks were underrepresented. Both soft and hard versions of the cultural theory figured in the solution offered. On the one hand, the rotating credit association turned out to have contributed to Asian commerce on the Pacific Coast, whereas the African rotating credit association had dropped out of the cultural repertoire of American Blacks during the period of enslavement. At this juncture, the Asians' ability to solve the chronic problem of capitalization provided a cultural resource for business proprietorship which American-born Blacks simply lacked. Similarly, traditions of extended kinship and filial piety encouraged Asian family business, but the same traditions did not favor Southern-born Blacks. In these two cases, then, "orthodox" Black-Asian cultural differences seemed to account for gross differences between groups in rates of business proprietorship.

On the other hand, linguistic and regional heterogeneity of Asian immigrants encouraged the formation of solidarity subgroups which additionally facilitated the collective development of business enterprise. Supported by the spirit of *Landsmannschaft,* Japanese and Chinese communities sprouted nepotistic trade guilds which regulated business enterprise in the interest of the coethnic membership. Informal association also channelled business-related values, information, and skills in the Asian communities so that high rates of business activity naturally resulted. At this level, Chinese-Japanese cultural differences seemed unimportant. Both Asian communities relied upon situationally engendered social solidarity to prop up the small business system upon which the whole group's livelihood critically depended. The contribution of this solidarity to the overall business activity of the immigrants is a reactive meaning of entrepreneurship in this context.

An exclusively reactive treatment of ethnic entrepreneurship appeared also in Bonacich's theory of "middleman minorities."[6] Agreeing that disadvantage imbued minorities with a motive for self-employment, Bonacich's situational formulation offered a new and ingenious union with the entrepreneurship theory. In her view, exclusion enhanced minority solidarity, and minority solidarity, in turn, engendered a clannish cooperation in business. The business competition of clannish minorities further aggravated the hostility of the host population, thus intensifying the solidarity of ethnic minorities in business and further augmenting their collective advantage in this sphere. This formulation ignored unique cultural endowments (for example, the rotating credit association) which might contribute to ethnic overrepresentation in business. Hence, Bonacich's treatment altogether lacked a hard cultural side. Sojourning ethnics engaged in entrepreneurial behavior (hard work, thrift, clannishness) because of situational pressures rather than because of deeply rooted cultural proclivities. On the other hand, the sojourner theory postulated that entrepreneurial minorities operated as cohesive groups, the members of which behaved differently from nonmembers. Here the sojourner theory departed from disadvantage theory according to which the disadvantaged operate as solitary individuals and do not differ from the nondisadvantaged in behavior.

COLLECTIVE AND INDIVIDUALISTIC STYLES OF ENTREPRENEURSHIP

At this point the orthodox, reactive, and mixed treatments of minority entrepreneurship converge around a dimension of analysis which distinguishes recent interpretations from older ones: the issue of collective versus individualistic styles of entrepreneurship. The cultural theory of entrepreneurship traditionally depicted an individualistic style of business management. In this version, cultural influences affected individuals in the course of primary socialization during which they introjected the distinctive values and motivations of their group. When group values and motivations encouraged business success, a minority produced adults who succeeded in business. The prototype of this model is Weber's Protestant sectarians who espoused the values of diligence in a calling, thrift, profit, and individualism. These values and the attendant motivations caused adult sectarians to prosper in business, but they were supposed to do so as noncooperating individuals. Individualism was a prime tenet of Calvinist religion so economic cooperation was in principle repugnant to the life ethic of believers. Of course, Weber was aware that most people are not Protestants. Indeed, the radical individualism of the sectarians was precisely the quality that distinguished them from traditional merchant classes and endowed their enterprise with its uniquely bourgeois character. Subsequent studies of business enterprise in moderation lost track of this restriction. Indeed, McClelland even concluded that the needs for achievement and affiliation were mutually repugnant. Yet, as Waterbury pointed out, ethnic traders combine a relentless search for profit with communitarian ties.[7] The objection Waterman turned up is theoretically important. The root of the trouble is the uncritically accepted, post-Weberian assumption that business management must be individualistic. In reality, this assumption substitutes a deviant minority (Protestant sectarians) for the world's majority pattern and thus reverses the empirical weight of cases.

Textbook treatments of this issue emphasize individualistic value and motivational effects. There is, of course, no question that ethnic values and motivations do affect individual behavior. Recent research only proves that there exists a largely ignored dimension of collective action which goes beyond individualistic value or motivational effects, the dimension of collective action. Collective styles of entrepreneurship depend upon group resources in which business owners can only participate insofar as they maintain an active, adult participation in community life. For example, a rotating credit association requires cooperators to establish a reputation for trustworthiness in the ethnic community, and this reputation depends, in turn, upon active involvement. In the same sense, an ethnic informational network confers benefits upon business owners, but to obtain this benefit an owner needs to belong to the network. Isolates cannot share network information so this resource only benefits participants in community life. Trade guilds may also regulate and control internal competition, but the benefits of ethnic collusion "in restraint of trade" only accrue to members. Isolates cannot share this collective resource. Taking account only of value and motivational effects completely ignores the dimension of collective action which may and in most cases does also supplement the business position of entrepreneurial minorities.

The sociological issues emerging from this review of recent entrepreneurship literature are both elementary and advanced. The basic issue is whether or not structural disadvantage is a sufficient explanation for intergroup differences in rates of business proprietorship. The sociological side of this issue hangs upon the claim that characteristics of groups (values, institutions, solidarity, etc.) affect economic behavior. A more advanced issue is, given intergroup differences in response to disadvantage, what is deeply cultural and what is reactive? At this more advanced level, a second problem is not whether but how intergroup differences manifest themselves in economic behavior. That is, do group influences encourage an individualistic, collective, or mixed style of business management? The advanced problem resolves itself into the manner of collective influence in the entrepreneurship of immigrant minorities. Here the sociological approach detects and classifies collective bases of action in what marginal utility economics has always regarded as the supreme field of action of economically rational individuals: private business enterprise.

Chinese and Japanese in North America have been persistently overrepresented in small business enterprise, and their historical experience has, therefore, provided a major source of evidence on ethnic entrepreneurship.[8] Recent immigration of Koreans to the United States has lately created a valuable opportunity to reexamine the social sources of Asian entrepreneurship. Like the prewar Chinese and Japanese, Korean immigrants in Los Angeles today are notably overrepresented in wholesale and retail trades even though these sectors have been in decline for several generations.[9] What causes this overrepresentation? Perhaps Korean business reflects only disadvantage in the labor force and class origin. This is the null hypothesis: ethnicity confers nothing. But there are ethnic possibilities. The most urgent theoretical issues are, first of all, whether Korean business reflects any collectivite effects at all, be these individualistic, collectivistic, or mixed. Second, the Korean case can provide a fresh view of orthodox and reactive sources of ethnic entrepreneurship insofar as ethnicity actually has any independent effect upon entrepreneurship.

KOREANS IN LOS ANGELES

Koreans have lived in Los Angeles since 1905, and the city's small community actually housed a government-in-exile during the Japanese occupation, 1905-46. However, in 1970, Los Angeles's Korean community numbered only 8,811, a quantitatively invisible ethnic minority. Since 1965-68, South Korean immigration to the United States has increased sixfold. This abrupt increase reflects the liberalization of U.S. immigration laws in 1965, fear of another Communist invasion, political and social ferment in the Republic of Korea, and the enduring political and cultural ties between the United States and Korea. The city of Los Angeles has received about 60 percent of the new Korean immigration to the United States.[10] The Southern California metropolis is the largest Korean settlement in the United States and the largest Korean settlement in the world outside Korea.

The number of Koreans now in Los Angeles is a matter of estimate. There are no reliable counts. In 1973 the U.S. Department of Health, Education, and Welfare conducted a field study of Koreans in Los Angeles. The Department's report declared the 1970 Census estimate of 8,811 Koreans "unquestionably a gross misrepresentation."[11] Korean newspapers, spokesmen, and clergymen noisily estimate the Korean population of Los Angeles County at about 85,000 in 1975. Korean spokesmen have a motive in exaggerating the number; by so doing they can maximize their political influence in municipal government and their ethnic visibility to the Department of Health, Education, and Welfare. Therefore, Terry and Stull's conservative estimate of 65,000 is safer because it's unbiased.[12] Either way, the Korean population of Los Angeles County is roughly 1 percent of the county total, a rule of thumb which neatly simplifies analysis.

The proliferation of Korean businesses in Los Angeles is obvious to the eye, especially along Olympic Boulevard in the heart of the city's developing Koreatown. Anyone can see that this newcomer minority has occupied more than their share of the city's storefronts and hamburger stands. Estimates of the Korean business population have thus far depended upon counting Hangul-lettered storefronts in Koreatown.[13] This research has indicated that Koreatown has more ethnic businesses than Little Tokyo, Chinatown, or the Fairfax Avenue kosher district. The finding is significant but obviously ignores the Korean businesses located outside Koreatown as well as businesses that lack storefronts facing the street. Partially to surmount this obstacle, we acquired copies of bilingual business and telephone directories compiled by a Korean publishing firm as a commercial venture. The 1975 Korean Business Directory and its 1976 supplement were coded for conformity to the Standard Industrial Classification employed by the U.S. Department of Commerce to describe the Los Angeles County business population.[14] Admittedly, the Korean directories understate the number of Korean firms doing business outside of Koreatown. Korean informants assured us that businessmen whose clientele were non-Korean were less likely than Koreatown businessmen to list their firm in the ethnic business directory, even though listing was free. Nonetheless, our procedure is a great improvement upon the method of counting storefronts in Koreatown and offers, in addition, the possibility of comparing the Korean business population to the county total.

Some results of this comparison appear in table 2.1. Interpretation of these data must be judicious. Striking overrepresentation of Koreans does appear in retail trade. Indeed, the margin of Korean overrepresentation in this industry (195 percent of the expected number) exceeds the margin of Chinese and Japanese overrepresentation (131 percent) in

TABLE 2.1   Korean Businesses in Los Angeles County, 1975

Industry	Korean Business Directory, 1975	Los Angeles County, 1973	Index (100 = Expected)
Agriculture	–	1,082	–
Contract construction	10	8,292	12.99
Manufacturing	34	16,831	21.48
Transportation and public utilities	20	3,140	68.74
Wholesale	102	10,729	102.04
Retail trade	550	30,584	193.12
Finance, insurance and real estate	45	11,306	22.25
Services	382	64,951	75.66
All industries	1142	127,706	83.49
Estimated base populations	65,000	6,980,000	

Sources: *Korean Business Directory 1975* (Los Angeles: Keys, 1975); U.S. Department of Commerce, Bureau of the Census. *County Business Patterns, 1973: California CBP-73-6* (Washington, D.C.: Government Printing Office, 1975), pp. 62ff.

1929—yet small business has been in continuous decline since 1929. Table 2.1 also indicates that Koreans are overrepresented in wholesale trade, too, although that margin of overrepresentation is minimal. On the other hand, our data do not support the media characterization of Koreans in Los Angeles as "successful in business." On the contrary, our data indicate that Koreans are underrepresented in most industries and that all their firms do not represent a full 1 percent of the county's business population. Therefore, Koreans have not struck it rich in business or demonstrated a rags-to-riches success story in the Alger tradition. They have, however, developed nearly twice as many retail stores in proportion to their number as have other Los Angeles residents. This phenomenon is sociologically interesting, but it is altogether too common a distortion to equate overrepresentation in retail trade with "success in business."

Still, why have the Koreans opened so many retail and wholesale businesses? The complete answer to this problem is complex. As expected, disadvantage in the labor market plays a major role in Korean proprietorship: Korean newspapers, spokesmen, and informants are unanimous in this refrain. Interestingly, discrimination plays a minor role in perceived disadvantage. The biggest disadvantage is inability to speak English. Only 10 percent speak English without difficulty. Koreans cannot obtain jobs in American firms because they cannot speak English. Therefore, Koreans conclude, they must open small businesses. Of course, class background also contributes to Korean enterprise. Korean emigration derives from highly educated, Westernized, Christian strata in urban Korea. In this respect contemporary Korean immigration is altogether different from pre-World War 2 Asian immigration. Korean immigrants are among the best educated people in Korea, and their level of education is much superior to that of the average American. "The median educational level is 16 years or the equivalent of an undergraduate college education."[15] The American median is in excess of twelve years. Kim even found that 70 percent of Korean proprietors were college graduates.[16] By contrast, American proprietors have only average educational credentials.

Informants acknowledge that emigres sneak capital out of Korea in excess of the $1,000 per person limit set by Korean law. After three years in Los Angeles, the income of Koreans in Los Angeles rises above the county median.[17] By dint of strenuous saving and closeted wealth, Koreans have amassed substantial personal assets upon which they draw for business capitalization. True, California branches of Korean banks have also lent some venture capital, but this sum has been tiny in amount relative to personal saving and Small Business Administration assistance. Nonetheless, educational background, personal wealth, and labor force disadvantage have permitted Koreans to flourish in small business, even during the adverse economic conditions of 1974–75. In this respect, the contrast of Koreans and Mexicans or Blacks in Los Angeles is misleading. The displaced peasantry of Mexico and the American South are also disadvantaged in the labor force, but these rural migrants brought with them no class resources of capital or higher education to offset the disadvantage. Hence, it is no surprise that Mexican and Black people in Los Angeles have not established in proportion to their number as many business firms as have college-educated Koreans.

SOCIAL SOURCES OF KOREAN ENTERPRISE

Without discounting or disputing these or other class and disadvantage sources of Korean enterprise, the purpose of this review is only to assess the existence and presumptive importance of ethnic sources of Korean entrepreneurship. Admittedly, a full treatment of this subject would require the weighting of various factors against one another in an effort to determine how much of the margin of Korean overrepresentation each contributed. However, it is sufficient for the purpose of this preliminary review of data still under analysis to run down the social sources of Japanese and Chinese entrepreneurship before World War 2. This comparison of prewar Japanese and Chinese with contemporary Korean business enterprise can yield a preliminary determination of whether there are presumptive grounds for supposing that ethnic business is a form of collective action or whether it is, as marginal utility economics supposes, only an aggregate created by independently calculating individuals.

Rotating Credit Associations. Prewar Chinese and Japanese immigrants made extensive use of rotating credit associations for the purpose of capitalizing business enterprise as well as for consumption. As the name implies, a rotating credit association consists of a group who pool their funds on a regular basis then rotate the total sum around the group until all members have received it. The rotating credit association has a long history in Korea, too. The Koreans call the institution *kye*. Kennedy finds "no indication" of the existence of *kye* before 1500, but thinks the institution is probably ten centuries old at least. Oh simply declares the *kye* "hundreds of years old."[18] Either way, this cooperative financial institution has a firm place in the cultural repertoire of Korean people.

However, the popularity of *kye* in Korea waxes and wanes in response to situational influences. Since World War 2, its popularity has increased to the point that their proliferation is seen as an obstacle to the consolidation of mainstream financial institutions.[19] Several sample surveys have documented the remarkable popularity of *kye* among urban Koreans. A 1963 survey disclosed that 43.7 percent of Korean households were members of various *kyes*. Oh's sample survey in 1971 reported 65.8 percent of households as active *kye* members. Only 18.8 percent of households had never been *kye* members. Member households invested approximately 26 percent of their monthly incomes in *kye*, an astounding rate of saving.[20] A Bank of Korea survey in 1969 disclosed that 72.3 percent of respondents were active *kye* members. Surprisingly, Kennedy's research found that Koreans with higher income and education were more likely to belong to *kye* than those with lower income and education and were also more likely to belong to more *kye* per individual. However, multiple *kye* membership is the standard practice among all strata of Korean society. Higher status Koreans are also those most likely to emigrate to the United States.

Several types of *kye* exist. Kennedy distinguishes five.[21] One of these was work-sharing and nonfinancial. Two involved mutual aid for consumption, especially weddings and funerals. The "industry *kye*" and "moneymaking" *kye* involved the payment of interest within the membership group and the investment of portions in farm or business. Memberships in a *kye* usually number about thirty, and, as elsewhere, members are typically kinsmen, friends, neighbors, or alumni of an educational institution. Kennedy attributes "the tendency to core" to the institutional necessity for mutual "trust which is the key to success."[22]

The *kye* is a popular financial institution among Los Angeles Koreans, too. With one or two exceptions, every Korean we have interviewed since 1975 has acknowledged the existence in Los Angeles of rotating credit associations, called this association *kye*, and known someone who is participating if not participating himself or herself. The largest *kye* we learned about circulates a rotating fund of $20,000 among 40-50 members, each of whom contributes $400 monthly over a fifty-month period. Consumer purchases are the commonest usage. Substantial conviviality accompanies many *kye*. Restaurants are common meeting places in Los Angeles as in Seoul. When shares are taken, recipients commonly apply as much as $200 of their net to providing food, drink, and entertainment for associates.

An illuminating progression turned up. In 1975, a Korean businessman told us he was past president of the Na U Club. The members of this club pool money for investment in the stock and bond market. In 1975, their portfolio amounted to $100,000, which our informant called "small potatoes" for this sort of group. Groups of this sort are common among Korean businessmen, he stated. The respondent's reluctance to describe in greater detail the workings of this institution make its classification problematic, but it appears to correspond to what Kennedy called an "investment *kye*."

In March, 1977, the Na U Club met at Hoban Restaurant in Koreatown, and the president announced the club's intention to form a "finance company" with a member-subscribed capital of $500,000. Describing the

Na U Club as "a fraternity of Korean businessmen," *The Korea Times* reported that the new finance company would devote itself to "helping Korean immigrants operate small and medium-size business firms."[23] Of course, this company is not philanthropic; the club's member-investors plan to collect interest from borrowers. Nonetheless, the club's intervention created an investment fund which would not otherwise have been available to Korean immigrants: Koreans are eligible to borrow this money. Thus, what began as a fraternity of rich businessmen turned into an ethnic business resource.

What is the utility of the *kye* for Korean small business? Oh reported that 40 percent of *kye* members in Korea used their portions for investment, but only 15 percent invested in a business.[24] Although a minority of *kye* members, business investors evidently made a significant contribution to the financing of small business in Korea. However, preliminary evidence does not indicate that money obtained in the *kye* moves directly into the capitalization of business in America. Kim carried out an enumeration of Hangul storefronts in Koreatown. He found no evidence that Korean proprietors were using *kye* for purposes of business capitalization. The principal sources of investment capital were savings brought from Korea, SBA loans, and a thrifty life in America. H. Kim compiled a list of fifty Korean firms in four U.S. cities. Of those questioned, only one acknowledged using *kye* as a source of capital for business investment.[25]

Preliminary though they are, these findings nonetheless suggest that *kye* is less important in Los Angeles than in Korea and also less influential in Asian-American business life today than were rotating credit associations among prewar Chinese and Japanese. Additional grounds support this inference. First, institutional credit is much easier for Koreans to obtain in Los Angeles than in Korea. As nonwhites, Koreans have access to government-funded business assistance organizations which offer counseling and low-cost business capital. For example, Asian, Inc. is a nonprofit organization funded by the U.S. Commerce Department. The corporation guarantees 90 percent of business loans for eligible borrowers. Koreans have been outstandingly successful too in obtaining low-interest loans from the Small Business Administration. Ironically, public intervention on behalf of their business prospects benefits only immigrants: Koreans who stay in Korea obtain no minority privileges there. Moreover, U.S. government solicitude for nonwhite business only began in the Nixon Administration as a result of Republican platform endorsement of "black capitalism." Prewar Asian immigrants could look to the U.S. government for no such help. Additionally, the elimination of discriminatory practices in American banking and even the proliferation of minority-owned banks have rendered mainstream financial intermediaries more reliable sources of credit to Asians than they were before World War 2. Public subsidies, accommodating bankers, and government contracts make venture capital easier for Asians to obtain through institutional channels and thus tend to reduce the Koreans' necessity to resort to *kye*.

However, the immigrants' personal savings are the central source. Korean immigrants arrive in the United States with undisclosed but substantial capital sums for business investment here. Personal fortune is the principal source of the money Koreans invest here; SBA loans rank a distant second.[26] Prewar Chinese and Japanese peasants did not arrive in the United States with a personal fortune. These people were of humbler social origin in their own societies. Hence, there is reason to suppose that affluent Koreans rely more upon their personal fortune than did prewar Asian businessmen who more frequently had to employ the rotating credit association for business capital.

How much Koreans need ethnic financial cooperation depends upon how disadvantaged they are in American capital markets. By virtue of their personal wealth and nonwhite status, a political asset, Korean small businessmen today occupy a more privileged position in American capital markets than American counterparts. In this sense, Koreans need ethnic financial cooperation less than most other groups. Therefore, there is no ground for surprise that they appear to cooperate less in finance than did prewar Asians who were genuinely disadvantaged. Despite these unpropitious circumstances, the financial behavior of Los Angeles Koreans still reveals unambiguous dimensions of ethnic cooperation. Confronting the same market opportunities, 65,000 randomly selected bourgeois of Los Angeles would not cooperate in finance by means of a *kye*, the Na U Club, or its ethnically exclusive loan company. Some financial behavior of Los Angeles Koreans is collective and cultural in the sense earlier defined.

Nepotistic Trade Guilds. Prewar Japanese and Chinese operated numerous guild-like associations of tradesmen. These particularistic associations often intervened in business life to regulate the size of the business population in the trade (i.e., exclude outgroups), inhibit price competition, monitor hours and work conditions, assist members in distress, declare holidays, and unite in politics. Contemporaries believed that the trade guilds contributed to the Asian communities' commercial prosperity. Regional, locality, and kinship solidarities provided the basis of association of these trade guilds as of prewar Asian communities in general. However, *Landsmannschaften* are rare among Koreans in Los Angeles. Terry and Stull describe surname associations, but our research has not confirmed their existence, much less their significance.[27] In these twin respects, Koreans differ markedly from prewar Asians. On the other hand, high school and college alumni associations are very significant, quasi-ascriptive bases of social association among Koreans. Apparently alumni solidarities carry over to the business world. Some respondents indicated that alumni are more likely to form business partnerships. More than 100 Protestant churches (mostly Korean Methodist and Presbyterian) exist. This proliferation represents a rate nearly eight times greater than among residents of Los Angeles in general (Table 2.2). The *New Korea* reported that churches were "of the evangelistic type which concentrate on the fellowship among churchgoers," but we found little fellowship.[28] Ministers we interviewed gave a deprecatory account of the communicants' solidarity. The ministers acknowledge a frantic competition for congregants. To attract congregants the clergy offer social services, especially translation, driver education, counseling, and job referral. Perhaps as a result, congregational solidarities are nebulous. They do not carry over to business life.

Although apparently free of borrowed locality, kinship, or religious solidarities (we are uncertain about alumni connections), numerous business and professional associations do exist among Los Angeles Koreans. Indeed, these associations are, in proportion to population, between three and thirteen times more numerous among Koreans than other Los Angeles residents (Table 2.2). At the same time, the memberships of these associations are small, and in no case do memberships include more than one-fifth of Korean firms actually engaged in the trade. Many associations are little more than a name and slate of officers. The officers of these associations have even been reticent about discussing membership statistics in the apparent belief that modest membership rolls diminished the importance of their group as well as the prestige of their office. However, when pressed, association spokesmen have acknowledged the restricted size of their memberships and the modest or negligible role their association accordingly has been able to play in the life of the trade. "There are no formal controls by any organized market association."[29] Interestingly, Korean association spokesmen recurrently compare their fledgling organizations to powerful trade and commerce bodies they enviously perceive in the Japanese and especially the Chinese communities. These evidently serve as models for Korean business leaders who look forward to achieving for their association the level of imperative coordination other Asians have already achieved.

In view of the modest membership of Korean business and commercial associations, these bodies can hardly be assigned responsibility for the existing overrepresentation of Koreans in business. Their contribution in this respect is probably positive but small nevertheless. On the contrary, we have the impression that the associations are desperately trying to attain control of the bustle of activity at the grass-roots level but that they have thus far been unable to develop the imperative controls they envision. Were they ever to succeed, the associations would be in a position to make a strong contribution to the prosperity and number of Korean firms in the various trades. But associations cannot be assigned responsibility for creating the existing business system. Here the character of the Korean immigrants has imported only a propensity for organization, but this propensity has set in motion long-range possibilities whose actual outcome is still in doubt.

TABLE 2.2 Korean Voluntary Associations in Los Angeles County, 1975

Type of Association	Number	Index (100 = Expected)
Business associations	11	317.9
Professional membership organizations	12	1304.3
Civic, social and fraternal associations	79	1083.9
Religious organizations	79	780.6
Charitable organizations	10	638.6
Nonprofit membership organizations	6	347.8

Sources: for number: *Korean Business Directory, 1975* (Los Angeles: Keys, 1975); for index: U.S. Department of Commerce, Bureau of the Census, *County Business Patterns, 1973: California CBP-73-6* (Washington, D.C.: Government Printing Office, 1975).

Family Firms. Cohesive nuclear and extended families formed the nuclei of many Asian firms before World War 2. Naturally, this cohesion is a sociological feature of East Asian culture, but its consequences apparently included the stimulation of multiple-owner business firms. True, the family firm and family farm are basic units of small business in the American business tradition, too. However, cultural traditions which keep together a higher proportion of husband-wife families lay the basis for a greater number of family firms. Additionally, the extended family system characteristic of the Chinese gave their firms easy access to a kinship pool whose members frequently operated as partners. Chinese firms had more owners than non-Chinese firms, and they hired fewer unrelated "hands."

Since World War 2, traditional extended families have become less common in urban Japan and Korea. This trend is pronounced among the educated, Christian, and Westernized strata from which Korean migrants were chiefly recruited. Even so, our preliminary analysis tends to show that Asian firms in general have more owners than non-Asian firms (Table 2.3).

TABLE 2.3 Ethnicity of Firms by Business Types in Hollywood Liquor Industry, 1975 (percent)

Business Ownership	Korean	Chinese	Japanese	All Businesses
Corporation	5.5	13.3	11.7	10.2
One owner	41.8	36.2	36.4	52.7
Two owners	50.5	43.8	45.5	33.9
Three or more owners	2.3	6.7	6.5	3.2
TOTAL	100	100	100	100
NUMBER	220	105	77	2,112

Source: Compiled by the author.

These data represent a complete tabulation of all applicants and transferrors who came before the Department of Alcoholic Beverage Control's Hollywood Division in 1975. Therefore, this data base does not provide a representative cross-section of liquor licensees in Hollywood. Instead, the transferrors' list includes all persons who sold a liquor license in 1975; the applicants list includes all new license applicants, all license purchasers, and all petitioners for administrative changes in an existing license. Of these, new applicants and license purchasers represented about 70 percent. The ethnicity of firms we inferred from the ethnicity of owners' surname. Although this data base does not represent a representative sample of Hollywood liquor licensees, the data do offer, we feel, a fair basis for estimating types of firms characteristic of ethnic groups in this retail industry. The reason is the restrictions the Department of Alcoholic Beverage places upon sale, relocation, or application for liquor licenses. No one is permitted to sell liquor without a license, and all changes in license status must pass through the ABC bureaucracy. The ABC bureaucracy is a bottleneck through which all licensees must pass at one time or another. Hence, there is no reason to suppose that the active firms in the ABC file for 1975 differed in respect to size composition from the inactive.

In general, the Asian-owned firms (Chinese, Japanese, Korean) reported fewer single-owner businesses than did all firms (Table 2.3). This difference characterized both applicant and transferror pools. Similarly,

TABLE 2.4 Same Surnames of Multiple Applicants and Transferrors and Predominate Ethnicity of Firms in Hollywood Liquor Industry, 1975

	Korean	Chinese	Japanese	All Persons
Multiple Applicants				
All same surname (%)	70.5	79.2	59.4	59.0
Number	95	48	32	700
Multiple transferrors				
All same surname (%)	96.2	92.9	100	88.7
Number	26	14	13	248

Source: Compiled by the author.

Asian firms indicated higher proportions of two-owner firms than liquor firms in general. The higher proportion of two-owner firms among Asians probably results from the influence of kinship, especially the husband-wife firm. Table 2.4 shows that multiple-owner firms were usually owned by persons sharing the same surname. These are presumably husband and wife in nearly all cases. Interestingly, the preponderance of same-surname pairs was greater among Asian than among all firms. This difference indicates that multiple-owner Asian firms were more likely than non-Asian to be "mom and pop" or, at least, kinship firms. Conversely, non-Asians were somewhat more likely to establish multiple ownerships by associations of persons with different surnames. However, Asian-non-Asian differences in this regard are slighter than the overwhelming propensity of all multiple ownership firms to enlist persons bearing the same surname.

Interesting differences between the Koreans and the other Asians also appear in table 2.3. Japanese and especially Chinese firms were much more likely to have three or more owners than were liquor firms in general. The imbalance confirms the view, based on prewar evidence, that Japanese and Chinese firms had more owners than non-Asian firms. But the Koreans do not reflect this Asiatic style of firm ownership. On the contrary, Korean firms are most numerous at the two-person (husband-wife) level, but they are actually fewer than expected among the three or more owner category. Thus, liquor industry data do not support the hypothesis that Korean firms benefit from the assistance of extended kinship systems; nor have our informants given us any reason to believe they did. The influence of the kinship system among the Koreans appears to concentrate at the two-person level, causing a proliferation of husband-wife firms.

These liquor industry results do show convincingly that Asians less frequently enter business as individuals than do others and that the two-person firm and multiple-owner firms predominate among Asians. Kinship systems (and demography) probably account for this Asian-American difference, but, whatever the cause, the effect reflects qualities of ethnic life. These qualities are increasing the size of Asian firm membership with consequences that are presumably advantageous, although the data in tables 2.3 and 2.4 do not strictly permit this last inference. Nonetheless, the data do offer grounds for asserting that orthodox cultural characteristics of East Asians in general (kinship systems) are affecting the structure and size of Los Angeles firms. Here is support for the view that cultural repertoires differentiate the ethnic business population.

Ethnic Homogeneity of Business Sales. When a buyer and seller are coethnics, their transaction is ethnically homogeneous. When buyer and seller are ethnically different, their transaction is ethnically heterogeneous. Thus, when Lopez sells his business to Mendoza, their transaction is ethnically homogeneous because both are Spanish. When, however, Lopez sells his business to Wong their transaction is ethnically heterogeneous because Lopez is Spanish and Wong is Chinese. Insofar as business owners operate as isolated, profit-maximizing individuals, they presumably transfer businesses without reference to ethnic background. Under this circumstance, business sales among coethnics ought to be no more frequent than the proportion of coethnics in the buyer or seller population. Conversely, strong preferences for coethnics in business sales are evidence that ethnicity influences the conduct of business.

Evidence bearing on ethnic homogeneity of business sales among prewar Asians is only indirect. First, there is a presumption of homogeneity arising from the clustering of Chinese and Japanese in the same trades. For example, Chinese hand laundries were frequently sold, but the ethnic identity of the laundry trade was so strong that non-Chinese virtually never purchased a Chinese hand laundry. Therefore, perfect homogeneity characterized the sales of Chinese laundries. Similar considerations apply to Japanese in truck gardening, gardening, and retail groceries. Second, Chinese commercial institutions had elaborated informal practices which strongly encouraged ethnic homogeneity. These practices included the requirement of Chinese witnesses at business sales, the collection of "goodwill" taxes by associations, and the permission of trade guilds to transfer ownership.[30] These requirements tended to enforce homogeneously Chinese participation in business transfer, thus excluding out-groups and protecting the Chinese community's stock of viable small businesses. The Japanese did not achieve an equivalent level of institutional control so this inference does not apply to them in equal measure.

The retail liquor industry in Hollywood offers considerably stronger and more direct evidence of ethnic homogeneity in business sales than anything previously available. The evidence is the complete record of all sales and purchases of liquor businesses (taverns, markets, restaurants, package stores purveying beer, wine, or spirits) in Hollywood during 1975. This record is complete because it is taken from the files of the Department of Alcoholic Beverage Control. California law assigns this agency statutory responsibility for investigating and authorizing all sales of liquor licenses. Although the department collects no ethnic information, the surnames of buyers and sellers offered a reliable basis for inferring the ethnicity of Asians.

The ethnic homogeneity of business transfers was extreme (Table 2.5). For example, 79 percent of Korean sellers found Korean buyers even though Koreans represented only 15 percent of all buyers. Similarly, 70 percent of Chinese sellers found Chinese buyers even though Chinese represented only 7 percent of all buyers. Conversely, "all other" persons were 74.4 percent of buyers, but this 74.4 percent accounted for only 7.5 percent of purchasers of Korean businesses and 11.1 percent of purchasers of Chinese businesses. This ethnic homogeneity of transactions greatly exceeds chance levels and is inexplicable on the assumption that buyers and sellers operate as isolated individuals in a market.

Two explanations obtrude. One is enhanced trust resulting from the mutual sympathy of coethnics: insofar as buyers trust coethnics more than others, they have a motive to seek out a coethnic seller less likely to cheat them. A second is convenience. Ethnics associate with one another and read the ethnic press. Ethnic social circuits carry information about available businesses so coethnics easily find one another. The result is ethnic homogeneity of business transfer. True, the process of information transmittal is utilitarian—ethnics choose the easiest modality. At the same time, the propensity of ethnics to associate with one another, a purely sociological characteristic, has created the communications matrix engendering this utilitarian behavior. Naturally, convenience and trust need not exclude one another: far more likely, in fact, ethnics prefer one another because they are more convenient to locate as well as more trustworthy. Either way, the process of business transfer reveals decisive preferences for coethnics which are impossible to explain without acknowledgment of the role of ethnicity in commerce.

TABLE 2.5 Ethnic Homogeneity of Liquor License Transfers in Hollywood, California, 1975 (percentages)

Buyers	Sellers			Buyers as % All Buyers
	Korean	Chinese	Japanese	
Korean	79.0	18.5	16.7	15.0
Chinese	9.0	70.4	0.0	6.7
Japanese	4.5	0.0	50.0	3.9
All Other	7.5	11.1	33.3	74.4
Total	100	100	100	100
Number	67	27	18	641

Source: Compiled by the editor.

Immigrant Motivations and Values. Prewar Chinese and Japanese immigrants were often sojourners who intended to return to their Asian homeland after accumulating sufficient money in the United States. The sojourners naturally worked hard and saved their money in anticipation of their repatriation. Hard work and thrift gave the Asians an edge in certain industries. Therefore, Bonacich concluded that sojourning had actually produced the middleman business system in which the Asian immigrants chiefly worked.[31] In this sense, sojourning set in motion situational forces which produced ethnic entrepreneurship: interaction of sojourning Asians and the native population combined to produce this effect which was not an emanation of deeply rooted cultural propensities of the Asian immigrants.

Koreans in Los Angeles have no intention of repatriation to Korea. They regard themselves as permanently in the United States. Therefore, sojourning plays no role in their ethnic commerce. On the other hand, Koreans still regard themselves as exceptionally hardworking, thrifty, and ambitious. True, wages in South Korea are only one-tenth those in the United States. Hence, Koreans regard U.S. wages, even in menial jobs, as highly attractive. Still, international wage disparities probably do not account for Korean entrepreneurship because other Asian (Philippines) and non-Asian (Mexico) countries send immigrants from low-wage areas who do not develop an ethnic business system. Many Koreans attribute their countrymen's industry and ambition to relative deprivation. That is, the Koreans now in America were once well educated and professional people in a status-conscious Asian society. In the United States their real wages are higher, but their jobs are menial and social prestige comparably low. Therefore, Koreans in America have a motive to regain the social prestige they held in Korea, and they work hard to this end.

Whatever the causes, we have the impression that Koreans do work longer hours than other Americans and that they are more frugal. These are admirable qualifications for small business enterprise in which the hours of labor are typically long and the money return meager. Indeed, but for these qualities, Koreans would have no economic basis in Los Angeles other than wage earning, and the general level of unemployment in the county has exceeded 7 percent for several years. Are industry and frugality imported cultural traits of Koreans or complex emergents from the migrants' class, ethnic, and political situation? The phenomenal industrial growth of Korea since 1967 has been based upon the hard work and dedication of Korean people. One supposes that these qualities carry over to the emigrants. On the other hand, the Koreans have not had a reputation for intelligence and industry for very long:

Korean productive energy tends to be intermittent rather than sustained. In consequence, the people have not shared the reputation for industriousness given to both Japanese and Chinese, or Germans in the West. Also the Korean mind does not have the intellectual turn, that quality of consistent willingness to reason which, for example, distinguished the Chinese or the Jews.[32]

The abrupt change of image of Koreans in the last decade is hard for a value explanation to comprehend because, as Ogburn liked to observe, a change cannot be explained by a constant. For this reason, the contribution of imported values to Korean enterprise is unproven—but not to be dismissed without additional evidence. On the other hand, there is ample sign that Koreans have motivations to work which distinguish them from other Americans and encourage their enterprise. Koreans work long hours, live frugally, and trade their way up the hierarchy of ethnic industries which stretches from corner grocery stores through gas stations, hamburger stands, and sewing shops, to real estate speculation, the current apex. The motivations of Koreans reflected shared experience and are, therefore, ethnic if only in a reactive sense. In terms of motivations to work, Koreans are a group apart from other Angelenos.

CONCLUSION

Why are Koreans in Los Angeles so heavily engaged in retail and wholesale business? A major contributing factor is the happy combination of labor force disadvantage and government subsidies for nonwhite business on one side and personal wealth and strong educational background on the other. The class background (education, wealth) of the Koreans provides able individuals. The unfavorable labor market and U.S. government policy provide motive and opportunity for business enterprise. One might argue that, given these situational encouragements, any rabble of wealthy immigrants would wind up in business self-employment today. Thus conceived, the explanation of Korean overrepresentation in commerce requires no invocation of ethnic business style, ethnic solidarity, or ethnic culture.

This economistic conclusion is a systematic distortion of a complex reality in the narrow interest of conceptual simplicity. In actuality, class and political determinants share influence with strictly ethnic characteristics of the Korean people. That is, the motivations and values, the social networks, clubs and churches, the family system, and modalities of financial cooperation constitute real and important influences upon the business conduct of Koreans. A polyglot amalgam of rich immigrants from a diversity of lands might share the class background and political advantage which encourage Korean enterprise in America today. However, such an amalgam would by definition lack the cohesion and specifically Korean character of the Korean people in Los Angeles. Education and wealth are class characteristics which can become the property of individuals. But the ethnic solidarity and culture of the Korean people reside in the community. Individuals share the business resources and participate in its benefits by virtue of ethnic identity and participation.

Comparing contemporary Koreans with prewar Japanese and Chinese, the grossest conclusion is the persistence of collective resources in ethnic entrepreneurship. Despite the great changes in the American polity and business system and the deteriorating position of small business, the Korean ethnic group still mobilizes resources which Korean individuals can then exploit to good effect in commerce. In this sense, the Korean ethnic community provides a matrix within which Korean individuals can find individual and collective resources from which to assure their own livelihood and the social mobility of the American-born generation. This conception of collective resources encompass the calculating individualism of marginal utility economics but encases this phenomenon in a social integument.

However, the comparison of Koreans and prewar Asians also turns up some intergroup differences. In general, the Koreans in Los Angeles today operate in nuclear family units whereas the prewar Asians operated much more frequently in larger units of clan, regional association, and trade guild. Compared to previous generations of Asian business owners, Koreans are Westernized, Protestant, and individualistic. The causes of these differences are apparent. As Lyman has emphasized, the imbalanced (heavily male) sex ratios of prewar Chinese and Japanese sojourners reduced the salience of the nuclear family.[33] Clan and regional associations took over the functions otherwise performed by nuclear families so that, especially in the Chinese case, the business enterprise of the immigrants transpired under the aegis of powerful and highly visible institutional controls. The non-sojourning Koreans in Los Angeles do not suffer an imbalanced sex ratio so they have no comparable propensity to substitute institutions for nuclear families. Therefore, the institutions of the Koreans, although numerous, are incomparably weaker in their mundane controls over business enterprise than were those of prewar Asians. Additionally, the Westernized and Christian Koreans have embraced religious values which are in origin Protestant, even Calvinist. The individualistic ethos these impart augments the general decline of extended kinship in the Far East since World War 2. Highly educated and Westernized, Korean immigrants today naturally seem more Westernized and ready for cultural assimilation than did generations of nearly illiterate and culturally conservative Asian sojourners in prewar California.

A taxonomy of ethnic influences upon Korean business (Table 2.6) reveals a tangled mixture of orthodox and reactive, collective, and individual influences. Yet, complex as it is, the table is an analytic simplification of a fluid reality. For example, Korean churches have a continuous impact upon the persistence of distinctively Korean values, and vice-versa. Nonetheless, the table illustrates the range and mixture of influences actually affecting Korean enterprise. The data thus summarized argue against the orthodox individualistic interpretation of business enterprise. True, values and motivations do, as the orthodoxy proposes, support ethnic business by encouraging individuals to fan out in solitary pursuit of profit. However, an orthodox, individualistic interpretation of Korean business in Los Angeles altogether ignores the still important collective and reactive dimensions of this complex phenomenon. Therefore sociological orthodoxy is too limited a view of ethnic business enterprise.

TABLE 2.6   Ethnic Influences on Korean Business in Los Angeles: A Taxonomy

Business Style	Ethnic Origins	
	Orthodox	Reactive
Collective	*kye* Korean churches alumni clubs family system	Na U Club finance company trade associations ethnic newspapers social networks reflecting ethnic solidarity
Individual	Korean cultural values and traditional motivations to work	Relative deprivation arising from immigration to high-wage country

Source: Compiled by the editor.

Just taking account of the collective and reactive dimensions of ethnic business is a big improvement upon orthodoxy. But bigger issues lurk behind these middling ones. Sociological studies of entrepreneurship have proceeded upon the presumption that ethnic solidarities taper into oblivion in the face of the economic and cultural rationalization of modernity. This is a special case of the general view of ethnicity as a residual and declining force in advanced societies. Hechter has recently demonstrated how dubious is this long-cherished assumption.[34] Korean business activity also has a cautionary effect upon the orthodox view that ethnic solidarities have no place in advanced economies. These solidarities still play a substantial role in Korean business today. True, the Korean results do not entirely contradict the modernization hypothesis. After all, Koreans offer a closer resemblance to individualistic orthodoxy than did Asian businessmen of a generation earlier. Thus, the direction of observed change has been the predicted one. On the other hand, the rate of change is slower than predicted, and the actual correspondence between the Korean business system and individualistic orthodoxy is less than expected. There are also grounds for arguing that the evolution of American society, the most advanced industrial society of the world, created structural needs for groups like Koreans who fill systematic gaps in welfare capitalism.[35] The cautionary conclusion of this research in progress is, therefore, that even if modernization theory be in principle correct, the rate of change is slower than expected, actual change to date much less, and ethnicity likely to remain an independent force in economic and social life for a long time to come. Conceptualizations of ethnic business activity still need to take into account its collective and reactive dimensions.

LAWRENCE A. LOVELL-TROY

CLAN STRUCTURE AND ECONOMIC ACTIVITY
The Case of Greeks in Small Business Enterprise

A common theme in American culture is that small business ownership is an expression of the agrarian ideal of individualism. As such, many Americans conceive of entrepreneurship as a manifestation of the American dream and aspire individually toward this status. Actually, there is much in American history to support these ideas. For example, C. Wright Mills referred to American society during the first century of its existence as being characterized by independent proprietors and farmers pursuing their material interests in a capitalist system of self-balancing competition. Referring to this as a society of small entrepreneurs, Mills claims that its single most important feature was that a substantial proportion of the American people owned the property with which they earned their living.[1]

Although the social and economic facts of existence in America have changed through the years, such that the independent proprietor is no longer characteristic of many Americans, the ideology which arose early in American history has not changed significantly. Economic adaptations to society are still often seen in individualistic terms. Indeed, the "self-made man" who takes a risk, opens a business, and attains success is still the epitome of the American dream and is revered as the individualistic symbol of the success of the capitalist economy.

This essay is a revised version of a chapter in the author's doctoral dissertation. The author wishes to acknowledge the financial assistance provided by the Graduate School of the University of Connecticut which facilitated the collection of much of the data. Harold Abramson, Scott Cummings, William D'Antonio, Floyd Dotson, and Mary Lovell-Troy offered helpful suggestions on various drafts of this essay.

This individualistic view of economics is found in social and economic theory as well. For example, Schumpeter set the tone for much economic research on entrepreneurship by emphasizing the importance of the individual, innovating entrepreneur in economic development.[2] Similarly, Weber's analysis of Calvinist sectarians in the forefront of European economic development led other researchers to seek out other, comparable cultural supports for individualistic economic activity, ultimately disregarding much historical evidence for collective approaches to economics.[3]

Importantly, the experience of immigrants in the United States has often been seen as offering support for the individualistic conception of the American dream. For example, Vidich and Bensman argue:

In responding to the opportunities that America offered, the immigrant affirmed the validity of and gave added impetus to the economic optimism and expansiveness that characterized an expanding industrial society. In being converts to the American way, the immigrants supported and deepened the American dream. They became true Americans.[4]

The individualistic conception of the American dream notwithstanding, some research of late has suggested the importance of collective approaches to small business ownership, especially among ethnic groups. Summarizing a large body of comparative literature, Edna Bonacich has commented: "Communal solidarity plays an important role in the economic position of middleman groups. Family, regional, dialect, sect, and ultimately ethnic ties are used for preferential economic treatment. The primordial tie of blood provides a basis for trust, and is reinforced by multi-purpose formal and informal associations."[5] Bonacich is arguing here that ethnic groups frequently use the collective supports found in their ethnic ties to assist them in economic adaptation. Contrary to the paradigm of entrepreneurship based on individualism, then, Bonacich is suggesting a collective response to economic opportunity.

Ivan Light has also specified collective responses to economic opportunity by describing the way in which the social organization of Japanese and Chinese immigrants facilitated small business ownership.[6] Light found that the most important units of social organization among the Japanese and Chinese in the United States, the *ken* and the *fong*, respectively, were actually organizations of clans based on the village, the region, and common kinship ties. Immigrants used the trust and morality ascriptively based in the clans to create and regulate small business activity. Since units of social structure which include large numbers of individuals defined as kin are common in Oriental societies, Light has shown that these immigrants used collective bases of morality, vested in their culture, to organize their economic activity in this country. Moreover, by focusing on the unbalanced sex ratios, the lack of a nuclear family structure, and the frequent discrimination which these immigrants faced, Light has shown the ways in which the Oriental ethnic groups developed reactive cultural characteristics and social structures to support further their entrepreneurial aspirations.

Therefore, recent research has called into question an exclusively individualistic conception of entrepreneurship by focusing on collective economic activity and thereby has cast doubt upon the individualistic conception of the American dream. The question remains, however, whether other ethnic groups in the United States also show collective responses to economic opportunity and, if so, are there intergroup differences in economic activity which nonetheless could still be considered collective? Moreover, if there are features in the culture of ethnic groups, whether orthodox or reactive in Light's terms, which assist ethnic group members in their economic adaptation to American society, how are they implemented; that is, how, specifically, do cultural supports facilitate small business ownership?

GREEKS IN SMALL BUSINESS

A good test of these issues may be the case of Greeks. Greeks have been migrating to the United States in large numbers since the turn of the twentieth century, with approximately 500,000 arriving between 1900 and 1924.[7] Significant numbers of Greeks also arrived in the United States as World War 2 refugees and displaced persons; and the 1965 liberalization of the U.S. immigration laws has led to what some have called a "new wave," with over 89,000 being admitted between 1967 and 1972.[8]

Throughout the twentieth century, Greeks have settled predominately in the urban centers of the Northeast and the Midwest and have been consistently concentrated occupationally in small business.[9] Greek street peddlers, shoeshine parlors, florists, fruit and vegetable peddlers, and confectionary stores were all extremely common throughout the region, both within the Greek communities and as isolated ethnic entrepreneurs.

The restaurant business, however, has been the most important trade to Greeks throughout the years. The expansion of the urban centers in which the Greeks settled created a need for businesses which catered particularly to the lunch needs of workers; and the increase in disposable income among the urban population in general created favorable conditions for the development of full-service, albeit often small, restaurants.

References to Greek restaurants are common throughout the literature, with particular reports from around 1920 of Greek lunchrooms in New York and restaurants in Chicago, San Francisco, and Tacoma, as well as in New Haven in the 1930s.[10] National statistics from the 1950s found Greeks still concentrated as workers and owners in restaurant businesses after World War 2, and others from 1970 have indicated that recent immigrants have continued the pattern.[11]

By the 1970s, however, inflation and an increasingly mobile population had undermined the conditions which had formerly been favorable to the establishment of full-service restaurants, and post-World War 2 Greek immigrants began to turn to the fast food industry. In New England, Greeks opened pizza businesses. Elsewhere, I reported data collected in Connecticut which indicate that up to 80 percent of the Greek immigrant families in the Greek communities in that state are self-employed in small businesses, with as many as 76 percent of them in the pizza business. Although I did not collect data on all Greeks in the state, a total of 58 percent of the Greek immigrant families in the four communities studied were self-employed in small businesses, with 64 percent of them in the pizza business.[12] In this essay, I will discuss in some detail the extent to which the contemporary Greek concentration in the pizza business in Connecticut is a result of a collective adaptation to economic opportunities.

Traditionally, studies in the area of ethnic group economic activity have typically used aggregate, historical, or survey data. As such, they document fairly well the concentration of particular ethnic groups in small businesses and offer suggestions as to the connections between the social organization and culture of ethnic groups and the resulting economic concentration, but they leave many questions unanswered. Specifically, studies based on such data have difficulty making the detailed connections between culture and social structure, on the one hand, and the actual entry of ethnic group members into particular small businesses, the actual process by which ethnic group members receive their training, and the particular ways in which ethnic group members receive financing for their own businesses, on the other.

For example, elsewhere in this volume Light reports data on the ethnic homogeneity of liquor license transfers in Hollywood, California. While the data are impressive in that they indicate a great deal of ethnic homogeneity in such transfers, the methodology used does not allow for an in-depth understanding of the process whereby such transfers take place. Light's explanation of this homogeneity falls on the dual concepts of intra-ethnic group trust and social structural convenience. Simply stated, coethnics trust each other more than outsiders, and they associate with each other more as well. While these explanations are certainly plausible, his data reveal little information about the process.

The data I will present concerning Greeks in Connecticut were collected in 1975 using a two-stage methodology which yielded information on these unanswered questions. First, the extent of Greek concentration in the pizza business was determined by compiling lists of such businesses from the Yellow Pages of the twenty-five telephone directories in the state. The Assessor's Offices in the 107 towns in which pizza businesses were found were then contacted to learn the name of the owner of the personal property in the respective businesses. The ethnicity of the proprietors was then determined from their names.

In the second stage of the research process, I attempted to contact the proprietors of all pizza businesses within a two-county area of the state for interviews. Out of forty attempts, contacts within thirty-one nuclear families resulted in interviews with a total of forty-one Greeks in the business. These interviews elicited information on the processes by which they immigrated to the United States and ultimately came to open their own businesses. Particular attention was paid in these interviews to contacts between our respondents and other persons in the Greek communities in the state and specifically to other family members. In addition, twenty other persons knowledgeable about Greeks in business in Connecticut were interviewed, including Greek community leaders and distributors of pizza business material. In sum, through the ethnographic procedure of open-ended interviewing in a particular geographic location which includes a large number of ethnic group members in a particular business, information was obtained on the social processes by which recent immigrants initially find employment in the New World, acquire the training needed to open small businesses of their own, and arrange for capitalization of their new businesses.

SOCIAL AND ECONOMIC ORGANIZATION AMONG GREEK IMMIGRANTS

When immigrants move to a new society, they must involve themselves in the social and economic conditions of their new home. Nevertheless, the norms and values by which they interpret their new surroundings are influenced by their socialization within the culture of their previous society. Their self-conceptions as well as their interactions with their new environment change to the degree to which they begin to adapt their culturally derived definitions of reality to new conditions. Light has conceptualized these changes in culture as "reactive." In analyzing the behavior of ethnic group members in a society, therefore, attention must be focused on the culture within which they were socialized and the changes in that culture brought about by life under new conditions.

The particular aspect of culture that concerns us here is the degree to which economic responses to new conditions are shaped in a collectivist orientation, in an individualistic one, or in some mixed fashion. The two ideal types, perhaps, are seen in the contrasting cases of the Protestant sectarians analyzed by Weber, who used cultural supports to direct their economic activity in an individualistic form, and the Oriental entrepreneurs analyzed by Light, who used their cultural supports to create a collective economic response. I will argue below that Greeks in Connecticut show a somewhat mixed entrepreneurial response, not nearly so individualistic as would be predicted by traditional economic theory but not as collective as that found among Light's Orientals either.

In Greece, the most important unit of moral community is the nuclear family, and Greeks feel obligations most strongly to these individuals.[13] Obligations to others, such as members of their extended families, and to friends and neighbors, take second place and are only fulfilled when they do not infringe on the rights, duties, and obligations which they feel to their nuclear family. This, in Light's terms, is the cultural baggage, or cultural asset, that directs Greeks in a particular manner economically, and it differs sharply from the collectivist, familial obligations felt by the Orientals studied by Light.

It is the thesis of this essay that the nuclear family is the most important entrepreneurial unit among Greek immigrants in Connecticut but that these families are also united into clan structures which facilitate the entrance of the specific nuclear families into business. The clan, then, becomes the key element tying Greek immigrants and their families into larger units of ethnic social structure. Therefore, although the Greek entrepreneurial response is based fundamentally on the nuclear family and consequently might be conceived of as a version of family capitalism, the sociocultural adaptation of Greeks to American society is based on the clan structure, which provides economic assets to Greeks that would have been unavailable to isolated family units.

The Greek clan itself is a loose structure formed through the migration process. When an immigrant family sponsors its relatives for admission to Connecticut, a clan forms, centering on the original immigrant. Because of provisions in the U.S. immigration laws, sibling ties are the most important kinship ties for the migration of new immigrant families.[14] The sibling tie, therefore, becomes the primary relationship by which various nuclear families are united into clans. Moreover, as we will see below, the sibling tie also becomes the most important kinship bond within which Greeks fashion their economic adaptation.

It is important to remember, however, that while clans as units of social organization in Greek immigrant communities in Connecticut do exist and are referred to as such by the immigrants themselves, they do not command the degree of moral solidarity found in the Greek nuclear family. Immigrants feel obligations to members of their clan, particularly to those whom they have sponsored for admission to the United States, but these obligations are secondary to those felt for members of their nuclear families. Economically, this means that relatives are helped only to the degree to which such assistance will not impair the functioning of their own businesses or the profit to be made there.

In the remainder of this essay I will demonstrate the economic function of the clan structure by discussing the employment histories of several of my immigrant respondents in Connecticut within the context of their clan membership. In this way, it will become apparent that the Greek entrepreneurial pattern falls somewhere between the collectivist and the individualist extremes. Moreover, I will demonstrate that by depending on ties within one's clan and ethnic group a Greek immigrant may more easily open a small business and, therefore, may more easily realize the American dream than could Americans not so bound within the ties of ethnicity.

I have selected two specific clans from the nineteen discovered in Connecticut for discussion, based on the completeness of knowledge about the various individual nuclear families of which they are composed. In the discussion that follows I will present data which focus on three particular phases through which Greek immigrants must move on the way toward becoming self-employed: (1) finding initial employment after migration; (2) obtaining specific training in the pizza business; and (3) capitalizing one's own business. At each step, the key issue to be resolved is whether the economic response of the Greek immigrants I interviewed is more collective than individualistic. Following the presentation of these data, generalizations will be offered which will also take into account data obtained from my other respondents.[15] Through this analysis the value of the methodology used will become apparent in that it allows us to fill in tentatively the gaps in our knowledge about the specific relationship between the culture and social structure of ethnic group members and the ultimate establishment of their own businesses. We turn now to the description of the two clans selected for detailed discussion.

THE PALASSIS CLAN

In the late 1940s two brothers, Nick and Spiro Palassis, came to the United States from the Greek island of Lemnos. While in Connecticut, they both married women who were recent immigrants from the neighboring island of Samothrace. Although I could not determine what jobs Nick and Spiro previously had, they formed a partnership in 1962 and opened a pizza business in New London, Connecticut. Although I did not interview either of them directly, it is likely that they received training in the pizza business from one of the first Greek immigrants in the state to open such businesses. If this is the case, small business ownership became an option for members of this clan through the contacts which Nick or Spiro had within the Greek community. Their response was collective in the sense that they formed a partnership, thereby uniting two nuclear families economically. Nevertheless, it was more individualistic than the cases of the Orientals discussed by Light because the partnership was not enclosed within a larger unit of moral community.

This partnership lasted until 1965, when Spiro and his wife left Connecticut to return to Greece. Three years later, finding that they did not like living in Greece anymore, they returned to New London. At this time, Spiro took a job in a factory but soon left it. The push from his culture toward self-employment was apparently quite strong, and he was not satisfied working for someone else. Therefore, Spiro and his wife opened another pizza place, this one in Jewett City, a small town just north of Norwich. It is interesting to note here that Spiro did not return to his former partnership with his brother Nick but opened his own business as an individualistic economic response.

In 1962, the same year that Nick and Spiro opened their first pizza business, Nick's wife's brother, Sam Volaitis, jumped ship in Boston while in the Greek Merchant Marine. His purpose was clearly individualistic: "My sister could make invitation to bring me over. My sister was here at that time. But I came here on a ship from the Philippine Islands. I wanted adventure. I was eighteen at the time." Through his sibling tie, he was brought into the local Greek community and found a job working in a Greek-owned restaurant, making about thirty-five dollars a week. He admits that his pay was low because the owners knew he was an illegal alien and therefore did not have to pay him much. This suggests a collectivist response to employment but within an individually exploitative context. During this period Sam married an American woman but was soon reported to the immigration authorities and deported. He returned legally in 1966 as the husband of a U.S. citizen and was divorced within a few months.

When Sam returned to the United States, he already knew about the possibilities available to him in the pizza business, but he had individualized professional aspirations. Ultimately, however, the pizza business was the path of least resistance. He reported:

When I came here the second time, I worked in a factory. And I didn't want to get involved in this kind of [pizza and restaurant] business. I wanted to go to school here. So I went and registered at . . . College, and then I was going to go to another college. But I couldn't afford it. I didn't have an apartment. I didn't have a car. I didn't have anything. I had to work, and I wanted to go full-time to school, but I couldn't afford it, so I didn't do it.

So after living in Connecticut legally for six months, Sam quit school and started to work in his sister's pizza business. As during his earlier, illegal stay in Connecticut, his sibling tie was again used as an economic contact point. Soon, he became a partner by buying into his sister's business.

At the time of my interview with Sam, he had just returned from a vacation to Greece. During this visit to his hometown on Samothrace, he met and married a Greek woman. She is now working in the pizza business with her husband, brother-in-law, and sister-in-law. Another of Sam's sisters works in the pizza business on weekends, although I learned nothing else about her. In addition to Sam and Nick, there is another partner in the business named Eleftherios, but I was unable to interview this man. According to other informants, he is an immigrant from the Greek region of Epirus who first worked as a dishwasher in Nick's and Spiro's pizza place before buying in as a partner. As such, he represents an exception to the pattern of a kinship-based small business.

While Spiro Palassis and his wife were in Greece between 1965 and 1968, they sponsored Mrs. Palassis's brother and his wife, Mr. and Mrs. Theodoros Sarantos, for admission to the United States. Since their official sponsor, Mrs. Palassis, was not in the United States at the time of their immigration in 1967, the Sarantoses first went to Ohio, where Theodoros had other relatives. The only jobs they could find there, however, were as poorly paid dishwashers in Greek-owned restaurants. Sam Volaitis, who knew them on Samothrace, told them to come to New London and work in his and Nick's pizza business. In this instance a regional tie operated as a clan contact, suggesting that an Old-World friendship may be a functional equivalent to a kin tie.

A year later, Theodoros's sister and brother-in-law returned from Greece and soon opened the business in Jewett City. The Sarantoses began working for them immediately, suggesting that kinship may be stronger than Old-World friendship, nonetheless. After five years, Spiro and his wife decided once more to return to Greece, this time to retire; so Theodoros and his wife took over the business. Mr. and Mrs. Palassis, however, have kept ownership of the property to ensure a continued income from the rent paid by her brother and her sister-in-law. This transaction recalls Light's findings regarding ethnic homogeneity of liquor store sales. The fact that the Sarantoses continue to pay rent to the Palassises suggests more of an individualistic economic transaction than may be implied from Light's data.

Since the Sarantoses have become U.S. citizens, they have sponsored Mrs. Sarantos's three brothers for admission to the United States. Two of them and their wives work in the Sarantos's pizza place. The other one works in a factory. When I asked why one brother was working in a factory, Mrs. Sarantos replied: "I can't use more. I need girls, but not guys. I need plenty waitresses here. 'Cause [her brother] likes to make more money, I can't pay him more money." It is apparent, therefore, that the Sarantoses have maintained their business as an independently owned pizza house. They have brought relatives into the business as employees but only when they could afford to pay them. In all, eight people work in the Jewett City pizza business. Six are Greek, and all six are in the Sarantos's extended family: Mr. and Mrs. Sarantos and two of her brothers and their wives. The other two employees are Americans: a counterworker and a food server.

The Palassis clan includes two other nuclear families. Nick's and Spiro's sister married Angelo Demetrios in Greece, before they immigrated to Australia to work in a business with Angelo's brother. This partnership did not work out, so Nick or Spiro sponsored them to come to the United States. Once here, they expanded the network of pizza businesses in this clan by opening one, having first been trained at Nick's business in New London.

The final nuclear family to be discussed in the Palassis clan has been in Connecticut since 1958. In the late 1950s George Pappas was in the Greek Navy and was sent to the submarine base in Groton for special NATO training. While he was there, he met Mary, a second-generation Greek-American, who is Nick's and Spiro's cousin. In 1958, George and Mary went to Greece, where they were married after he obtained a discharge from the navy. They then returned to Connecticut, where George found a job in a factory, where he stayed for seven years, and Mary returned to her bookkeeping job. Their family life was characterized by a thrift which in itself is an expression of George's cultural background in Greece. He told me, "The first four years, this is no exaggeration, when both of us was working, we used to save five hundred dollars a month."

In 1965, George was refused a promotion in the factory, which he felt he deserved. He expected to be able to enter the Engineering Department, while the company would have paid him to go to school at night.

When he heard that they gave the job to somebody else, he quit. At this time, however, George and Mary were not living within a clan structure of recent immigrants; rather, their friends were second and third generation Americans of various ethnicities. Accordingly, George did not have contacts within the Greek-immigrant community which would have facilitated his entrance into the pizza business. However, he did have the cultural background of Greek ethnicity which predisposed him to self-employment in the restaurant business. Therefore, as an individual with no ethnic ties, George looked in the newspaper for a new job. He reported:

I go home, pick up the day's paper. "Luncheonette for sale." I come down here. "How much?" "Five thousand." "You got it." "Tomorrow, pay me." "What are you going to do?" "I'm gonna do something here." I'm a Greek with five grand. If I lose it, I lose it. If I don't, everybody is going to respect me 'cause I got good business. And I did it. That's it.

George taught himself the restaurant business and maintained his shop as a luncheonette for six years. Then, in 1971, his wife's cousin, Spiro Palassis, taught him how to make pizza. He incorporated this food into his menu, and now most of his profit comes from the pizza he sells, although he still has a thriving business selling eggs and sandwiches for breakfast and lunch. Except for one summer employee, a cashier, he essentially works in the business alone. His wife comes in a few hours a week to keep the books, and his brother, whom he sponsored for admittance as soon as he became a citizen, works some nights. Still, he remains very much an individualistic business man. He acknowledges receiving help from his wife's cousin but downplays it, maintaining his independence ferociously. He argues:

I do all the work. I enjoy it. I'm my own boss. I don't take nothing from anybody. . . . Business is good. You know why? Because I'm alone. I work myself. If I have to put two or three people to work, I'd make nothing. I'd have to pay them. The expenses would be higher. And what am I going to do? I'd be running around doing nothing. I gotta be here. This is my shop.

In sum, therefore, the Palassis clan includes Nick and Spiro Palassis and their wives, although Spiro and his wife had returned to Greece by the time of my field work; their sister and her husband, the Demetrioses; their cousin Mary and her husband George Pappas; Nick's wife's sister, and brother Sam and his wife; Spiro's wife's brother and sister-in-law, the Sarantoses; and finally, Mrs. Sarantos's three brothers and their wives. At the time of my interviews, there were four separate pizza businesses which supported most, but not all, of these families. One of these businesses is a partnership, jointly owned by two nuclear families within the clan and a third from outside the clan. Another business is owned independently by a nuclear family in the clan, and it employs two others, while paying rent to a third. The final two businesses are owned independently.

This pattern of business ownership illustrates the central theme of this essay, that the Greek immigrant entrepreneurial pattern is mixed: it contains elements of collective economic response, but it also shows a strong individualistic strain. Businesses tend to be owned by individual families, or at most small partnerships, and others within the clan are often employees, rather than co-workers. Nevertheless, the clan structure itself, as a lateral extension of sibling ties, is a quasi-collective form of social organization which functions to facilitate entrepreneurship among its members.

THE LYKOUDES CLAN

George Lykoudes entered the United States in 1963 on a tourist visa and simply never left. He claims he was allowed to stay as a displaced person because his parents were refugees to Greece from Turkey. George's brother and two sisters also immigrated at around the same time, each one accompanied by a spouse.

Like some of the respondents from the Palassis clan, George shows a mixture of individualistic and collectivistic economic response to conditions in America. He migrated first to Springfield, Massachusetts, where, being a trained mason, he found several construction jobs in Springfield and Amherst. He soon hurt his back, however, and could no longer depend on his masonry for a livelihood. In 1965, then, Lykoudes formed a partnership with a sister's husband and two Greek immigrant friends to manage a restaurant in a large hotel in Niantic, Connecticut. Only one of these four immigrants had any restaurant experience prior to this partnership, however, indicating again the strong push toward the restaurant business in the Greek immigrant cultural adaptation to America.

These four Greek immigrants stayed in this restaurant for only a year, before selling out. It would seem that the individualism noted elsewhere about Greeks might have overridden the collectivist partnership. Lykoudes claims: "We didn't get along with the owner. I guess she sold the place and she wants the place back. And it was getting too much. We were working eighteen, seventeen, sixteen hours a day, seven days a week." His brother-in-law, George Syriotes, offered a different interpretation of the breakup of the partnership: "We didn't work out together. Each person had his own ideas. We couldn't work together." Upon leaving the restaurant, the partners went their separate ways economically. Lykoudes bought two fast food stands at the beach in Rhode Island and worked masonry in the winter. Syriotes returned to his previous trade and worked for a furniture company, installing wall-to-wall carpeting.

Then, in 1968, through contacts within the Greek community, Lykoudes heard that a pizza house in Groton that had been owned by a fellow immigrant was now for sale. He told me:

I knew the place, 'cause I knew the fellow, and when I used to go down to the beach I used to stop here and ... and I like the area. I liked the spot. And he was getting kind of tired. He couldn't handle it very well. And I hear he want to sell. So I come around, and I say, "Hey! You want to sell?" He say, "Yeah." I say, "If you want to sell, I'm interested." ... At the end of the summer, he says he want to sell. So I come around to find out what he was asking, and I bought the place. I paid $24,000. I got it from working on construction and on the beach. I paid half of it down, and the other half in a year's time.

Although Lykoudes learned of the business opportunity from contacts from the Greek community, his obligations to his family members led him to bring his brother Peter and his brother-in-law, George Syriotes, into the business with him. Peter has stayed with his brother, although I was never quite clear about whether Peter was a partner or an employee. Still, these brothers have developed the business into one of the most profitable pizza businesses in Southern Connecticut. A second-generation Greek-American banker reported that the bank offered to buy the business and pay George $500 a week salary to run it. Lykoudes declined, saying he could not afford it.

George Syriotes stayed with the business as an employee for three and a half years before finding a pizza business of his own. He told me that he bought his business with a $15,500 bank loan but refused to answer further when I asked him about any financial help he may have received from his brother-in-law. In the absence of more data, therefore, I am forced to conclude that he received none and that his clan ties provided him with no specific financing.

George Lykoudes's other sister has never worked in pizza businesses because her husband, Stephen Ziogas, quickly opened a tailor shop after they immigrated. Six years later, when the Ziogases became citizens, they sponsored his brother Steve for admission. Steve Ziogas had been living in Australia, working as a mechanic in garages since 1964. Just prior to being sponsored to come to the United States, he and his family returned to Greece, where he tried to open his own garage. The business never worked out, and he came to Connecticut as soon as his brother could sponsor him.

Steve's first attempt at economic adaptation in the United States was individualistic. He found a job as a car mechanic, using the skills he brought with him from Greece and Australia. He quickly saw, however, that mechanics make very little money as employees so, not knowing how to start a garage in the United States, he went to work in pizza businesses. Like Sam Volaitis in the Palassis clan, the pizza business was the line of least resistance. Employment found from contacts within the Greek community offered a more stable and secure means of making a living than using individually acquired skills. First, Steve worked for his brother's brother-in-law, George Lykoudes, for a couple of months. Then he found a more permanent and higher-paying position in one of the largest pizza businesses in the area, which was owned by a Greek immigrant who was not related to him at all. He was introduced to this proprietor, however, by a mutual Greek friend. After about a year as an employee in this business, he bought his own place.

Steve's first pizza business was acquired financially by personal thrift and good fortune. As a business in a poor location, it cost him only $3,000, and none of this money was acquired through ethnic contacts. An insurance settlement from an accident paid him $2,500, and the remainder he had saved during the first year that he had been in the United States. Within three years, he managed to earn back his investment plus additional money, which allowed him to put a down payment on a new pizza business in a better location. At the time of my interview with him, his new business had been open a few weeks and was not yet making a profit. Nonetheless, he was confident that it soon would. From his view, why should it not be successful? Are not other Greeks able to make it in this business?

The final families in the Lykoudes clan to be discussed here illustrate again the mixture among Greeks of collective and individual economic response. When George Syriotes, Lykoudes's brother-in-law, became a U.S. citizen in 1971, he sponsored his sister and brother-in-law, the Stavretises, and their daughter Kathy, for admission to the United States. The entire Stavretis family worked for Syriotes for about a year. Then, in 1972, the Stavretises formed a partnership with Kathy's fiance, a Greek immigrant whom she met here in the United States, and bought a pizza business. By 1975, when I interviewed John and Kathy Geannopoulos, the business was earning about $24,000 a year profit, which was split evenly between the Stavretises and Geannopouloses.

In sum, then, the Lykoudes clan includes George and Peter Lykoudes and their wives; their two sisters and their husbands, the Syrioteses and Ziogases; George Syriotes's sister and her husband, the Stavretises; their daughter Kathy and her husband, John Geannopoulos; and, finally, Stephen Ziogas's brother Steve and his wife. As we saw in the Palassis clan, small businesses supported the families, and these businesses are independently owned or at most are small partnerships. As indicated above, I am uncertain whether George Lykoudes has included his brother Peter in his business as a partner. The Stavretises and Geannopouloses do have a partnership, while Steve Ziogas owns his own pizza business, and his brother Stephen owns his own tailor shop.

CLAN STRUCTURE AND EMPLOYMENT

Before addressing the generalizations drawn from the descriptions of the Palassis and Lykoudes clans, I wish to emphasize once more the importance of the sibling tie in the development of the clan structure among Greek immigrants in Connecticut. In the Palassis clan, all immigrants who are considered part of the clan, except George Pappas, are brothers or sisters of the original immigrants or their spouses, or they are the siblings of the spouses or members of their families. The Lykoudes clan is also formed from the sibling ties in the Lykoudes family of orientation. Each of the Lykoudes sisters brought her husband into the clan, and each husband brought his sibling into it as well. Kathy, a daughter of one of these siblings, then brought her husband into the clan.

We see, therefore, that clans among Greek immigrants in Connecticut cities are formed from the serial sponsorship of each successive immigrant's siblings. In the case of George Lykoudes, his immigration led to the migration of a minimum of five other nuclear families within eight years, 1963-71. At first, all of George's brothers and sisters who wanted to come did so. Then, once they had been in the United States for six years and had become U.S. citizens, George's two sisters' spouses brought over their own siblings. In this way, Greek immigrant clans are enlarged every six years, until no more brothers and sisters who wish to emigrate are left in Greece.

The key issue addressed in this essay, however, is not the structure of the Greek clan system. Rather, it is whether the economic response of Greek immigrants within the clan structure is more collective than it is individualistic. As stated above, I argue that the Greek response is somewhat mixed. It is not nearly as collective as that found among the

Orientals studied by Light, but on the other hand it is certainly not as individualistic as the traditional theories of entrepreneurship have suggested. As such, it may be conceived to be quasi-collective in nature.

As Light suggests, disadvantages in the labor market, such as poor English, inadequate education, and discrimination, have often been seen to have led foreigners to turn toward small business ownership as a solution. The alternative, orthodox cultural view is that immigrants bring with them specific cultural skills that predispose them to pursue small business ownership within particular fields. Finally, the reactive cultural view suggests that the minority situation encourages ethnic solidarity which in turn creates a collective propensity to respond in specific, institutionalized ways leading ultimately to self-employment.

Although the Greek immigrants I studied were disadvantaged in the American labor market—few spoke English at the time of their migration and most had only six years of elementary education in Greece—this disadvantage alone does not explain their concentration in a particular small business. Alternatively, few brought with them skills that would have led them to predominate in the pizza business, much less the restaurant industry, over the previous three-quarters of a century of Greek migration to America. The structure of their ethnic communities, however, did facilitate their entrance into the restaurant industry by providing them with a secure passage from the status of migrant to that of entrepreneur. Still, their ethnic community structure is not nearly as cohesive as that found in the Oriental communities studied by Light, and, therefore, the economic adaptation of Greek immigrants is less collective in nature than was the case among the Orientals.

It would be perhaps most efficacious to analyze the data presented in the clan descriptions above in terms of the three economic processes required for an immigrant to move from the status of an initial migrant to that of a self-employed entrepreneur. These three steps are (1) the way in which new immigrants find initial employment in the United States; (2) the way in which immigrants acquire training needed in a particular small business; and (3) the form of financial assistance made available to immigrants when they do open their own businesses. Each step will be analyzed to indicate that although Greeks do use institutionalized networks within their ethnic communities to assist them, these networks are not as cohesive as those reported for Orientals and, therefore, the Greek immigrant response is less collective in nature.

Initial Employment. When new immigrants enter the United States, their first priority is to find work. As new migrants, however, they are often at a disadvantage in the labor market. If they do not wish to be employed as unskilled laborers, therefore, they must fall back on skills they brought with them, if any, or they may utilize resources available to them from their ethnic community. Using personally acquired skills in the search for the initial job would be an individualized response to the problem, as would relying on unskilled factory work. Using contact points within the ethnic community to find employment in an "ethnically predominated" industry, however, would be a collective response to the problem.

Two generalizations emerge from the two clan descriptions regarding the conditions under which Greeks pursue an individual or a collective response to the problem. First, if a new immigrant's migration sponsor has a small business at the time of his or her migration, it is likely that initial employment will be found in this business. Second, if a new immigrant's migration sponsor does not have a small business at the time of his or her migration, it is likely that initial employment will be as an unskilled factory worker or in a job calling for already possessed skills.

As noted above, migration sponsors are most often siblings. A collective response to initial employment, therefore, reduces to a question of working for one's sibling. In the Palassis clan, Nick's and Spiro's sister and her husband, the Demetrioses, began working for Nick in his business immediately upon settlement. Sam Volaitis, Nick's wife's brother, first worked in a factory; but he specifically wanted to go to school and, therefore, he chose an individualized path. Interestingly, he only lasted six months in factory work before beginning to work for his sister and brother-in-law. The collective response in this case was the easier and more secure path. Finally, two of Mrs. Sarantos's brothers and their wives are working in the Sarantos's business in Jewett City. It is only the Sarantos's inability to pay the other brother enough money that is preventing all three of her brothers from working there. This case suggests the limits that may be applied to the collective response in the sense that self-interest of the sponsor is paramount over the collective interest of all siblings.

In the Lykoudes clan, only the Stavretises, George Syriotes's sister and brother-in-law, migrated at a time when their sponsor was self-employed. As we would expect, the Stavretis's first job was working for George Syriotes. The collective response to the problem of first employment is available, therefore, only when one's sibling is self-employed.

The individual response is likely when one's sibling is not self-employed, and, consequently, the most important contact point within the ethnic community does not lead to a lucrative position. From the Palassis clan, George Pappas worked in a factory for seven years because his direct immigration sponsor, his American-born wife, did not have a small business. Similarly, Mr. and Mrs. Sarantos went to Ohio and first worked in restaurants as unskilled laborers before coming to Connecticut because their sponsor, Theodoros's sister, was not even in America at the time. It may be interpreted, however, that the Sarantos's response was collective in that they settled with other relatives and found employment in a Greek-predominated industry. Their exception to the generalization is partially accounted for by the fact that their migration was atypical; their sponsor was not in America. It is important to note, however, that they did not go to New London to seek employment with Theodoros's sister's sister and brother-in-law, Mr. and Mrs. Nick Palassis. Although these people may all be considered to be in the same clan, the lack of meaningful ties over so large a social distance suggests the lack of solidarity within the clan structure.

From the Lykoudes clan, George Lykoudes began work as a mason, George Syriotes as a carpenter and carpet layer, Stephen Ziogas as a tailor, and Steve Ziogas as a car mechanic, all these being trades these men had in Greece. In most of these cases, the sponsor for immigration did not have a business at the time of the sibling's entrance into the United States. The one exception, Steve Ziogas, again suggests the limits of the collective response. Stephen did have a tailor shop at the time of Steve's migration, but this business would not support two families, and there was no work in it for others to do.

Other evidence from my data supports these generalizations. Only seven of the thirty-one immigrant families interviewed in the pizza business in Connecticut had siblings in the pizza business at the time of their migrations. Six of them found their first employment in America in the pizza business. The seventh, Sam Volaitis, turned to pizza within six months. On the other hand, of the twenty-four immigrants who did not have a close relative in the pizza business at the time of their migration, only one began his American job history in the pizza business.

The majority of those immigrants without family in the pizza business started working as unskilled factory workers. Their situations may be better understood with reference to the position of one of my respondents, who reported the choice he had when he started looking for a job for the first time in the United States:

My brother-in-law [a second-generation Greek-American] called up the place [a factory] and asked if they had any jobs. He asked me if I want to work the restaurants or I want to work in a factory. The first question, of course, was money. I say, "What do they pay?" first. He say, "In restaurants, you make about $25, and you going to eat there." I says, "How about in the factory?" He says, "That factory there start at about $1.35 an hour." So I figured out that I might make sixty or seventy dollars. So I says, "I go to the factory."

This respondent allows us to understand better that even though working in a Greek-owned restaurant would be conceptualized as a collective response to the problem of initial employment, it is not necessarily a favorable one. Greeks have found employment in restaurants in the United States since the earliest years of the Greek migration to the New World; and this fact is well known in the rural Greek villages. What is also well known, however, is that such employment pays little and has not been a secure step in the ladder toward self-employment. Therefore, an individual response to the economic problem of first employment is often preferred to a dead-end position as a dishwasher in a Greek restaurant, even though the latter may be easier to attain.

Learning the Business. All of the immigrants interviewed, with the exception of two Greek Orthodox priests, eventually did open their own pizza businesses, and all were taught how to make pizza and operate such a business by other Greeks. As such, they used resources found within the Greek community. It may be conceptualized, therefore, that Greeks show a collective response to the problem of acquiring training prior to opening one's own business. The process by which they acquired the training needed for this business, however, varied according to their relationship with others in the business. This variation itself suggests that the Greek immigrant response to this problem in general is not as collective as would be suggested by Light's findings with regard to the Chinese and Japanese.

I will explore this variation further by stating two generalizations which emerge from the description of the two clans and then support these with reference to additional data that were collected. First, immigrants with siblings in the business acquire the needed training from these kin. Second, immigrants without siblings in the business learn from a Greek immigrant friend or while working as an employee in a Greek-owned pizza business.

Those immigrants with siblings in the business tend to acquire the skills needed quickly and easily. Nick and Spiro Palassis were the first in their clan to learn the business, but, as indicated above, I could not determine how they learned it. Sam Volaitis learned from Nick, his brother-in-law. Angelo Demetrios and his wife also learned from Nick, who is Mrs. Demetrios's brother. Theodoros Sarantos and his wife acquired the skills from Mr. and Mrs. Spiro Palassis, who are Theodoros's sister and brother-in-law. Finally, two of Mrs. Sarantos's brothers and their wives are currently learning the business from her.

George Lykoudes, the first in his clan to learn the pizza business, learned it from another of my respondents, who is not related to George. Once he did acquire the skills, he taught his brother Peter and his brother-in-law, George Syriotes. The Stavretises learned from Syriotes, who is Mrs. Stavretis's brother.

With the exception of Nick and Spiro and George Lykoudes, the first in each clan to learn the business, all other respondents with siblings in the business acquired the skills quickly after migration while working in their siblings' establishments. Those without siblings in the business must wait longer, and they have a more difficult time. Only two immigrants from the clans discussed above were in this position. Steve Ziogas's brother is a tailor, and his wife has no other family in Connecticut. Therefore, in order to learn the pizza business he worked as an employee in one of the large pizza businesses owned by Greeks in the area. Similarly, George Pappas had a luncheonette for six years before he started to make pizza there. His wife's cousin, Spiro Palassis, was the man who taught him how. Interestingly, George was taught to make pizza nine years after his wife's cousins started their business and thirteen years after he started living in Connecticut. Immigrants with closer relatives in the trade rarely have to wait more than a year.

Support for these generalizations and more detail concerning the second one can be found through analysis of how all thirty-one immigrant families learned the trade. Thirteen learned from a close relative, either a sibling, a spouse's sibling, or, in two cases, a cousin. None of the other eighteen had relatives as close as a cousin in the pizza business. These immigrants generally tended to learn the trade in two different ways. Eleven of them approached Greek immigrant friends who had pizza businesses and requested that the friends teach them. These immigrants often worked part time without pay in order to acquire the skills. They all had other jobs which paid them enough to live on but not enough for them to be happy. One respondent reported, "When I started working at [the factory], I started to work in the pizza places also. I met some Greek people, asked questions. Sometimes I went to help. They said, 'Teddy, we need you there.' Most of the time, I didn't get paid. . . . They showed me. They taught me." Another said, "When I came here, I was working a few years in the factories, different places. I was working for five years in one place. After that, a friend of mine had a pizza house, and I decided to go into the same business. . . . When I had a chance, a day off, a few weeks, I went there to work to learn the business." One more admitted:

I had a half a dozen friends in the pizza business. Everyone of them was doing well. Groton, New London, New Britain, Hartford. Every time I visited them, they were putting in more time than I was in the factory, but their benefits were better.

So, for me, I checked into what it would take to get an electrician's license: time, school, tests. That would have took years and I had my wife, my daughter, and there was no way I could support the family and go to school the same time. So I decided to give it [pizza] a try.... I went to friends, on nights that I had off, to learn the business without pay.

A second way in which immigrants without relatives in the business tended to learn was by working as full-time employees in other pizza businesses. Four respondents held jobs that would not pay them enough to live on while they spent time learning the pizza business. Therefore, they applied at some of the larger, Greek-owned pizza houses for full-time work. Most often, these immigrants were introduced to their prospective employers by mutual Greek friends. Finally, of the three respondents in the residual category, two hired Greek immigrants to teach them the business, while the third learned through a process I did not discover.

Summarizing the findings, immigrants with relatives who have pizza places learn the business from their relatives. The data from the clan descriptions show that they often learn the business as soon as they immigrate to Connecticut. Those immigrants without relatives in the business, however, tend to approach friends who are apparently quite willing to teach any other Greek immigrant how to make pizza. These immigrants are often working full time in factories or other jobs and simply learn the trade while working for their friends at night. Finally, other immigrants find full-time jobs working in large, Greek-owned pizza places, which have enough business to ensure that full-time employees are always needed.

Therefore, Greek immigrants acquire the skills of the pizza trade in a collective mode. The variation in their responses, however, may be understood with reference to their relationships to their clan structures and their ethnic community. As suggested earlier in this essay, the Greek clan is the key element tying Greek immigrants and their families into larger units of ethnic social structure. Moreover, the clans themselves are created from the serial sponsorship of siblings for admission to the United States. The clans, then, become important units of moral solidarity and, as such, define limits of moral obligation that are expressed economically through the training provided for the newcomers in the pizza business. The extent of such obligation is seen in the speed and ease with which new immigrants acquire these skills after migration.

Those immigrants who wish to enter the pizza business but who lack clan ties to this trade have a more difficult problem acquiring the training. They solve this problem, though, by pursuing contacts within the Greek community. They approach friends to teach them, or they find jobs which will provide them with an opportunity to learn. That the moral obligations found within the Greek community as a whole are weaker than those found within the clan structure is seen by the differences between the paths followed by immigrants in these two positions. Those with clan ties begin their employment histories in the pizza business and then move on quickly to open their own. Those without clan ties most often work in factories or in other jobs while they learn the business during their spare time.

The subsequent behavior of those respondents who entered the pizza business without family to teach them supports the notion of the moral importance of the clan structure and its economic effects. Of the eighteen respondents in this position, ten trained all of their own and their spouses' siblings as soon as they could. Six others reported that they had no other relatives in the United States or in Greece who wanted to enter the business. Reliable information was not obtained from the other two. It is clear, therefore, that the moral obligations found within the clan are quite strong, and assistance in training is normative.

Financial Assistance. All aspiring entrepreneurs must overcome one last hurdle in the process of opening a small business: capital formation. Somehow, they must acquire the necessary capital to finance the establishment of their own businesses. Some research suggests that this hurdle is a major one for many Americans seeking to realize the American dream. How did the Greeks interviewed overcome this hurdle, and was it a collective or an individualized response to the problem?

At first glance, data from the clan descriptions suggest that this step is individualistic. None of the immigrants in the two clans was assisted financially by a relative. In the Palassis clan, George Pappas found his luncheonette independently of his family and financed it from money that he and his wife had saved during the seven previous years. I did not determine the financial considerations under which Sam Volaitis bought into his sister's business, under which the Demetrioses established their own, or under which the Sarantoses took over their business from Mrs. Sarantos's sister and brother-in-law.

I do have more information on the finances of the Lykoudes clan. Steve Ziogas financed his first pizza business from an insurance settlement and his second from the profits of the first. George Lykoudes financed his business from his previous jobs at the Rhode Island beaches and his masonry. George Syriotes took out a bank loan to buy his business, and the Stavretises also took out a bank loan, which was co-signed by another of my respondents not related to this clan.

Other data collected support the conclusion that relatives do not assist financially newer immigrants when they establish their own pizza businesses. Of the sixteen immigrants from whom I obtained reliable information on this topic, only one claimed to have been helped financially by his relatives; and in this case his relatives were second-generation Greek-Americans. Two others claimed to have borrowed money from friends. Of the thirteen others, seven saved enough money from working in factories, often by working as much overtime as they could get, five others received bank loans, and the final one used an insurance settlement.

Therefore, in the matter of capital formation, kinship ties within the clan structure do not appear influential. From the examples discussed, it appears that thrift, hard work, savings, and investment provide Greek immigrants with the capital needed, and although such values may be found in the Greek culture, each immigrant appears to solve the problem independently.

Other data collected, however, suggest that a collective response does occur but on the level of the ethnic group rather than the clan. There are three forms that this collective response takes. First, sympathetic Greek-American bankers often feel an obligation to assist new immigrants with loans, despite the fact that they have no credit rating. One told me:

Immigrants that haven't really established themselves more or less filter to me [for loans]. I really don't know why. [But] I don't think I've missed anyone yet for a loan for a house, for the business, or for personal loans. They have all been very faithful and honorable in their obligations. I have no reservations about giving these people loans. They come over, and they don't have any credit, [but] I know they're going to make it. Even though the auditors go crazy once in a while! But they do. They always make it.

This respondent also confirmed that many of the immigrants save large amounts of money in a relatively short period of time and then invest in a business. He referred to one recent immigrant who has been working as an employee in a large pizza business for a year and a half and has $9,000 in his savings account.

The second form of collective response to the problem of capital formation also involves bank loans, but with non-Greek bankers. In a small number of cases, an established immigrant may co-sign a loan, which the newer immigrant may need to establish a business. Although this rarely occurs within the clan structure, other moral ties seem to circumscribe this practice. In the three cases about which I have reliable data, the co-signer was a second-generation father-in-law in one case, and fellow immigrants from the same region of Greece as the respondents in the other two cases.

The final form of collective response to the problem of capital formation is actually the most common and therefore the most important. In this form, one's sibling or employer extends his or her credit with distributors of pizza ovens, foodstuffs, and paper goods to cover the new business. For example, one of my respondents was employing three recent immigrants in his pizza business at the time of our interview. He indicated he would help them in any way he could when it came time for them to open their own places. When I asked him if he would finance them, he responded: "I don't have the [money]. I just bought a house, and I bought my partner out. If I had a few thousand dollars, yes, I would. I am going to help them with anything I can. If I have the money I would give it to them. If I don't have, my credit is good." Since few immigrants with businesses have several thousand dollars at their disposal, the extension of their own credit with the distributors turns out to be the most common form of economic assistance by which an established immigrant may assist his or her sibling or employee. As such, new immigrants solve the problem of capital formation in this collective fashion. They do not have to save large amounts of money to cover these costs but will be offered credit based on the good name of their trainers.

Another respondent explained clearly how this process works:

This guy, I helped him a lot. Because when he started, he couldn't speak very good English. And I gave to him all my salesmen. You know he was here. [He worked for this respondent for two or three years.] I gave my reputation to him. I was responsible. You know, if he don't pay, I pay.

It is most interesting to note that this respondent and his trainee are not related, nor are they tied together by village or regional bonds. Their one common link is their ethnicity, and this is deemed enough.

The owner of a bakery equipment company, who claims to have sold pizza ovens and other equipment to about five hundred Greek pizza businesses since the 1950s, confirmed this pattern. He said:

Our record with the Greek pizza houses ... has been virtually ... untarnished. These people's words are their bonds. We can never get a credit check on these people for our banks. The banks took our word for it that the guy was good because we knew him when he worked for Bill or George ... or whoever it happened to be.

Therefore, Greek immigrants do receive financial assistance when they open their own businesses and, as such, show a collective response to the problem of capital formation. The most common form of financial assistance which is given to newer immigrants is that the relative or employer who trained them extends his or her credit to cover the newer pizza businesses. This pattern occurs among relatives and non-relatives alike. Therefore, although the clan structure seems to be relatively unimportant for this step, the bonds of ethnicity and the obligations felt within these bonds provide immigrants with an option unavailable to others in America wishing to open their own businesses. Of course, the clan structure can play an important role in those cases in which a new immigrant buys into, or takes over, the business of an older relative. These immigrants simply find the passage from being trained to opening their own business easier than do others without family in the business. From my research, however, I would conclude that it would be a rare Greek immigrant who, once trained in the pizza business, did not move on to open his or her own establishment, whether or not the immigrant has relatives in the business.

SUMMARY AND DISCUSSION

This essay has presented some of the data collected among Greek immigrants in small business enterprise concerning how these immigrants enter small businesses. Contrary to the individualistic conception of the American dream, these data suggest that Greek immigrants use collective responses to the economic problems which must be overcome in order to achieve upward mobility from the status of unskilled laborers to that of self-employed entrepreneurs. As such, the findings cast doubt on the traditional economic views that suggest that entrepreneurship comes about from the strivings of self-sacrificing individuals who persevere, using such traits as personal thrift, a spartan life style, and rugged individualism.

The data presented above show that Greek immigrants rely heavily on their clan structures in their path toward entrepreneurship. Those immigrants with siblings who are self-employed in small businesses begin working for them, acquiring in the process the skills needed for opening their own businesses. Once trained, they then establish themselves in business using the credit umbrella provided for them by their kin. For these immigrants, then, the clan structure provides a secure path toward self-employment, and their economic behavior in this process may be conceptualized as collectivistic.

Greek immigrants who settle in the United States when their siblings are not self-employed have a more difficult time becoming entrepreneurs themselves. Nevertheless, they too follow an established path using the contacts available to them within the ethnic community. Although their first jobs are likely to be as unskilled factory workers or as tradespersons practicing a skill they had in Greece, it appears that many eventually become self-employed in small business, irrespective of their particular training. The data presented above suggest that they approach Greek friends to teach them the required skills or work full time as employees in the larger businesses of other Greeks. Once trained, they too are provided with credit umbrellas by their teachers to carry them through the early, difficult period of self-employment.

The path toward self-employment followed by these immigrants without contacts in their clan structures to small businesses is longer and more difficult than that followed by the siblings of established entrepreneurs. For them, the less moral bonds of ethnicity must be used to smooth the economic path. Because the bonds of ethnicity among Greeks in general are not as solidary as those found exclusively within the clans, such a path is more insecure and therefore requires more individual effort, initiative, and risk.

At the outset of this essay, I asked whether intergroup differences in collective economic adaptation may be found to exist and, if so, how they might be explained. The data presented here suggest that there is a difference in collective economic behavior between the Greeks I studied and the Orientals studied by Light. Light found that the Orientals used the trust and morality ascriptively based in the clan structure but extended throughout the ethnic community to create and regulate economic activity.[16] I found that the situation among Greek immigrants in Connecticut cities is somewhat more individualistic. The clan structure does serve to channel newcomers into small business by providing a smooth path based on collective resources. But the meanings which these immigrants apply to their clans are different from those applied to the Oriental clans. Consequently, the economic processes of Greek immigrants are more individualistic than are Oriental immigrants.

The clan among Orientals is conceived to be a tight unit of collective solidarity. The morality and trust found in this unit apply equally to all members of the clan and lead to economic behaviors oriented toward collective interest. Clans among Greeks, on the other hand, are more diffuse. They are formed from the combination of nuclear families of siblings brought together through the migration process rather than from a collective identification with a surname grouping, a village, or a region. Consequently, the morality and trust are localized in the nuclear family and are extended to members of the clan only when such extensions do not interfere with the Greek conceptions of nuclear family self-interest. Therefore, the economic response of Greeks is more individualistic by nature, that is, it is much more like the response expected from traditional, individualistic views of capitalism than is the response of Orientals.

An important example of this individualistic economic behavior is my finding that Greek immigrants will only assist members of their clan economically when such assistance does not conflict with the interests of their nuclear families. This means they will not employ their siblings nor finance those whom they have taught if such behavior will reduce the profit from their businesses beyond what they consider reasonable. This individualized conception of profit and loss differs sharply from the collective concerns of the Japanese and Chinese studied by Light and places the Greek economic response much closer to the individualistic, orthodox models of entrepreneurship.

Nevertheless, the point should not be lost that Greek immigrants do show a collective economic response. As noted above, this response is most secure and most automatic within the clan structure, as newcomers are led to depend upon group resources. A collective response is also found, however, among those immigrants tied to the resources not by a clan structure but merely by bonds of ethnicity. These immigrants still use collective resources, but their position is much more individualistic. Obligations within the ethnic group are not as strong as those within the clan, and, consequently, much more personal initiative is required if an immigrant in this position is to share in the group resources.

Ultimately, then, the issue of intergroup differences in collective economic behavior falls upon the concept of the strength of obligations found within units of social structure. At the collective extreme, Oriental immigrants to the United States feel a great deal of obligation to others within their clan structures, and the depth of these obligations leads to a cohesive sense of collective interest which spreads throughout the ethnic community. The Greeks I studied are somewhat less collective in moral and economic behavior and feel a strong sense of obligation only to those within their nuclear family. Nevertheless, Greeks do feel obligations to assist their siblings, and thus a quasi-collective interest is created at this level. Greeks generally do not feel obligations to others who are not in their clan structure, however. Accordingly, unaffiliated Greeks may take advantage of group resources but it is up to them to initiate the process. Since others will not feel obligated to help them without being asked, an unaffiliated Greek may only depend on collective resources if he or she initiates it individually.

In conclusion, this essay has demonstrated that intergroup differences exist in collective response to entrepreneurship. The Greek response is not nearly as collective as that found among Orientals, but it is certainly not as individualistic as traditional modes of capitalistic economic behavior as depicted by Schumpeter, Weber, and the American dream. Moreover, the essay has suggested that the variation in collective modes of economic response may be explainable in terms of variations in the strength of obligations found within units of ethnic social structure. Specifically, the less collective entrepreneurial pattern displayed by Greeks, in comparison to the Orientals, may be explainable in terms of weaker family and clan obligations. Greek nuclear families operate businesses independently, or at most in partnerships of two or three families, while Chinese and Japanese seem to have operated businesses which were tied together by a strong network of collective, ethnically based morality.

PART TWO

ORGANIZED RELIGION AND COLLECTIVE ENTERPRISE

O. KENDALL WHITE, JR.

MORMON RESISTANCE AND ACCOMMODATION
From Communitarian Socialism to Corporate Capitalism

MORMONISM AND AMERICAN CULTURE

As an indigenous movement, Mormonism embodied a unique synthesis of American religious and secular culture. Accommodating Christian beliefs and nineteenth-century science, Mormon theology, though assuming a posture of biblical literalism, was radically liberal.[1] It fused religious eschatology with secular reform. The optimistic assessment of human potential and the notion of progress so characteristic of American culture became the foundation of the profound this-worldliness of Mormon theology. In short, the Mormons captured American hopes and expectations in their theology. They assumed an obligation to build the Kingdom of God as the ideal society based upon principles of equality and cooperation. This new social order, which was to be the ultimate realization of American destiny, would begin with the implementation of communitarian socialism. However, the reaction of others forced the Saints to reevaluate their early social ideals. Additional social experimentation required even greater social isolation, which in turn led to further disillusionment. A radical consciousness emerged implying that only separatism could fulfill Mormon expectations for American society. But Mormon separatism further alienated other Americans and, largely due to its success, created the conditions for its own destruction. The extreme choices of accommodation or annihilation could hardly have been more apparent when Mormon leaders exchanged collectivism, theocracy, and polygamy for capitalism, democracy, and monogamy. The "peculiar people" were readily assimilated into mainstream American society. This paper examines the Mormon economic experience from an early honeymoon with American culture, through discord and separation, to a reunion symbolized by an era of corporate capitalism.

Upon publishing the Book of Mormon, which Joseph Smith claimed to have translated from ancient records, the Mormon church emerged as the divine restoration of primitive Christianity. Not to replace the Bible, the Book of Mormon was a companion volume—a new scripture—containing the religious and social history of pre-Colombian inhabitants of the Americas. Its appeal was probably less a function of its explanation of Hebraic origin for the American Indians than its conception of American destiny and legitimation of Caucasion immigration, conquest, and domination of Indian land. The Book of Mormon identified America as "choice above all other lands" and promised it to the faithful in the "last days." The "elect" were to "gather" from all nations to build the Kingdom of God in preparation for Jesus's Second Coming.

By identifying the "gathering" as his basic doctrine, Joseph Smith ensured his place in history and the success of his church. Nothing is more central to American consciousness than immigration. It is, according to Commager, the "oldest" and "most universal" theme in our history.[2] Being an immigrant or descendant of immigrants is the one experience shared by all Americans, excluding only the American Indians. The Book of Mormon, which identified even Indians as descendants of immigrants, celebrated the immigration theme in its own story of the migration from the ancient Holy Land. Joseph's subsequent emphasis on the gathering of "modern Israel" from the nations of Babylon retheologized the American experience and legitimated the utopian nationalism of nineteenth-century Americans.

It is no accident that American society—with its preoccupation with work, achievement, and mobility—sired a religious movement which proclaimed, even more boldly, the American gospel. Mormonism projected the fluidity of the class structure, celebrated in American cultural myths, into the beyond. A pluralistic metaphysics in which matter, time, space, good, evil, and intelligence exist independent of God rendered even the divine task one of mastery. Man's objective was no less. God earned his status, according to the doctrine of eternal progression, and man must do the same. This is succinctly expressed in a popular Mormon saying: "As man now is, God once was; as God now is, man may become."

How does man become like God? Only through work, in which he acquires the requisite knowledge and skills for controlling the elements, develops the proper moral character, and participates in the appropriate rituals, can he realize his destiny. Where could the American conception of work and value of achievement obtain more ultimate expression than in a doctrine proclaiming that God earned his status and demanding no less of man? It is hardly surprising that a theology preoccupied with process instead of final states—with the quest rather than the end, the pursuit rather than the goal, "becoming" rather than "being"—would make work the sacred repository of ultimate meaning. However, a collective rather than individualistic conception of American destiny finally distinguished the Mormon version.

Since their theology maintained that Jesus would only return to a community built upon equality, order, and cooperation, the Mormons were able to fuse the religious enthusiasm embodied in Christian eschatology with the immediacy of secular reform. Millenial hopes and expectations became the basis of a this-worldly theology, and the energy religion so often projects onto another world became the basis for a collective transformation of this world. Mundane activities were infused with religious significance, and building the good society became a social obligation. A religion which could not save man in this life could hardly expect to do so in the next. So, in theology and practice, Mormonism repudiated the classical Christian discontinuity between the religious and secular.

COMMUNITARIAN SOCIALISM AND THE DISENCHANTMENT WITH AMERICAN SOCIETY

Nowhere is this repudiation of discontinuity more evident than in early Mormon economics. The conversion of Sidney Rigdon, a Campbellite minister, leader of a commune, and "the most successful revivalist on the Western Reserve,"[3] brought knowledge of the economic experimentation of the Owenites, Rappites, and Zoarites into the new church. That Rigdon soon convinced Smith of the necessity for a communistic foundation for the Kingdom of God may be inferred from the latter's immediate revelation on the "Law of Consecration and Stewardship."[4] Though some scholars interpret this revelation as a concession to capitalism—apparently because of its repudiation of the "common-stock principle" associated with Rigdon's commune and its unique conception of property—the thrust was socialistic. Individuals were to "consecrate" their property to the Lord, that is, deed it to the church, and then receive an "inheritance" or "stewardship" which may be more or less than the original donation. Inheritances were to be allocated according to need and worked for the sustenance of the individual (if single) or family. All "annual increase" (surplus) was to revert to the bishop's storehouse for redistribution in the community, additional stewardships, or collective enterprises needed to build Zion.[5] In other words, the economic equality required by the

Kingdom of God would result, first, from pooling and redistributing property and, second, through preventing the private accumulation of wealth by channeling all surplus into a common storehouse.

It was Mormon economics that suggested the first break with American society. Initially failing to perceive the radical challenge inherent in communitarian socialism to a society becoming more preoccupied with individual competition and laissez faire capitalism, Mormonism embraced cooperation and collectivism. Additional revelations warned against disunity and inequality. "Be one, if ye are not one, ye are not mine" (D & C 38:27); and "It is not good that one man should possess that which is above another, wherefore the world lieth in sin" (D & C 49:20). Perhaps the Mormon position was most forcefully argued by Apostle Orson Pratt:

Unequal possession of that which God has made for the benefit of all His children is sin. All nations, kindreds, and people are in sin because of this inequality. The Saints are still in sin so far as they approve of this unequal possession; and we shall remain in sin until we make exertions to put this inequality away from us. We must be one, not only one in heavenly riches, but one in earthly riches.[6]

It was this socialistic impulse that revealed Mormonism's emerging conception of the ideal society as a corporate antithesis of the laissez faire capitalist model of American society.

Consequently, to embrace the new gospel was not to join another church. On the contrary, it demanded leaving Babylon, "gathering" to Zion, and building the Kingdom. Though the location for the New Jerusalem, the capital city of Zion, had not been revealed, the Saints began gathering in Ohio. During May 1831, a small community at Thompson implemented the Law of Consecration (with the resulting social system known as the United Order); but litigation, in which two of the wealthier members left the order and successfully sued for the return of their "consecrated" properties, forced the community to disband.[7] In the meantime, revelation identified Jackson County, Missouri, as the center of Zion; so the Thompson Mormons migrated to their new holy land in July 1831. Though the Ohio experiment had only begun to assume its structure, it enabled even the poorest Mormons to migrate from New York to Ohio and from Ohio to western Missouri.

Implementation again began immediately. The Saints established the "bishop's storehouse" to receive and distribute "consecrations" and "inheritances" (stewardships). When the order was fully organized, each family—in accordance with Joseph's "Plat of the City of Zion,"[8] would receive a building lot in the city, with farmers granted additional land outside of it. Tools and other resources, including licenses and public service positions, would be allocated so individuals could serve group needs according to their interests and abilities. Individuals apparently enjoyed some latitude in the disposition of their stewardships, and thus the notion has been encouraged that the United Order was not socialistic.[9] But they could neither expand their operation without the bishop's consent nor control the market for personal gain. With the annual consecration of all surplus (i.e., its return to the bishop's storehouse) the church controlled investment, economic planning, and the distribution of resources.

Within a year, three to four hundred Mormons had gathered to Zion, and most received their inheritances; by the following year, July 1833, over 1,200 resided in Jackson County. Though Hamilton Gardner, in one of the earliest objective analyses of Mormon communism, doubted that the United Order reached the point where any member obtained a surplus from his stewardship,[10] at least the "consecrations" generated sufficient revenue to purchase several thousand acres of land, establish the first weekly newspaper west of the Missouri River, maintain stores, and operate a transportation system. Arrington et al., in an analysis of the extant deeds of consecration or stewardship, found a range from $34.25 to $316.52 and a total of $1,210.97 in consecrated properties.[11] While it is impossible to determine the representativeness of these data, we know they constitute the deeds of only seven out of several hundred. By pooling their property the Mormons obtained the resources to acquire thousands of acres of land in western Missouri.

Even so, consecrations were not sufficient to provide inheritances to all who were entitled to them. Serious poverty, which one contemporary critic suggested was "little above the condition of our blacks"[12] and another saw as "their best prerequisite for the reception of their expected Saviour,"[13] precluded any quick realization of Mormon dreams. Litigation challenging the legality of Mormon property relations forced compromises and hindered economic development, while internal disputes over the determination of consecrations and inheritances threatened the Order. Despite these problems, its initial success probably posed a more serious threat to its own survival.

Indeed, in the hostile reaction of the settlers, it is possible to detect considerable envy as well as fear. They found it difficult to compete with a people whom they claimed were "characterized" by the "profoundest ignorance, the grossest superstitions, and the most abject poverty."[14] Their writings imply that indolent and destitute Mormons were acquiring all the land, controlling the economy, and threatening to dominate political institutions. The notion of a conspiracy among

Mormons, Blacks, and Indians, reinforced by the settlers' prejudices, gained credence from Mormon social relations. If a congregation of "settlers, vagabond Indians, renegades, traders, and Negro slaves"[15] at the first Sunday service in Jackson County frightened the settlers, publication of an article perceived as an invitation for "free people of color" to immigrate to Zion literally infuriated them and precipitated the hostilities O'Dea has called the "Mormon Missouri War."[16] Within a year, the Mormons had abandoned Jackson County.

The Mormon experience in Missouri, during the next six years, recapitulated Jackson County. While the citizens of Clay County welcomed the Saints for "temporary asylum," their position remained too tenuous for the United Order. Soon asked to leave Clay, they acquired a county of their own (Caldwell) in 1836. For a while this appeared to be the solution. Saints gathered from the United States and Canada, and the community prospered. Within two years, they had some 250,000 acres divided into 2,000 farms in the county, and they had built 150 houses, four dry good stores, three family groceries, several blacksmith shops, and two hotels, excavated for a temple, and constructed a schoolhouse also to be used for a church, townhall, and courthouse at Far West.

The United Order was not reestablished, partly because of rapid population growth and some external conflict; however, several properties were consecrated for public use, and the "lesser law" of tithing was revealed (D & C 119). Since revelation blamed greediness of the Saints for an apparent failure of the United Order, the "lesser law" was to operate until the Saints prepared themselves to live the "higher law." The new revelation required an individual to consecrate all surplus, everything beyond his family's needs, upon conversion and then 10 percent of all annual increase thereafter. The surplus was again redistributed to the poor and used for collective ventures.

With the arrival of most of the Kirtland Saints in Far West, the Mormons began spilling over into neighboring counties. The denial of the right to vote to a Mormon in Gallitan precipitated civil war. Several thousand troups prepared for battle; the Missouri legislature appropriated $200,000 to quell the "Mormon Rebellion"; and Governor Boggs issued his infamous order demanding that the Mormons "be exterminated or driven from the state." Before leaving Missouri in 1838–39, 12,000 to 15,000 Mormons were driven from their homes; over forty lay dead; Joseph Smith was in chains on charges of treason and sentenced to be shot; and approximately $2 million of Mormon properties had been confiscated.

Though the Missouri experience fostered notions of emergent nationality and ethnicity inherent in early Mormon consciousness, it was the move to Illinois and subsequent experience there that portended a thoroughgoing separatism. The Illinois legislature, believing the state to be badly in need of immigrants and capital, enthusiastically granted the Mormons a charter for their new city of Nauvoo. Rarely did a city enjoy such political, judicial, and military autonomy, but this did not lead to a revitalization of Mormon socialism. The consecration of surplus properties and the contribution of 10 percent of profits maintained public works and enabled some redistribution of resources. However, abortive efforts to obtain compensation for stolen properties and redress for the Missouri persecution only convinced Mormon leaders of the necessity for separatism. Nauvoo's isolation and autonomy encouraged grandiose dreams of an empire in Texas, Oregon, California, or the Rocky Mountains, greater emphasis on apocalypticism, and theological and institutional innovations. In fact, it was Nauvoo that sowed the seeds of Mormon separatism. As Flanders argues:

The pattern of much that was basic to Mormon society in the West began in Nauvoo: forms of social organization and control, the union of ecclesiastical and civil government, the notion of an independent Mormon nation-state within the American Federal Union, peopling a new country with convert-immigrants, and the polygamous family system. Utah had its roots in Nauvoo.[17]

Even the assassination of Joseph Smith, their greatest disappointment, became a symbol of the ultimate sacrifice of the individual for the group. The Prophet's martyrdom enhanced the Saints' determination to build an autonomous social order.

SEPARATISM: THE PURSUIT OF ECONOMIC AUTONOMY

Following the death of Joseph Smith, the Mormons began reorganizing under factional leaders. Brigham Young, apparently the most convincing, led the largest faction, and the choice, as Flanders suggests, became one of retaining U.S. citizenship or remaining "a literal citizen of the Kingdom of God."[18] Preparation for the famous migration to the Rocky Mountains consumed most of the latter's time and energy. With the escalation of mobs and persecution, land and houses sold for ridiculously low prices, and the Saints soon fled. The famous exodus to Utah required greater centralization of social organization and extensive cooperation. Organizing 15,000 people into two large divisions, each subdivided into companies of one hundred, fifty, and ten, revealed ingenuity. Cooperation resulted in the construction of bridges and roads and the planting of crops to be harvested by subsequent parties. When it appeared that resources might not be sufficient, President Polk, who during war with Mexico believed the Saints might serve national interests, created the Mormon Battalion and thus inadvertently enabled the use of salaries and clothing allowances for supplies for the Mormon exodus. Moreover, to a people who already identified with the ancient Hebrews, this migration was easily interpreted as the exodus of modern Israel, led by another Moses, to a new Promised Land. The symbolic value of this trek should not be underestimated. It reinforced a collective identity that would sustain the Saints in the economic challenges soon to confront them.

Facing the harsh environment of the Salt Lake Valley, Brigham Young immediately reminded the Saints of their basic economic principles. Individuals, strictly speaking, did not own property but acted as "stewards" over nature. Clearly the most immediate application of the Mormon conception of property was the public ownership of water and timber in which everyone was to enjoy equal access. As Brigham declared, "There shall be no private ownership of the streams that come out of the canyons, nor the timber that grows on the hills. These belong to the people: all the people."[19] Private land, specific lots, were selected through a lottery and distributed according to principles of equality, productive use, and small holdings. The Mormon priesthood, which directed the lottery and managed the public resources, also directed economic policy toward the goals of political and economic independence. Brigham Young explicitly articulated Mormon economic objectives:

We do not intend to have any trade or commerce with the gentile world, for so long as we can buy of them we are in a degree dependent on them. The Kingdom of God cannot rise independent of the gentile nations until we produce, manufacture, and make every article of use, convenience, or necessity among our own people. We shall have Elders abroad among all nations, and until we can obtain and collect the raw material for our manufactures it will be their business to gather in such things as are, or may be, needed. So we shall need no commerce with the nations. I am determined to cut every thread of this kind and live free and independent, untrammeled by any of their detestable customs and practices.[20]

It was possible for the Mormons to implement their economic system, with its deviant conceptions of property and cooperation, largely because of the territory's ambiguous status. While the war had ended, the negotiations with Mexico had not decided the fate of this land. Consequently, it was not subject to U.S. territorial law, and the Mormon theocracy was able to determine economic policy, control political activity, and govern social life. The organization of the Free and Independent State of Deseret signaled the open establishment of a political Mormon empire. Even the subsequent granting of status as the Territory of Utah in 1850 failed to eliminate theocracy.

Colonization and immigration were the primary means for building the Mormon Empire. Deseret, originally conceived as most of today's Western states, included portions of California, with a seaport at San Diego, and numerous communities linking the Pacific Ocean with Salt Lake City. Within ten years, ninety-five colonies, mostly surrounding Salt Lake, had been established; and before colonization efforts ended over five hundred Mormon communities dotted the western United States, Canada, and Mexico.[21] Frequent rebaptism of those "called" to establish new settlements gave additional religious significance to the colonization program, encouraged greater cooperation, and again underscored the this-worldly nature of the Mormon religion. While Mormon leaders urged colonization to solidify political power and guarantee economic autonomy, the population required for the program came partly from polygamy and primarily through immigration. At no point in Mormon history did the "gathering"—the fundamental doctrine of early Mormonism—receive greater emphasis nor correspond so closely to social reality. The elect, who were gathering from Babylon, provided the labor for building the Kingdom of God.

Since Mormonism appealed largely to economically oppressed classes, its converts often lacked the resources to migrate to Zion. The problem was obviously compounded for Europeans, especially in England and Scandinavia, where people were ready for the "gospel of America."[22] However, the cooperative values and collective institutions which characterized Mormonism readily adapted to the new task. Having established the Perpetual Emigrating Fund to aid exiles from Nauvoo in their journey west, Brigham Young, in 1851, extended it to assist European converts. Initially financed by "consecrations," tithing, and donations, those receiving assistance were to repay the fund upon their successful establishment in Zion. Though never self-sufficient and sometimes requiring infusions from general tithing and occasionally debt cancellations, its success easily may be inferred from the fact that the Perpetual Emigrating Fund assisted approximately 100,000 poor Mormon immigrants before the federal government demanded its abolition in 1887.[23]

The efficiency of Mormon institutions appeared through the entire immigration process. Before leaving their native lands, English and Scandinavian converts began to exchange their national identities for a Mormon identity as they sang hymns equating their homelands with

Babylon and Utah with Zion. Using missionaries as coordinators, officials matched each convert's occupational skills with needs in Mormon communities. Brigham Young, during an attempt to industrialize part of Utah, requested British missionaries to send "blowers, moulders, and all kinds of furnace operators to immediately immigrate to the Valley without delay,"[24] and thousands of the English immigrants that settled Mormon communities came with skills, at an optimum age (median 22), and as members of stable families. Mulder shows that artisans, craftsmen, and farmers outnumbered unskilled laborers among Scandinavian immigrants and concludes that they were even better suited for the tasks confronting Zion than the "urban British migration."[25] With this extensive coordination, it is hardly surprising that the number and names of immigrants were typically known in Utah before they left their native lands.

Not only were skills matched with the needs of Mormon communities, but the entire operation, including shipping agencies, chartered vessels, outfitting places on the frontier, and experienced leadership, was run by the church. Charles Dickens's fascinating description of eight hundred Mormons on board the Amazon documents the rapid emergence of a functional social structure. Within a couple of hours, they had "established their own police, made their own regulations, and set their own watches at all the hatchways."[26] Daily language, civic, religious, and cultural indoctrination—which was apparently unique in intensity and effectiveness—guaranteed their rapid assimilation into Mormon culture. Upon arrival in Utah, new immigrants either assumed jobs previously matched with their skills, adopted new occupations, worked on public projects, or went on "missions" to establish new settlements. Extensive socialization activities continued until they were absorbed into the social structure of Zion.

If geographical and climatic conditions of the Great Basin initially forced the Saints to cope with subsistence, their leaders nonetheless reinforced the goal of economic autonomy. Through long-range planning, controlled land use, and the regulation of natural resources, they established the foundation of the Mormon economy. Brigham Young, who initially favored agriculture and home industry, opposed trading because it would force Mormons into the national economy. They would become suppliers of raw materials that would have to be repurchased at a "comparative disadvantage." However, the California gold rush of 1849 and 1850, which may have saved the Mormon economy, transformed Salt Lake City into a "half-way house" for California immigrants. This created both product and commodity markets for the Saints and provided some of the capital for the domestic industrialization efforts of the early 1850s. With an influx of British immigrants, the Mormons began their iron, textile, and sugar industries. If the latter initially failed, it provided the knowledge and skill that subsequently made sugar one of Utah's most profitable industries. The influx of gentiles, stimulated by the gold rush, destroyed many of the geographical boundaries that reinforced Mormon isolation; so church leaders acted to sharpen the social and cultural boundaries. They opposed mining, attempted to reinstate earlier forms of socialism, denounced dissenters, and rebaptized many of the Saints in order to "renew" their covenants. In short, the Mormon reformation, a form of revivalism, further delineated the boundaries between Mormons and gentiles and reaffirmed the primacy of group norms over individual desires. It demonstrated that it would take more than gold and an influx of gentiles to destroy Mormon separatism.

Space prohibits analysis of the numerous collective endeavors of Mormon society, which include irrigation, cooperative farming, resource management, industrial development, and public works. Yet the cooperative ethic, which underscored all of these, may be illustrated by a specific examination of the institution of tithing. During the 1850s and 1860s, it performed the economic functions of contemporary public and private institutions. Every ward (parish) and settlement had a tithing office to receive and distribute goods and services. Regional offices linked local tithing offices to the General Tithing Office or Bishops Store House in Salt Lake City. The latter served as a supply center and coordinated the overall operation. The Saints, who were expected to give one-tenth of their property upon joining the church and one-tenth of their income thereafter, paid tithing in property, produce, livestock, labor, cash, or a product (e.g., shoes from a shoemaker). Since most nineteenth-century tithes were paid in kind, especially through these two decades, major tasks of tithing offices involved the collection, storage, and redistribution of tithes. An institutional tithe, which anticipated the modern corporate profits tax, was collected from shops, stores, and factories, but its financial contribution was meager until the 1870s to 1880s.[27]

The significance of tithing as an economic institution is reflected in its multifunctional role. Providing capital for industrial development had less social significance than the redistribution of resources. Immigrants assigned to public works projects received compensation primarily in produce and commodities. Local tithing offices expended one-third of their resources, when their economic base permitted, on local operations, the poor, and Indians. They sent the remaining two-thirds to the General Tithing Office. Moreover, tithing offices functioned as exchange institutions. Individuals who brought eggs and cattle, for instance, could take out wheat and shoes, or receive credit to pay people who tithed with their labor. The extension of both producer and consumer credit and the option of "saving" usurped the role of banks. Individuals and businesses sometimes borrowed by withdrawing more tithing products than their credits justified and, on other occasions, saved by accumulating more credits than they withdrew. Tithing credits functioned like a modern check as individuals living in one community transferred their credits, on written orders, to support friends or family members in another community. "Tithing scrip," which became a medium of exchange, acknowledged the deposit in one tithing office and requested the withdrawal from another, with the General Tithing Office as the central coordinator. With the expansion of the tithing system, standard due bills which could be redeemed at tithing offices, also became a limited medium of exchange in the mountain west. They were even occasionally accepted by non-Mormon merchants, though typically at reduced value. So well organized and extensive was the institution of tithing that a group of northern Utah Mormons travelled to Southern California and back by depositing grain in the General Tithing Office and withdrawing commodities along the route, thereby saving cash for purchasing milling machinery in California.

Mormon economic policy emphatically opposed national trends, and the mounting "campaign against Mormonism was," as Arrington argues, part of "the rising national campaign for private property, the free market, competition, and unrestrained enterprise."[28] The 1865 Whig platform's denunciation of polygamy and slavery as "twin relics of barbarism" and Democratic President Buchanan's subsequent dispatching of 2,500 troops to control the Mormons may well have been motivated less by marriage patterns than by economic interests. Utah gentiles, who sought free markets and urged private enterprise, perceived Mormon institutions as a direct threat. They encouraged national politicians and Eastern capitalists to help destroy the Mormon Empire. While some advocated political and economic coercion, others were convinced that "natural" developments would destroy Mormon separatism. A particularly significant portent appeared with the completion of the transcontinental railroad in 1869, which brought more and cheaper Eastern goods into the Great Basin economy. Church leaders denounced those whose conspicuous consumption was based on trade with gentile merchants, and they reaffirmed a boycott of non-Mormon businesses. The School of the Prophets, a sort of council of economic advisors, and the Relief Society, a women's auxiliary, emerged to implement the boycott and to convince the Saints to avoid unnecessary expenditures. In order to reduce the consumption of tea, coffee, alcohol, and tobacco—of which Brigham Young had previously encouraged local production—the School of the Prophets and Relief

Society organized a complete boycott. It was under these conditions that the Word of Wisdom, which today requires abstinence, was transformed into a moral principle.

With the general failure of the boycott and the emergence of internal dissent favoring accommodation, the Zion's Cooperative Mercantile Institution (ZCMI) emerged to protect the Mormon economy. Some Utah communities had experimented with mercantile cooperatives, apparently imported from England via missionaries, but the threat of absorption into the national economy and the foundation of cooperative values and collective institutions were excellent conditions for their implementation among the Saints. Eighty-one cooperative stores were in operation within six weeks after the opening of ZCMI. If the appearance of a cooperative in small communities signaled doom for noncooperating local merchants, those in Salt Lake City created significant losses for local merchants. However, expanding markets created by the completion of the railroad, especially the new mining communities, saved many non-Mormon businesses.[29] At the same time, the cooperative movement reaffirmed Mormon values.

In fact it inspired a resurgence of early Mormon socialism. Many Saints believed the cooperatives would prepare them for the restoration of the Law of Consecration and Stewardship. During the 1870s, the United Orders—communitarian socialist experiments built upon principles of the original revelation—sprang up in several Mormon communities. Arrington et al list 222 different orders established during the 1870s and acknowledge that others will "undoubtedly" come to light with further research. Perhaps the most successful, famous, and thoroughly socialist was Orderville in southern Utah. Lasting for several years, it abolished private property, established communal meals, recreation, and rituals, and became self-sufficient. Though several factors contributed to its eventual disintegration, the energy devoted to the conflict over polygamy may have been the most crucial. These United Orders, according to Arrington, succeeded in promoting thrift which enabled capital accumulation for purchasing machinery and equipment, creating employment for the Saints and assuring more rapid development of resources, particularly "in areas where Utah had a comparative disadvantage."[30] For at least a decade, this resurgence of communitarian socialism reinforced Mormon separatism.

After Brigham Young's death in 1877, and the failure of several of the United Orders, his successor eased trading restrictions and established Zion's Central Board of Trade. As a cooperative effort, the board of trade encouraged greater private business but not without imposing constraints designed to serve public interests. Each valley, county, or stake (diocese) established a local board with representatives to meet with the central board during general conferences of the church. Central coordination replaced local self-sufficiency. Zion's Central Board of Trade created hundreds of jobs through obtaining contracts for the construction of railroads; it established a centralized marketing agency for exporting farm produce as far away as Montana and San Francisco; it imported farm implements, wagons, and buggies from the East; it regulated prices and prevented excessive price and product competition; and it negotiated reduced freight rates for the importation of foreign commodities and the exportation of local products. During 1844, the year of its greatest success, the board of trade collapsed because of the intensification of government harrassment of the Mormons. Be that as it may, this decade saw Mormons implementing their fundamental values. Officials reduced debts to the Perpetual Emigrating Fund, wards, and delinquent tithing by one-half; some Mormon capitalists and banks cancelled debts; and Mormon leaders redistributed wealth—primarily in the form of sheep, cattle, and wheat—in favor of the poor.

If confrontation with the state had strengthened the Mormon resolve for separatism through most of the nineteenth century, the intensification of governmental harrassment during the 1880s was simply too much. Polygamy, which assumes a central role in most explanations of this conflict, was actually a symbolic issue. Though Puritanical Americans who could care less about the Mormon economy or polity became indignant over this "barbaric" marriage practice, considerable evidence suggests that the issue of polygamy was simply a convenient means of mobilizing the resources to destroy Mormon separatism.[31] The radical challenges posed by the economic and political assumptions of the Mormon Kingdom of God threatened the American economy and denied the legitimacy of the nation-state. It was economic and political institutions, not polygamy, that justified accusations of Mormon rebellion. That Congress was more interested in controlling the Mormon economy and destroying the political power of the priesthood is easily inferred from the provisions of the anti-polygamy legislation itself. From the early Anti-Bigamy Act of 1862 to the Edmunds-Tucker Act of 1887, the legislation imposed extraordinary constraints on economic and political activity, including the disincorporation of the Mormon church, limitation of ownership of property to $50,000 for nondevotional purposes, disenfranchisement of significant segments of the Mormon population, the placing of territorial political power under control of federally appointed officers (non-Mormons), the abolition of women's suffrage, and the dissolution of the Perpetual Emigration Company with the confiscation of its resources in order to prevent Mormon immigration.[32] Since bills never enacted into law contained even more extreme economic and political constraints, it is that much more apparent that the anti-polygamy campaign extended well beyond polygamy.

That governmental prosecutions of polygamy (cohabitation) and the Saints' resistance profoundly affected the Mormon economy can no longer seriously be doubted. With most of their leaders in prison or hiding, business establishments were abandoned or operated by inexperienced wives and children. Cooperatives which fell under control of a few individuals were later converted into private enterprises. The socialistic communities which had survived into the 1880s were dismantled; and Zion's Board of Trade no longer regulated Mormon business. This was, as Arrington argues, a period when

> almost every business history, in short, shows stagnation; almost every family history records widespread suffering and misery. Above all, the church, as the prime stimulator, financier, and regulator of the Mormon economy, was forced to withdraw from participation in most phases of activity. The Raid, in other words, was a period of crippled group activity of every type, of decline in cooperative trade and industry—a period when, above all, church economic support was essential but not forthcoming—a period when planning would have saved much, but when the planners dared not plan.[33]

Last ditch efforts to save their economic resources saw the Mormons establishing private trusts to hold church property; signing the title of meeting houses, tithing offices, granaries, herds, stores, and irrigation projects over to local wards and stakes; and selling of livestock on church ranches in Idaho, Arizona, and Wyoming to Mormon capitalists. However, these efforts failed, and a compromise with the government resulted in the surrendering of "well in excess of $1,000,000."[34] With Mormon property falling under federal receivership and the Supreme Court upholding the Edmunds-Tucker Act, the Saints were left with the choice of accommodation or annihilation.

ACCOMMODATION: AN ERA OF CORPORATE CAPITALISM

The manifesto of 1890, in which Mormon leaders committed the Saints to "practice" plural marriage no longer, marks the public acknowledgment of accommodation. Using the precedence of the Supreme Court ruling in the 1862 anti-bigamy act, the declaration reaffirmed Mormon belief in the divine origin of plural marriage but now forbade its practice. A belief in upholding the laws of the land—not previously a preoccupation of Mormons—was juxtaposed with the practice of polygamy to reaffirm commitment to a principle which would not be lived as long as it was forbidden by law. By dichotomizing belief and action, a significant departure from traditional Mormonism, the manifesto legitimated the change from a posture of resistance to accommodation without repudiating polygamy. The same dichotomy between belief and action, which enabled the mystification of basic Mormon doctrines, was employed to justify political and economic assimilation.

The Mormons could not have exchanged polygamy for monogamy, theocracy for democracy, and communitarian socialism for corporate capitalism so easily without profound changes in their theology. A new ideology was necessary to legitimate a new social arrangement with the larger society. The old social order—embodied in the notion of the Kingdom of God as a concrete political and material entity—was being built in the land of Zion upon values of order, unity, and equality. The gathering of the faithful was the means for building this empire, the administration of which would be turned over to Jesus upon his Second Coming. However, it was this theology of the Kingdom of God and the gathering that became a major casualty of accommodation along with, of course, the social institutions for which it had provided meaning.

The Kingdom of God was perhaps the easiest conception to change. Since there were theological contexts in which the church and the Kingdom of God were synonomous, the mere lack of discourse about political and economic aspects—basic to the original conception—tended to blur the distinction. When the church and the Kingdom of God were not regarded as synonomous, the latter became an other-worldly kingdom to be established at some undetermined point in the future, usually after Jesus's return. Material objectives became spiritual ideals. Mormon leaders transformed the Kingdom of God into a mystical entity. Losing its specific, material meaning, the Saints relegated the Kingdom of God to the realm of metaphysics. It is worth noting that apologetic histories throughout this century, either by ignoring the traditional conception of the Kingdom of God or imposing contemporary meanings on it, have reinterpreted Mormon history. By treating "political Mormonism" as the bogeyman of apostates and anti-Mormons, apologists have absolved the Saints of any responsibility for their historical conflicts and transformed the Kingdom of God from a material entity into a metaphysical ideal.

The conception of Zion underwent a similar transformation. If early Mormonism avoided the pitfall of fixing the Second Coming in time, it was not so cautious with space. The Second Coming would occur in Zion, which was identified by revelation as western Missouri. Several elusive phrases in the Book of Mormon eased the difficulties of relocating

Zion as the Saints were periodically compelled to do; and various explanations for "redeeming Zion," whereby the Saints would return to Jackson County to reclaim their lost property, or relocating it, for instance in the "tops of the mountains," occurred throughout the nineteenth century. After the manifesto, two other themes predominated. Zion was first conceived as all of North America and later as the "pure-in-heart." The latter, which is the predominant conception today, again transformed concrete material meanings into passive nontemporal and nonspatial forms. Zion is no longer a place, a specific location; it is an attitude, a state of mind. Zion is the pure-in-heart.

With Zion no longer a specific place nor the Kingdom of God a concrete reality, the gathering became meaningless. Mormon separatism had ended. Having acknowledged the legitimacy of Babylon, it was no longer necessary to "gather out of her midst." Consequently a policy of urging the Saints to remain in their native lands to build the church replaced the most fundamental doctrine of early Mormonism. Incidently the language shifted from building the Kingdom, the ideal society, to building the church, an institution. Neither the gathering, nor the Kingdom of God, nor Zion made sense without the prospects of an independent Mormon Empire. Accommodation destroyed their theological meanings and social functions, and it has made the Mormon diaspora official policy since the turn of the century.

Political and economic capitulation soon followed the manifesto. The Mormon "Peoples' Party" disbanded. Church authorities literally divided the Saints among the Republican and Democratic parties in order to increase their prospects for statehood. Economic institutions underwent two immediate phases of accommodation. The first, which began in 1882 with the opening of manufacturing and retailing to private enterprise, led to an increase in both Mormon and gentile businesses. Mormon institutions, including most of the local manufacturing and mercantile cooperatives, were secularized or sold to private interests. In fact, the trading of shares leading to greater concentration had advanced sufficiently that the noted economist Richard T. Ely, writing in 1903, could observe that the Mormon experience was no longer "wholly encouraging to believers in cooperative principles."[35] The second phase, according to Arrington, appeared with "the arrangements made to finance new companies in the 1890's." Though the church failed to withdraw from economic life as the gentiles hoped, it departed radically from the past by using its credit and resources to assist private endeavors and by "actively soliciting financial assistance from outsiders." A major consequence of this strategy was the eventual absentee ownership and control of the Utah economy by Eastern capitalists.

If completion of the transcontinental railroad in 1869 portended the end of Mormon separatism, as many scholars believe, then construction of the Hotel Utah, near the turn of the century, symbolized Mormonism's new era of corporate capitalism. Rural Saints especially rebelled against the use of tithing funds to build a luxurious hotel whose clientele would be mostly wealthy gentiles. The selling of liquor, forbidden to loyal Mormons, underscored the pecuniary preoccupation of priestly leaders and aggravated traditional Mormons. Indeed, the hiatus became so wide that President Joseph F. Smith defended the hotel and bar at a general conference.[36] With the Hotel Utah as a visible symbol of economic accommodation, the prophetic era of Mormonism came to an end.

The church wasted little time, as construction of the hotel illustrates, in implementing capitalist techniques. Mormon leaders repurchased properties of which the church had previously disposed and joined with capitalists to finance additional enterprises. By the mid-twentieth century, the church, according to *Business Week*, was probably "the biggest— and certainly the most diversified aggregation of capital in the Mountain West."[37] In addition to extensive nonprofit enterprises, the church owned or controlled insurance, sugar, and publishing companies; retail and wholesale distribution outlets; a newspaper and radio and television stations; banks and securities corporations; hotels and motels; cattle ranches; textile mills; food processing concerns; irrigating companies; an airline; and extensive real estate. By 1958, the church either had the controlling interest or owned corporations worth an estimated $200 million and fixed assets in "hundreds of smaller, nonprofit, 'welfare' enterprises" of $30 million.[38] The last public report of expenditures, which included nothing about income, occurred for 1955 with a total outlay of $86 million.[39] In 1962, Morgan, in a controversial article, quoted the mayor of Salt Lake City as saying the church made over $365 million a year.[40] Significant estimates for 1975 place income at $3 million a day, or over $1 billion annually. While $550 million are attributed to tithing and other contributions, the gross business income apparently exceeds $450 million without even considering "rental of commercial buildings and apartments, real estate transactions, interest and dividends from investments not made public, large individual donations, or royalties to the Tabernacle Choir for its record albums."[41] Even excluding the enormous capital investment in welfare holdings, these analysts claim that the church's assets place it among the fifty largest corporations in the country. Jeffery Kaye, from his recent study of Mormon economic activity in California (which incidentally describes several conflicts over tax exempt status of Mormon properties), concludes that the "Mormon church wields more economic power more effectively than any other organized religion in the world."[42] While it is extremely difficult to evaluate Kaye's generalization or to determine the extent of Mormon capitalism, there can be no doubt that the contemporary church is a multinational corporation in the most profound economic sense.

Not surprisingly, ideological justification and opposition to the labor movement accompanied the emergence of corporate capitalism. Traditional Mormonism, as should be obvious, repudiated economic inequality and regarded capitalism as a sin. In the late 1800s, Mormon leaders still warned the Saints of the adverse consequences of capitalism. A document signed by the First Presidency and the Council of the Twelve Apostles in 1875 read:

A condition of affairs existed among us which was favorable to the growth of riches in the hands of few at the expense of the many. A wealthy class was being rapidly formed in our midst from those of the rest of our community. The growth of such a class was dangerous to our union; and, of all people, we stand most in need of union and to have our interests identical. Then it was that the Saints were counseled to enter into cooperation. In the absence of the necessary faith to enter upon a more perfect order revealed by the Lord unto the Church, this was felt to be the best means of drawing us together and making us one.[43]

By the first decade of this century, many Mormon officials had come full circle. Reed Smoot, an apostle and conservative Republican, represented Utah in the Senate and worked aggressively to foster the image of Mormons as fiscal conservatives and laissez faire capitalists. Mormon leaders began to equate the economic freedom of laissez faire capitalism with Mormon theological notions of free agency. They subsequently denounced the New Deal as the harbinger of socialism and have since associated even the most meager efforts of government intervention in the economy or public expenditures that might enhance economic equality with tampering with a divinely constituted social order.[44] While heaping accolades on free enterprise, they attribute all manner of social evils, including crime, delinquency, divorce, illegitimacy, and civil disobedience, to expansion of the welfare state. This identification of free-agency with capitalism and characterization of reform movements as attempts to get "something for nothing" has enabled Mormon leaders to legitimate inequality and abandon a fundamental goal of traditional Mormonism. Those scriptures equating inequality with sin—for instance, "It is not good that one man should possess that which is above another, wherefore the world lieth in sin" (D & C 49:20)—are seldom heard from Mormon pulpits today.

The relative economic equality in early Utah—at least one-fourth more equal than the nation according to Arrington's analysis—and the church's official identification with the worker would have made unions less necessary. Even so, the first one, a local typographical union, appeared with Brigham's blessing in 1852. For several years the church supported unions, only becoming suspicious with the large influx of gentiles associated with mining. The church newspaper in 1855 declared:

The capitalists and mighty men of the earth should notify the Lord that he made a mistake when forming the balance of the human family, and petition that they be made with bones of iron, sinews, nerves, ligaments and muscles of steel, and flesh of brass. Then they could labor for them without food, rest, or shelter, and would not have to answer for not "multiplying and replenishing the earth"; neither would the magnates then have to account for the terrible oppression they are meting out to their fellows, often depriving them of the enjoyment even of the pure air and light of heaven and of the pure water of earth, of the privileges of properly raising families, of the necessary society of friends, of all or nearly all of the chances for mental improvement, crushing them down to constant physical work and toil, with little or no remuneration. For this cause we suggest to the corrupt wealthy of the world that they consider and practice upon the idea that their fellow beings are flesh and blood like themselves, that they have a right to a fair share of the bounties bestowed by a kind creator, and cease using human beings as though they were made of iron, steel, and brass.[45]

This statement clearly challenges the position of contemporary Mormon leaders. Their speeches and editorials in the Mormon press continually endorse the Taft-Hartly Act, Utah's right-to-work legislation, and the employer's right to hire whomever he wishes. The latter presumably allows him to reject union members. So adament is the position of church leaders that during the Johnson administration's attempt to repeal the Taft-Hartly Act, the First Presidency attempted to influence the votes of the three Mormon senators and eight Mormon congressmen. Five replied rebuking the Mormon presidency for impropriety.[46]

However, the Mormon authorities seem to have convinced most of the Saints. Davies, from a national sample of Mormons, found an inverse relationship between union membership and active involvement in the church. Moreover, the higher the position in the Mormon hierarchy the less the involvement with unions. Only 16 percent of the bishops and none of the stake presidents were union members. It is hard to imagine any general authority (the highest ecclesiastical positions) who would identify with a union. Perhaps this general economic conservatism can also be inferred from Davies's data on party identification. While the general membership only slightly favored the Republicans, the greater the involvement in the church, the greater the identification with the Republican Party. The relationship with leadership was even more pronounced. While 55 percent of the bishops identified with the Republicans, 89 percent of the stake presidents did so.[47] There is no doubt that party identification among the general authorities, who are not included in Davies's data, would be well over 90 percent Republican. Surely this opposition to labor, the legitimation of free enterprise, and the corporate capitalism of the church attest to Mormon assimilation into American society.

But what of Mormon values? How have they fared accommodation? While economic equality was abandoned, the values of work, achievement, and education survived. Losing much of their collective character, they remain profoundly this-worldly and are legitimated by a thoroughly American ideology. Consequently, many Mormons pursue business careers. Research by a management consulting firm found, when population was controlled, that more presidents of the nation's largest 471 corporations were born in Utah than any other state. Preliminary analysis suggests they were also disproportionately from Mormon backgrounds. Remarkable "achievement in high-level government executive positions" followed. Both have been explained as "part of a larger achievement of excellence."[48] Despite the disproportionately high number of Mormons in the upper echelons of business, bankruptcy data indicate there also may be a disproportionately high rate of failures. Personal bankruptcy in Utah, according to the University of Utah Bureau of Economic and Business Research, has been higher than the national average for several years. Since a strong cultural emphasis on personal success is likely to encourage greater risk taking, we may expect higher rates of both success and failure.

Mormon values have probably also contributed to greater relative income for the Saints. Data are not readily accessible, but some research indicates that the Mormons are above the national average. A study based on 1962 data found that being a Mormon did not contribute to greater income after education and occupation were controlled.[49] Unless other Mormon values or Mormon affiliation were assumed to increase opportunities for greater income within the same occupation, then we should not expect being a Mormon to make any difference. However, it does not follow that Mormonism has not contributed significantly to educational differences—as we will soon discover—which in turn affect income differentials. Carlson's projections for national and Mormon income differences in the year 2000 assume that the median income for Mormons during 1968 was $1,174 higher than the national median. If his assumptions are correct, there will be over $4,000 difference by 2000.[50] It appears that the values of achievement and industry have enabled the Mormons to compete with other Americans.

Nowhere has Mormon achievement been more impressive than in education. Here was a fundamental value that required little reinterpretation during accommodation. Utah has consistently led the nation in educational achievement. Census data show that it ranks first among the states in the percentage of its population completing high school between 1950 and 1970. E. L. Thorndike's initial study of the origin of scientists appearing in the 1938 edition of *American Men of Science* found Utah easily the most productive state.[51] His subsequent inclusion of *Leaders in Education* and *Who's Who in America* guaranteed Utah the same status.[52] Most recently Hardy has examined states in which Ph.D. recipients received their baccalaureates from 1920 to 1961, and found that Utah ranked first in the behavioral and social sciences, second in education, third in the physical sciences, and sixth in the arts and professions. For all fields combined, Utah ranked first throughout the period.[53] Even if Hardy has overgeneralized from these and similar data to establish a value complex for explaining these relationships, there is little doubt of the Mormons' remarkable educational achievement.

Nor is it surprising that the this-worldly nature of Mormonism, embodied in values associated with education and economic success, would manifest itself in politics. The years of political conflict, from at least 1833 to 1890, sharpened the Saints' political skills. Even a vindictive Congress, which refused to seat one elected official and almost a second at the turn of the century, failed to inhibit Mormon political involvement. While the Saints have often been charged with dominating political processes, seldom have they been accused of political apathy. Gaustad found four times the Mormon representation in the 1968 Senate than their population would warrant, but representation in the House was consistent with their population.[54] Mormons, he concludes, generally have disproportionate political influence. I have calculated the percentage of those among the voting age population who actually voted in the presidential elections from 1960 to 1972 and found the Utah mean of 75.4 percent to rank first among the states. These data not only illustrate the Mormon involvement in political life but document the extent of their assimilation into American society.

That Mormons fared better during accommodation than many other minorities does not mean that their most unique values and institutions have survived. Indeed, Mormon collectivism and the quest for economic equality, as this paper argues, became casualties of accommodation. Even so, vestiges of Mormon cooperation remain. The contemporary welfare program, which may have more symbolic than actual value, reflects both the conservatism of accommodation and the cooperative values of an earlier era. Emerging during the Great Depression, it received accolades from conservatives who found in it an alternative to the New Deal. It was they who contrived the myth that none of the Saints were on the public dole.[55] Some liberals, on the other hand, saw the program as a reactionary tactic to reduce the influence of the federal government—a return to nineteenth-century Mormon protectionism.[56] Both were overstatements. The Mormon welfare program was a response to immediate circumstances, but it drew heavily upon Mormonism's past. The acquisition of stake farms and ward projects, which relied on voluntary labor, simply returned to economic modes long familiar to the Saints. Collection of fast offerings—the cost of meals missed during a twenty-four hour fast which were redistributed to the poor—and tithing were hardly novel. Nor was the use of the Women's Relief Society and men's priesthood quorums to organize the work and distribute the resources. Today this program is large, but it probably does considerably less than is popularly believed. In 1971 it depended upon 3,990,515 hours of voluntary labor; 478 stake projects producing agricultural products, processing farm produce, baking goods, or manufacturing articles; and $8,635,000 in fast offerings, $5,487,800 in grants from church funds, and $3,600,000 in donated commodities. It currently provides resources for the poor Saints and general disaster relief around the world. However, a distinction between the "worthy" and "unworthy" poor and a stigma associated with the Mormon program forces many to seek public welfare.

The perseverance of cooperative values is most pronounced among rural Mormons where social relations reinforce them. O'Dea and Vogt found, in a comparative study of two very similar communities, that the one built upon cooperative Mormon values mobilized the energy and resources to complete several tasks which the community founded upon "rugged individualism" failed to do.[57] Leone, who recently found similar patterns in Arizona communities settled by Mormon colonists, also argues that the ecclesiastical structure which involves Mormons in a variety of positions prepares them for a world with considerable occupational mobility.[58] However, as the Mormon population becomes less rural, the pressures of accommodation intensify, threatening the last vestige of traditional Mormon social practice.

CONCLUSIONS

This transition from communitarian socialism to corporate capitalism— from resistance to accommodation—reveals the remarkable adaptability of Mormon institutions and beliefs. If the Saints themselves fared better than other minorities, they did not reenter mainstream America without considerable cost. The cooperative values and collective institutions of traditional Mormonism, which at the very least could serve as a critique of the excessive fragmentation and competition of American life, no longer guide the Saints. Nor does the vision of the Kingdom of God as an attainable social order. It has been relegated to the realm of metaphysics, referring at most to an other-worldly entity to be established by God at some remote point in the future. The social institutions that would make the Kingdom of God a concrete reality have long been abandoned. By replacing polygamy, theocracy, and communitarian socialism with monogamy, democracy, and corporate capitalism, the Latter-day Saints appear to have become even more committed to the modern institutions of Babylon than their fellow citizens. Today they are among the least likely to transform American society into a more humane social order.

FRANK RENKIEWICZ

THE PROFITS OF NONPROFIT CAPITALISM
Polish Fraternalism and Beneficial Insurance in America

"Seed to seed and there will be a measure," concluded one Polish-American propagandist for fraternal insurance in 1901. Proverbial and parochial wisdom perhaps, it epitomized the myth of the Polish immigration: the bad times and the implied failure of leadership in the old country, the formula of hard work and saving which brought success, and the uncertainty and narrowness of the victory for a better life in the new land. The very repetition of the premises of the myth gave it a kind of validity: "It was not good times that brought us to America. Practically all of us came here for bread, and all of us must fight for it"; and, "Today we are lifting ourselves out of material helplessness and have won a high position. . . . The best way to this is thrift." And again, "Let Polish savings go into Polish hands and into Polish industry. Let these savings circulate among the Poles and we will all benefit."[1]

Insurance fraternals, the institutions which did most to articulate the basic myth of the immigration, were rooted in the modern history of Poland, particularly in the growth of a secular national consciousness and the liberation of the peasant from serfdom, as well as in the circumstances of an industrializing society in the United States. The first of these factors chronologically, modern Polish nationalism, had its origins late in the eighteenth century among the gentry and gentry-based intelligentsia of the politically decadent Commonwealth of Poland. Its spirit animated many of the reformers among them who sought to modernize the nation's political institutions and, somewhat less so, its social structure. They failed in their immediate purpose—to preserve the Polish state against the grinding rivalries of the surrounding great powers—and Poland disappeared from the political map (if not from the politics) of Europe between 1795 and 1918.

The effort to explain the partition of Poland generated a long and bitter debate among Polish politicians and intellectuals. One of the chief explanations lies in the countryside where most Poles lived until the 1950s. Rural Poland in the eighteenth and nineteenth centuries exhibited an extraordinary range of social conditions: a few aristocratic families at the top with holdings and a style of life eclipsing that of many kings; a gentry, the largest in Europe, whose acute sense of social superiority masked wide differences in material position; and a peasantry, enserfed but holding the seeds of a complicated class structure of its own. The ordinary clergy, which provided such intellectual leadership as existed, was drawn without much regard to class from the lower gentry and better-off peasants. Integral to Polish society, but somewhat outside this class structure were Jews (as rural innkeepers, petty traders and bankers, urban craftsmen, and workers), Germans (in rural colonies and towns in the west), and Lithuanian, Podlesian, Ruthenian, and Ukrainian peasants in the east. Many Jews and eastern peasants had been partly Polonized through centuries of contact with Poles or control by Polish landlords.

For about a century, from 1770 to 1870, most leaders of Polish society—both nationalists and accomodators to foreign rule—reflected the interests of aristocratic and gentry landlords and remained largely indifferent to the peasantry's economic goals. Though much discussed by political and social activists, the end of serfdom was accomplished between 1808 and 1864 at the instance of the foreign powers which had partitioned Poland. The inability of native leadership to resolve the peasant question weighed heavily in the failure of repeated efforts to overthrow foreign rule from 1794 to 1864. The Polishness of the peasant was long embodied, therefore, not in some secular concept of the nation, but in the special kind of Catholicism which had developed since the militant Counter-Reformation of the seventeenth century, a mixture of folk-family culture predating Christianity, a messianic historical tradition which portrayed Poland as the eastern outpost of Western Christianity, and a pattern of liturgical and devotional practice centering on the Virgin Mary, heroic or long-suffering saints, pilgrimage (especially to the great shrine of Czestochowa), and great public feast days, such as Corpus Christi. A language as varied regionally as devotional practice provided the indispensable and uniquely Polish vocabulary of religious-cultural expression.

The great migration of Polish peasants from 1870 to 1930 followed very much from the unforeseen results of peasant emancipation and coincided with the growth of national consciousness among ordinary country people. Peasants quickly discovered that the abolition of serfdom and personal freedom did not confer economic advantage in the form of land ownership, increased competition among employers for their services as laborers, or alternative nonagricultural employment. However, late in the nineteenth century, the market forces which themselves had been altered by emancipation provided remedies. Chief among these was the acquisition of land by a minority of well-off peasants. It was the only investment that made sense to the peasant (as it remains in socialist Poland where most farm land is still privately owned in small or medium-sized units). The peasants—guided at first by intelligentsia and enlightened landlords and, later, on their own initiative—turned also to economic and political cooperation. Their struggle for genuine independence took many forms: consumer cooperatives, savings and loan banks, agricultural associations (for the purchase of machinery, seed, or breeding stock), the education of the young (both male and female to promote economic progress and prevent denationalization), and conservative populist political parties. Most of these social mechanisms had their formal origins in western Europe, but they were entirely consistent with Polish conditions and thinking after the failure of the last "romantic" uprising of 1863-64. The Polish village, in which even the most private elements of home and family were matters of communal concern, already provided a stable framework for spontaneous social action and innovation. Under the slogan "organic work" the Polish national elite elaborated an apolitical program of social progress through economic self-help, a kind of conservative reformism. "We want to extend work and learning in society," wrote Aleksander Swietochowski, a leading ideologue of this positivist and realist school, "to discover new resources, to utilize existing ones, and to concern ourselves with our own problems and not those of others."[2] By 1914, upper-class peasants had acquired considerable experience in cooperative social techniques and in the purchase and management of real estate through private or state banks. In the tradition of Polish rural life, they found many would-be imitators among the majority who made up the lower ranks of their class.

The alternative to upward mobility on the land was geographic mobility. Migration, a normal part of Polish life after 1870, followed several main channels: rural and seasonal within Poland itself, to the growing cities of Poland, westward to the industrial German Rhineland (Belgium and France after 1919), eastward to central Russia and Siberia, and overseas to the semi-jungle of southern Brazil and the farms and factories of the United States. Though interrelated, each line of migration had its special character. For example, the departure of country people and the growth of prosperous big farms in Poznania and West

Prussia in 1870-90, was followed by seasonal migration from adjacent Russian Poland to work in the newly intensive agriculture. Then, the growth of heavy industry in western Germany diverted Prussian Poles from the United States almost entirely after 1890. They were succeeded by a flood of immigrants from the Russian and Austrian provinces, a movement halted temporarily by World War I and then finally by restrictive U.S. laws in the 1920s and the onset of the Great Depression. Most overseas migrants from Russia and Austria came from the lower peasantry. By contrast, the hundreds of thousands of Russian Poles who travelled overland to the interior provinces of the tsarist empire included a high percentage of artisans, small entrepreneurs, and educated and professional folk.[3]

Altogether, some 3.1 million ethnic Poles emigrated through 1914. Perhaps as many emigrated and returned to the homeland, and several times that number were affected through family and village connections, a ratio which varied widely according to regional rates of migration. Record keeping by political and not by ethnic origin being what it was in the United States prior to 1910, it will never be known how many came to this country. The most recent analysis puts the number between 1.1 and 1.8 million, probably about halfway between the two.[4]

Within a decade in any place settled by more than a few families, the outlines of a social structure and its institutional expression—the local Polonia—were apparent. There has always been disagreement about the core institution in American Polonia, a matter of more than academic interest since the answer presumes a certain ideological approach to the community. The parish is commonly accepted as the institutional focus of Polish-American society, a kind of reworking of the European village into a form suited to the early urban, industrial economy of the United States. Upwards of 800 Roman and National Catholic parishes since the first Polish foundation in 1854 were created to meet every conceivable social purpose. However, there is reason to think of the parish as only one expression—important but subsidiary nevertheless—of the Polish-American village-neighborhood or commune. Every parish for long was established on lay initiative, usually by some society which gathered money, purchased land, recruited a priest, and (normally) worked with local non-Polish episcopal authority. Furthermore, many organizations and facilities, like the Polish Homes which proliferated in the second generation, existed separately but in symbiotic relationship with the churches. Polonia, like Poland itself, has long included non-Roman Catholic elements which, however grudgingly it is conceded by some, must be counted central to its society and history. These have included in modern times socialists and National Catholics as well as, more traditionally, the Jews, Germans, Ukrainians, and Lithuanians who were linked to Polish as well as to their primary ethnic culture. There was in fact a single Polonia, both local and regional, with complementary secular and religious dimensions, each with its special functions and hierarchy and each eager to influence the other. The tension between them, which has its roots in Poland, probably contributed to the immigrant peasants' further identification of themselves as Polish. Fraternalism tried to accommodate this diversity in Polish life more fully than did the parish (even as, ironically, it adjusted to American culture).

Cooperative institutions, loosely similar in spirit to the ones growing up in the Polish countryside but adapted to the circumstances of urban life, were soon apparent among the new migrants. The Prussian provinces (western Poland) were the homes of the earliest models of organic work, rural as well as urban. Workers in Upper Silesia, the oldest industrialized region of Poland, turned in 1850-70 to the mutual aid society for protection against the stresses of their environment.[5] Perhaps coincidentally, Upper Silesia was the home also of the earliest peasant migration to the United States and of many of the founders of the first mutual aid societies and the Polish Roman Catholic Union in America.[6] (The leaders of the other early major American fraternal, the Polish National Alliance, often came from Russian Poland with its century-long tradition of insurrection and ethnically diverse population. Their outlook—nationalist, liberal, and cosmopolitan—contrasted sharply with the clerical, inward-looking, and narrowly Polish orientation of the Union.)

Polish-American fraternalism with a beneficial character emerged formally in the young immigrant colony on Chicago's near northwest side in the late 1860s. As in Silesia, the low level of mobility in industrial society strongly disposed the immigrant to pool his resources, reinforcing the old village custom of mutual aid as a means of paying funeral expenses. The first of the breed in America, the St. Stanislaus Kostka Society, was founded in 1864 and reestablished in 1866. Led by staunch Roman Catholics like Peter Kiolbassa, Chicago's foremost Polish lay leader for nearly forty years, it proposed also to create the first Polish church in the city. Within a year, a similar and rival group, the *Gmina Polska* (the Polish Commune), challenged the society by trying to convert the planned parish into an autonomous stronghold of Polish nationalism. The nationalists lost this first round—the leadership of such persons as the pioneer publisher Wladyslaw Dyniewicz notwithstanding—and St. Stanislaus Kostka Church, which opened in 1871, fell under the control of the Romanist Congregation of the Resurrection and the autocratic Vincent Barzynski, its pastor from 1874 to 1899.[7]

Soon afterwards, in 1873, building on a suggestion of Jan Barzynski, the priest's editor-brother, the clerical party organized what became known as the Polish Roman Catholic Union of America (the PRCU). A federation of parishes and an alliance mostly of priests, though it has long called itself the mother of Polish-American fraternals, the PRCU held two conventions in 1874 and 1875, enacted a set of rules at the second meeting, and informally adopted Jan Barzynski's *Gazeta Katolicka* (Polish Catholic Gazette) as its organ. Dedicated to the protection of the immigrant and the preservation of Roman Catholicism, the new organization lacked the cement of a sufficiently strong common material interest among its members. Divided further by localism in Chicago and Detroit, the PRCU led only a shadowy existence until 1886. The benefit societies appearing in the parishes in the 1870s still functioned autonomously, collecting various fees (membership, insignia, monthly) and levying special assessments on the occasion of a member's death.

Meanwhile, in 1872, the Chicago nationalists regrouped as the St. Joseph Mutual Aid Society and established Holy Trinity Church nearly within earshot of St. Stanislaus. A long struggle for control with Father Barzynski ended in their favor in 1893 through the intervention of Rome and the Apostolic Delegate in Washington. In 1879, they and their allies in Philadelphia and New York prompted a public proposal from Agaton Giller, a distinguished exile in Switzerland, to unite the American Polonia. The basis of their action was a secular and realistic analysis of the Polish cause in light of the new peasant emigration, the failure of the insurrection in 1863-64, and the continuing transformation of Polish society. In the spirit of organic work they concluded that the nation would be served best through the education, social and economic progress, unification, and integration into American political life of all Polish immigrants. Presumably a prosperous and partially acculturated though not assimilated Polonia would provide a base for the revival of Poland when conditions warranted direct action. Events in World War I proved the judgment of Giller and his American colleagues not far wrong, and their definition of the social role of the immigration still governs broadly the thinking of their successors in the Polish National Alliance (PNA). At a meeting in Philadelphia in August 1880, several societies who shared these views laid the foundations. The first diet or convention in late September in Chicago and incorporation (as the United Polish National Benevolent Society) in December promised a good beginning. After the second diet in 1881, the nationalists established the weekly newspaper *Zgoda* (Harmony) in New York City, which also served briefly as national headquarters.[8]

If the St. Stanislaus Kostka Society was the prototype for the early local benefit society, the PNA was to become the model for national fraternals. Its first constitution in 1881 stood midway between the ideal of an ecumenical nationalist alliance and the reality of self-sufficient local lodges, something less than a scheme for the centralized insurance operation of even the early twentieth century. It proposed to carry out an ambitious program of material aid to the immigrant through an initiation fee and monthly dues of five cents per member of constituent groups. The possibility of membership by entire parishes and church communities was left open. A separately financed Association of Posthumous Relief was created to share the burden of a death benefit with the local societies, raising its money through a one dollar initiation and an assessment of one dollar from each member at the death of a member.[9]

The administrative structure of the alliance has been one of its enduring features. Membership was open to all persons (males, in fact) of Polish descent through lodges (themselves flexibly defined institutions). Supreme power rested in an annual (now quadrennial) diet representing all members through lodge delegates. The unicameral diet derived its name, some officers (such as a marshall) and some procedures from the *Sejm* or Diet of Poland, albeit a reformed and more efficient or Americanized version of that ancient parliament. A censor, a unique officer, presided at the Diet, headed a commission which judged the frequent disputes for power and representation and saw to it that the alliance and its publications remained true to their purposes. He was a kind of elected judge and constitutional monarch, frequently a powerful force but also illustrative of the Polish tendency to diffuse authority and render an institution weak. The administrative officers were headed by a president, but the general secretary, the only full-time salaried officer at first, was responsible for routine management. In time the officers formed an executive board or Central Government. Aside from the office of censor and with the addition of part-time regional directors and administrators in the early twentieth century, the PNA system became the model for Polish fraternals.

Though the Polish National Alliance set the pace for Polish-American fraternalism in the long run, it remained quite small and the center of painful contention during its first fifteen years. Catholic clergy like Father Barzynski and Buffalo's John Pitass, who objected to the PNA's secular definition of Polishness, launched the severest attacks. The resentment over the failure to exclude church independents, "atheists," "infidels," Jews, anarchists, socialists or Masons—the names by which the enemy was known varied a great deal—led finally to a secession of moderately nationalist clericals under Father Dominic Majèr of St. Paul in 1889-90.

Organized formally in 1895, the Majer group eventually split along regional lines when it reoriented itself toward its eastern areas of strength between 1905 and 1915. One branch incorporated as the Polish Union in the United States (Wilkes-Barre, Pennsylvania); the other as the Polish Union in America (Buffalo, New York). Both steered clear of the strong ideological commitments of the PRCU and the PNA.[10]

The argument over the admission of socialists was in effect a debate over the social and political ideology of the alliance and the Polonia. The nascent socialist movement in Poland in the 1880s and the parties growing out of it in the 1890s abandoned the philosophy of gradualism and self-improvement in favor of immediate, radical social change and direct resistance to the partition governments on class grounds. Urban industrial workers and Marxist ideology (usually) provided the basis for action. Eventually Joseph Pilsudski emerged from the ranks of the Polish Socialist Party to lead the internal struggle for Polish independence during the World War. The left was voted both in and out of the PNA in the 1880s and 1890s. Finally, after 1900, it found a more comfortable home in the Alliance of Polish Socialists (allied with Pilsudksi's PPS), the Polish section of the Socialist Party in the United States and, also, after 1919, in groups associated with the Communist Party of the United States. The American Polish left insisted on focusing on Poland's affairs and the class struggle and eschewed the fraternal or insurance principle entirely. In that it was truer to the romantic revolutionary tradition of the early nineteenth century than any other political grouping in Poland. As a result, however, the left never won many formal adherents in the Polonia though it had an important role in the struggles to shape the community's policy toward Poland in both World Wars and to organize the Polish-American worker in 1935-45. Its influence was limited also by the PNA and PRCU which, rhetorically and sometimes administratively, supported economic justice for the Polish-American worker. The separation from the socialists, when it was finally voted early in the twentieth century, effectively allied the PNA with the National Democrats in internal Polish politics and dulled the edge of American clerical anger.[11]

Both the PNA and the PRCU were afflicted throughout their early years with internal geographic and personal rivalries. These were resolved after a fashion in the PNA by reincorporation as an insurance corporation in 1887 and by settling publications and headquarters in Chicago in 1888, by then the most populous center of American Polonia. Erasmus Jerzmanowski, a wealthy New York businessman-inventor and the chief figure in the Eastern wing, abandoned the struggle in 1896 and returned to Poland. Easterners who might have been expected to join the PNA often enrolled afterwards in the Polish National Alliance of Brooklyn and the

Association of the Sons of Poland, both founded in 1903, which were particularly strong in the metropolitan areas of northern New Jersey, southern New York and western Connecticut. The two Polish Unions continued to grow in the other centers of Polish settlement in the East, northeastern Pennsylvania and western New York.[12]

The clerical forces, as they regrouped to meet the challenge of the PNA, encountered many of the same problems. Father Vincent Barzynski, working closely with Peter Kiolbassa and other lay allies in 1886–87, imitated the alliance by converting the PRCU into a federation of (parochial) societies and creating a separate Death Benefit Fund. The fund offered a $600 benefit to members and $300 to their wives, and all societies soon enrolled in the program. The union adopted an official newspaper organ: *Wiara i Ojczyzna* (Faith and Fatherland) in 1887, and *Naród Polski* (The Polish Nation) in 1897. A separate Association of Polish Priests, resembling the original PRCU, was organized in 1887 to look after such matters as a Polish Catholic immigrants' home in New York City. It promptly affiliated with the union. As a result, the PRCU enjoyed a spurt of growth through the early 1890s, paying out about $36,000 by 1891, and building a reserve fund of $10,000 by 1892. However, its financial position was undermined by new conflicts with church independents, the depression of 1893–97, ineffectual administration, unrealistically low dues, and the practice of insuring wives through husband-members. Complaints that the union was not meeting its obligations to pay benefits and included no one outside of Chicago in its top leadership followed a predictable regional pattern, and three new insurance federations appeared from its ranks in 1895 alone: the Association of Poles in America (Milwaukee), the Alliance of Poles in America (Cleveland), and the Polish Roman Catholic Association (Detroit). The Polish Beneficial Association (Bridesburg, Pennsylvania) in 1900, the Alliance of Polish Catholic Youth (Chicago) in 1894, and the Polish Alma Mater (Chicago) in 1910, completed the roster of smaller, clerically inspired fraternals.[13]

Only near the end of the century did Polish fraternalism begin to measure up to the size of the immigration. By then, the effort to unite Polonia ideologically had been practically given up (to be renewed during the war periods to pursue humanitarian and certain political goals with respect to Poland). The lines of difference among clerical factions, church independents, nationalists, and socialists had been marked out if not yet entirely institutionalized. New and more business-oriented leaders (men and women of the post-Barzynski, post-1863 generation) introduced administrative and legal reforms which permitted the fraternals to take advantage of U.S. business law and reflect more accurately the immediate needs of the immigrant community. The PNA continued to set the pace by reincorporating under the hospitable laws of Illinois in 1896 as a fraternal insurance company, freeing it and the PRCU, which followed suit in 1898, to operate in many more states.

The two majors, again with the PNA slightly ahead, also adopted more realistic assessments, restricted the upper age of those whom they would insure (in this period it was usually in the range of 16 to 45), and ended the practice of insuring wives through their husbands. The PNA finally adopted the graduated scale of assessments recommended by the National Fraternal Congress and was the first Polish fraternal to join the congress, considerably expanding the scope of its operations and testifying to its financial soundness. Revised constitutions in 1909 (for the PNA) and in 1913 (for both the PNA and PRCU) reflected the movement for change. A system of state divisions and community councils further rationalized and bureaucratized their management by 1910. Aside from administrative convenience in the rapidly growing fraternals, the addition of regional directors to the central governments and the state divisions provided new outlets for local leadership and minimized the perennial rivalries growing out of geography and proximity to national headquarters. Increasing salaries, perquisites, and reimbursements for travel made participation in governance more attractive and, it was argued, more efficient. Nearly all other fraternals followed eventually in their steps.[14]

Increasingly, categories of persons not previously insured or difficult to insure were brought within the Polish system. Women were the largest such group. The fraternals, products of a formally male-oriented society, did not at first admit them as regular members and insured them instead through their husbands for smaller amounts. The system was pegged to the loss of a male breadwinner as *the* family calamity against which protection was needed. Also, it was difficult to assume that women could meet assessments independently since they were employed more irregularly and their major earnings as housekeepers (maintaining family and boarders) were integrated into family income disposed of by the male head. Consequently, there was little formal provision for widows, young women at home, and for the increasing number of single working women after 1890. The new religious congregations—the Felicians were the largest of them—offered some services to these women, but they were temporary and did not offer much in the event of death. As staunchly Catholic organizations, the religious communities were also limited ideologically, an important consideration in all early ethnic foundations.

After several tentative efforts beginning in 1884, several women's groups in the Chicago area federated in 1898 in the Polish Women's

Alliance. The PWA's early history paralleled that of the Polish National Alliance. The founders, women like Teofila Samolinska, Anna Neuman, and Stefania Chmielinska, also held a secular view of the Polish nation. They believed that the emancipation, education, and protection of women would strengthen and extend the national culture through the influence of women on the family and upbringing of children. Their successors, such as Emily Napieralska, the Progressive who dominated PWA administration from 1910 to 1935, shared this outlook but focused more on the business aspects of the organization. Within a decade of the founding of the PWA, the major older fraternals revised membership rules to admit women fully, elected females to their boards of directors, and organized women's departments (the PRCU somewhat later) run by women in order to draw upon the pool of potential members. Three other smaller and regional women's fraternals appeared at about the same time: the United Polish Women of America (Chicago) in 1912; the Association of Polish Women of the United States (Cleveland) in 1913; and the Union of Polish Women (Philadelphia) in 1920, successor to the Polish White Cross established by Helen Paderewska to aid the Polish army during the Great War.[15]

The other major pool of uninsured were children and youths under fifteen. They were particularly difficult to insure since they could not be considered conventional members of the fraternals. The commercial companies lobbied successfully and long against allowing the fraternals in effect to insure nonmembers. Partially, the community overcame the problem through the foundation of special youth-oriented associations like the Alliance of Polish Catholic Youth and, under the direction of Father Francis Gordon, Barzynski's successor as senior Polish cleric in Chicago, the Polish Alma Mater. Coverage was extended finally to children by the majors in most states from 1919.[16] Every interest group and every region in Polonia became a focus for a fraternal insurance program early in the twentieth century. Religious independents, most of whom coalesced around Bishop Francis Hodur and the Polish National Catholic Church, founded the Polish National Union in 1908 to complement their church work with insurance and other secular social services.[17] The Falcons, a gymnastic federation and perhaps the most ardently Polish patriotic organization prior to 1920, found themselves without much social purpose after the restoration of the Polish state and the decline of immigration to the United States. They also turned to insurance as a source of purpose and cohesion, beginning temporarily within the Polish National Alliance from 1905 to 1914, and then separately after 1924, when most independent groups formed the Polish Falcons of America with headquarters in Pittsburgh.[18]

Commonly, during the era of their greatest growth, the fraternals offered benefits of $100 or more, $500 and $1,000 being the normal maximums. Low rates were the rule due to the relative absence of pressure for conventional profit, the low administrative costs of a mostly part-time management, and later, to tax advantages as nonprofit institutions. The PRCU, for example, estimated in 1905 that its members paid thirty-five cents each year in administrative costs compared to $1 to $2 for comparable commercial operations. A steady barrage of propaganda in the fraternal press and all manner of sales contests and promotions after about 1915 supported the work of an increasing number of sophisticated amateur agents. These men and women, usually the key persons in lodge and district organizations, were closely linked to local Polish business-legal-real estate interests. Personal contact and language—the very sources of ethnic community, in other words—gave them an unusual advantage with the immigrant generation. It is hard now to comprehend fully the need for a ritually and socially elaborate funeral, but if the frequent criticisms of sumptuous funerals and the prosperity of certain individuals (priests, undertakers, saloon keepers) who profited from them is any measure, then the need was great indeed. It is easier to understand the necessity of providing for a family in the months after death, and the argument for fraternal insurance as a means of thrift which strengthened the individual, the family, and the community was made repeatedly. It amounted to a kind of modernized peasant ethic of work, thrift, and communal strength.[19]

The statistics on growth after the turn of the century were impressive. Both majors experienced a modest expansion after the first reorganizations of 1886-87. The assets of the PNA rose from $1,444.76 in 1890, to $28,182.21 in 1895; those of the PRCU from $1,012.80 in 1887, to about $10,000.00 in 1893, before the reverses of the mid-1890s. The years 1895-1900 were the turning point, however. The assets of the PNA approximately tripled in value every five years from 1895 to 1915, then doubled every five years until 1930. Growing more slowly in the Depression, they were well over $24 million in 1935. Starting from a lower base, the PRCU did relatively as well or better, tripling its assets every four years from 1900 to 1911. After a slow start, the assets of the PWA grew between 50 and 300 percent every four years from 1906 to 1935, when they stood at about $4.5 million. By 1924, the fraternals had possibly about 350,000 members, or about 15 percent of the Polish-American population, not counting holders of more than one policy. In 1935, the number stood at about 650,000, or about 20 percent of all Polish-Americans, again not counting repeaters or making much allowance for the just developing third generation. Of course there were far more whose policies lapsed for some reason and were on the periphery of the system. Probably also the percentage of members in cities like Chicago or Milwaukee, where the organization and the advantages of fraternalism were more apparent, was considerably higher than the national average.[20]

The expansion of the fraternals was guided by some of Polonia's most talented men and women, individuals drawn mostly at first from the small, progressive, educated middle class, who were born or reared in Poland. John Smulski at the PNA or Stefania Laudyn-Chrzanowska and Emily Napieralska at the PWA were outstanding examples in this category. More interesting perhaps, the fraternals were administered often by persons with blue collar backgrounds, or by women for whom such opportunities were not available in "American" society, making them schools in business management as well as in communal leadership.

The example of Thomas Krolik is instructive. When he came to the United States in the 1880s, he worked first as a common laborer at a Chicago lumber company, then as a bookkeeper and foreman for the same employer. He served also for long terms as secretary of St. Stanislaus Kostka parish (with 50,000 members the largest Catholic parish in the world at one time) and as secretary of the St. Joseph Savings and Loan Association where he was accustomed to handling over $300,000 annually. Elected secretary of the PRCU in 1900, he was a member of the financial committee which completely reorganized the union and worked out a new assessment table which restored its fortunes. The success of Krolik and others had important implications for the future of Polonia's middle class. A recent study of top management in Chicago's major companies has documented the virtual absence of Polish-Americans. They were less well represented even than other major ethnic groups in the city. Discrimination by the "establishment" was the natural explanation, but lack of interest within the ethnic group may be equally or more important. The relative institutional completeness of Chicago Polonia, which the fraternals played a major part in creating, offered satisfying opportunities within the community. From this perspective, ethnic business activity did not hinder upward social mobility; it was less a trap than a trap door. Complaints of economic discrimination may reflect the ambitions of a younger, more Americanized generation than they do the history of Poles in the United States.[21]

Commensurate with their greater material prosperity, the fraternals expanded their social services, plowing back much of their "profit" into the community. Publicity and the general interest aroused by these projects have made them the best known works of the fraternals. The Catholic fraternals and their lodges (both Roman and National) contributed significantly to the maintenance of the Polish parish. Indirectly if not nearly as much as many hoped for, they supported efforts by the Polish Catholic Congresses (1896 and 1901), the Federation of Polish Catholics (1902), and the Association of Polish Priests to secure fairer representation for Poles in the hierarchy of the American Catholic Church and to protect the use of the Polish language. Both major fraternals initiated separate education programs in the first decade of the century. Scholarships or tuition loans for the education of children of members became the most substantial and most popular work of these departments. The PNA went a step further in 1912 by opening a technical high school in Cambridge Springs, near Erie, Pennsylvania (and, in 1978, by still supporting it as Alliance College). Their press was far more than house organs or community gossip sheets. Its practical information, editorial opinion, and imaginative literature socialized the immigrant to both American and Polish national culture, giving literary and literate leadership to an ethnic community. The *Alliance Daily,* founded (and still published) by the PNA in 1908, and the *Union Daily* of the PRCU from 1921 to 1939 were major vehicles of education broadly conceived. During the years of heavy immigration, the PNA and the Catholic clergy both maintained immigrant homes in New York City to facilitate initial adjustment or direct immigrants to the interior. Youth work, which expanded greatly to meet the needs of the second generation after 1920, demonstrated the value of insurance and sustained ethnic identification through scouting, camps, family recreation, and popular educational programs suited to the social background and aspirations of Polish-Americans.

Support for the Polish national cause, usually through separate coordinating agencies, was the fraternals' most dramatic action. Public relations efforts, such as the raising of statues to Polish heroes, protests, and petition to political authorities, congresses, and other forms of public demonstration became steadily more frequent after 1895. Work in this area reached a climax in World War 1 with an ambitious relief program for Poland, vigorous political pressure upon the Wilson administration for Polish independence through the National Department (the political arm of the Central Relief Committee), close collaboration with the National Democrats in Poland and with exiles like Ignacy Paderewski and Roman Dmowski in western Europe, assistance in recruiting and maintaining a Polish Army from America to fight the Germans in France and later the Soviets in eastern Europe, the purchase of Polish government bonds after 1918, and financial and political support for Polish claims in territorial disputes with Germany, Czechoslovakia, the Soviet Union, and Lithuania. The minutes particularly of the PNA Central and Diets in the early years of the century sometimes read like the deliberations of a government-in-exile as its leaders consider the effect of this or that event throughout the world upon the interests of Poland. For a brief while the American Polonia acted as the "fourth province" dreamt of by its founders—a community of Poles on neutral or undamaged ground, united as they never had been or would be, aiding Poland with humanitarian and political support.[22]

The root of these successes was the growth in real wages for the American worker from the 1890s to 1920s, benefiting even those who, like Polish-Americans, stood relatively low on the economic scale. The disposition of income reflected the historic values of the community. A portion was remitted to Poland, where it played a disproportionately large role in facilitating further immigration, the purchase or improvement of land, and, after 1918, the Polish international balance of payments. A large part went for consumer goods and neighborhood services, helping to sustain an ethnic middle class—a somewhat modernized, i.e., Polish-American, gentry—which had a strong interest in the survival of the community and its institutions. The most conspicuous investment was in churches and auxiliary buildings and services (schools, convents, rectories, orphanages, homes for the aged). This was, of course, more than an investment in a property and a staff whose services were used for only a few hours a week. It was symbolic expression—often the only one practical or imaginable on a large scale—of communal pride and consciousness and of the aspiration to institutional completeness. Its economic and cultural significance accounts in part for the intensity of quarrels for control of parish property, the selection of priests, the choice of building design, and the language of instruction.[23]

In the long run, the single largest and most important area of Polish-American investment was real estate—sound and safe (normally), if lacking liquidity. Early in their history the fraternals systematically encouraged rural colonization with some success. After the turn of the century, however, as their assets increased, they shifted their attention to a more practical goal for most Polish-Americans, the ownership of the one-family home on a small lot or the duplex typical of the corridors of Polish settlement which extended the boundaries of Chicago, Detroit, and other cities in 1900-30. Neighborhood savings or building and loan associations proliferated everywhere to finance the new blue collar neighborhoods. In Illinois, where laws early favored this means of home financing, there were 649 savings and loan associations in 1916; 246 in Chicago alone. About 209 of the state's total were clearly Slavic in control and location and at least 74 were Polish, all in Chicago or adjacent towns. The links among savings and loan associations, builders, sales agents, and fraternals have not been systematically documented, but there are frequent examples of the overlapping of interests and personnel. Most notably, until the 1930s, the fraternals invested the bulk of their capital in real estate, either by lending money directly to members (elaborately reported in minutes and reports) or by purchasing mortgages from banks and building associations. The Polish Women's Alliance in 1927 had tied up $1,350,000 of its assets of $1,540,000 in mortgages. The Polish National Alliance the same year had $14,207,000 in assets and $12,545,000 invested in mortgages. The bulk of their loans were for properties in the Chicago area and northwestern Indiana (Cook and Lake counties). Like the investment in the churches, the purchase of real estate by individuals tended to lock up capital and failed to produce the profit of more speculative investment or the social mobility of education. Nevertheless, it contributed and still contributes to the more valued goal of geographic and communal stability. The bitter fruit of the 1950s and 1960s, as the process of ethnic succession took its inexorable course in old neighborhoods, as property values fell and young people took flight, has done little to alter the impulse to buy and hold land. As a recent study puts it: the Polish-American community, compared to other European ethnic groups, is "low on mobility, high on ethnic institutional completeness, and high on segregation" scales.[24]

The growth in fraternal insurance and investment in real estate, however solid it looked, was still a form of speculation. Occasionally it created serious management problems—the conflict of interest for an officer who handled large sums in both the fraternal and in some related home service institution, or worse, the embezzlement or misappropriation of funds. The Great Depression revealed the fundamental weakness in the investment policy of the fraternals as the housing market collapsed and a record number of foreclosures on mortgaged property raised a question of their survival. The PNA for one held about $8 million in real property acquired through foreclosure by 1935, or almost one-third of its assets. Prudence and pressure from regulatory agencies since then dictated that the fraternals put the better part of their capital in government securities, a form of investment with which they had first become familiar during the bond drives of World War 1. By 1943, the PNA, under the influence of new leaders like censor Francis X. Swietlik of Milwaukee, had invested nearly $19 million, or over half of its assets in bonds and stocks. The proportion remained the same or higher as the PNA absorbed its share of the savings of wartime and the prosperous years that followed.[25]

An occasional financial scandal or rumor of scandal, self-serving salary increases and perquisites, factionalism, and complaints of stagnant and self-perpetuating administrations have continued to trouble some of the fraternals, including the largest. However, growth resumed in the late

1930s, though not at the same high rate as in the heyday of immigration and neighborhood expansion in 1900-25. The children's and especially the women's divisions showed the greatest strength after the number of adult male members reached a peak in the late 1920s. By 1975, when there were clear signs of a leveling off and decline, Polish insurance fraternalism still enrolled at least 700,000 members, something between 10 and 15 percent of the Polish-American population. With combined assets of over $300 million, it was far and away the largest of any produced by the immigration of 1880-1930, excceded among ethnic fraternals only by such giants of the older immigration like the Lutheran Brotherhood of America. About half the membership and assets were in the Polish National Alliance, making it the largest private Polish enterprise in existence.[26]

The major source of uncertainty for the fraternals since the Depression has been the emergence of the third and fourth generation of Polish-Americans. Their insurance may still be cheap, but the benefit is not nearly so attractive to a generation raised in the post-New Deal welfare state and accustomed to an inflationary economy. Moreover, institutional Polonia—still heavily influenced by second-generation descendants of the immigrants of 1880-1930 and the refugees of 1945-55—lags behind the development of the community. Many Polish-Americans, most of those in the primary settlements, have abandoned their old homes for new tract suburbs. These areas may be strongly tinged Polish, but they lack the institutions (fraternal lodges, for instance) of the old Polonia through which the fraternals did their basic social work and sold insurance. Some effort has been made to adapt to the new forms of ethnic clustering and ethnic identification of the more acculturated Polish-Americans. The administration of insurance programs has been centralized and streamlined so that they do not depend so heavily or at all on the lodges. Headquarters and offices have been relocated—the PNA has been the best example again of readjustment—nearer the new centers of ethnic population. The unheralded new economic immigration from Poland since 1955, meanwhile, has found the old lodge halls and the insurance system of some value.

Finally, however, the business success of the fraternals may prove to be their undoing as social agencies. The centralization of insurance transactions and the declining number of lodges may weaken grass-roots interest and ethnic identification. The allure of financial success, the preoccupation of regulatory agencies and trade associations with fiduciary responsibilities, and the competition of commercial companies seem at present to increase in proportion to the decline of the fraternals as vital ethnic institutions. Nonprofit status—their special advantage—may yet become another means of conventional profitability.

M. MARK STOLARIK

A PLACE FOR EVERYONE
Slovak Fraternal-Benefit Societies

Just twelve years ago Timothy L. Smith lamented that "the once promising field of immigration studies has fallen upon hard times."[1] Fortunately, this is no longer true. Even while Smith was making this statement, an "ethnic revival" was sweeping the United States, and it resulted in a proliferation of scholarly works on various aspects of the history of American ethnic groups. There is a gap in the story, however; no one has sufficiently analyzed one of the most important of all ethnic institutions that flourished in America—the fraternal-benefit society. By focusing on one people, the Slovaks, and primarily on their community in Bethlehem, Pennsylvania, this author will attempt to help fill this gap in American historical scholarship.

The Slovaks came to the United States from their nineteenth-century homeland in the Kingdom of Hungary primarily for economic reasons. Between 1720 and 1840 their population increased from 1,100,000 to 2,400,000, with no corresponding increase in their landholdings. Indeed, after serfdom was abolished in Hungary in 1848, most of the freed serfs actually lost the extra land that nobles had allowed them to work after landholdings had been fixed in 1767. As a result, the nobles, who made up 10 percent of the population, owned more than half of all the land, while the ever increasing peasant population had to look for other ways to supplement their subsistence income. Initially, Slovak men took to migrating from their homes in northern Hungary to the fertile southern lowlands and helped the landed aristocrats take in the harvest. Others wandered about Europe fixing household utensils and performing odd jobs. By the 1870s they had become a rural proletariat in search of work.

After the Civil War had ended in the United States and industrialization had begun in earnest, this country's labor shortage became acute. Until the 1880s immigrants from overpopulated western European states, such as Germany and Great Britain, stoked the American industrial plant. In that decade, however, both of these emerging industrial giants began to tolerate unions and pass social welfare legislation. Even though the United States still paid higher wages than did its industrial competitors, the fringe benefits that appeared for workers in progressive European countries served to keep them at home. Now American capitalists had to look for cheap labor elsewhere.

The countries of central, southern and eastern Europe—primarily Austria-Hungary, Italy and Russia—meanwhile, lagged behind the west in industrialization. Their economies were still largely agricultural, and they all suffered from a population explosion. It did not take long for scouts of America's railroads and coal mines to discover this untapped reservoir of labor and to lure a few thousand over by paying for their crossing and having them work on contract in the late 1870s and early 1880s. Even though Congress banned contract labor in 1885, it did not halt the flow of eager men who by then had heard of good jobs and high wages from friends who had previously made the crossing. The net result was that by 1890 the majority of immigrants entering the United States came primarily from central, southern and eastern Europe, and they dominated the immigration until Congress severely restricted it in the 1920s. By then 15 million had come from these areas, and among them were over 500,000 Slovaks.[2]

Since this was initially an immigration of agricultural laborers who had come to the United States to make their "fortunes" and then return home, they headed for those industries that paid the highest wages: coal, oil, and steel. As a result, the vast majority settled in America's industrial triangle—between Boston, Chicago, and Baltimore. The Slovaks were no exception, and fully half of them headed for the coal mines and steel mills of Pennsylvania. Here they lived in company housing in the coal regions or in row housing in the steel towns.[3]

Shortly after their arrival in the New World the Slovaks began to fraternize and organize. They started by living together in boarding-houses run by the as-yet-rare Slovak women in the vicinity of mine or mill. Later they set up more formal institutions called fraternal-benefit societies, and these in turn founded the parish churches. Family, lodge, and church, then, formed the basis of American-Slovak communities.[4]

When they began to organize, American Slovaks founded a variety of both local and national fraternals. These reflected certain divisions among the Slovaks, and by studying these differences one will discover the inner workings of the local and national Slovak communities in America. The lodges had very important individual, group and community functions that served as barometers of the strength, health and vitality of both the local and national bodies and, indeed, of the whole Slovak ethnic group in the United States.

EUROPEAN ANTECEDENTS

Contrary to what Oscar Handlin said about the American origins of lodges, when Slovaks in the United States organized their first fraternals, they often drew upon Old World examples. Guilds of craftsmen have existed since the Middle Ages and were not abolished in the Kingdom of Hungary until 1872. It comes as no surprise, therefore, that in 1883 a group of tradesmen from Slovakia who had settled in New York organized the "Persi Uherszko-Szlovenszky v Nyemoci Podporujuci Szpolek" (The First Hungarian-Slovak Sickness Benefit Society). Similarly, in 1888 a number of craftsmen in Bayonne, New Jersey, founded the "Prvý Bednarský Výpomocny Spolok" (First Cooper's Benefit Society). Both catered to skilled workers much as had the guilds of old.[5]

Even the unskilled had had organizations in Slovakia, and these, too, found roots in America. As early as 1460, for instance, the silver miners of central Slovakia had formed the "Society of the Most Sacred Body of Jesus." Similarly, miners in Hnilcik, Spis county, organized themselves into a "brotherhood" in 1858, while field hands in Trencín county founded the "Society of the Rosary" in 1881. To the Hungarian government it mattered not whether they were religious or secular organizations, however, because in its nineteenth-century paranoia about Slovak nationalism, which it dubbed "Pan Slavism," it quickly forbade them all. Nevertheless, Slovaks in America did remember such societies, as evidenced by the names they gave to some of the earliest ones that appeared: the Society of St. John in Bridgeport, Connecticut, in 1883, and the Society of Prince Rudolf in Bayonne, New Jersey, in 1887.[6]

THE RELIGIOUS, SOCIAL, AND GEOGRAPHIC COMPOSITION OF SLOVAK LODGES

Even though they had known three kinds of Old World fraternals, American Slovaks favored those of a religious nature. Very few among them were skilled workers, but the vast majority were very religious.

Thus, in a settlement such as Bethlehem, Pennsylvania, where the Slovaks organized nineteen fraternals (ten for men and nine for women) between 1891 and 1918, sixteen had a religious affiliation. Of these, twelve were Roman Catholic, two were Greek Catholic and two Lutheran —a good indication of the relative strength of each religious grouping.[7]

Not only did lodges reflect the religious composition of a Slovak community such as in Bethlehem, but they also revealed the social factors that played a role in their origins. An analysis of the membership roles of four Roman Catholic lodges shows that the men's Sts. Cyril and Methodius Society and the women's Assumption of the Blessed Virgin Mary fraternal, founded in 1891 and 1899, contained the richest and most influential leaders of the community from the start: the bankers George Zbojovský, John Gosztonyi and the saloonkeeper and developer George Slafkoský. While these men dominated the male lodge, their wives did likewise in the female counterpart. Membership in these fraternals carried much status. By contrast, the men's Sacred Heart of Jesus Society and the women's Nativity of the Blessed Virgin Mary lodge, founded in 1897 and 1898, respectively, had leaders of more humble means and attracted similar followers. Thus, the social stratification of a Slovak community could be revealed on the basis of lodge membership, at least for the first two generations.[8]

Geographic origins also played a role in the formation of lodges. Of the eleven Bethlehem Slovaks who gathered in the home of George Slafkoský on May 15, 1900, to launch the nationalist St. George's Society, six had come from the village of Siroké, Saris, and nine lived on Buttonwood Street. Thus, the majority had been neighbors in the Old World and the New. The women's counterpart, the Society of Mary Magdalen, founded in 1907, reflected the same origins.[9]

NATIONAL FRATERNALS

Such divisions did not confine themselves to small communities; in spite of efforts to overcome them, they persisted at the national level. P. V. Rovnianek, for instance, editor of the first and largest Slovak newspaper in the United States, *Amerikánsko-Slovenské Noviny*, tried to get all local lodges to affiliate with the National Slovak Society which he founded in Pittsburgh on February 15, 1890. Roman Catholic clergymen, led by Stefan Furdek of Cleveland, on the other hand, feared that Rovnianek's nondenominational society would become a hotbed for anti-clericalism, and they decided to go their own way. As a result, Furdek set up the First Catholic Slovak Union, headquartered in Cleveland, on

September 4, 1890. He also began to publish this society's newspaper *Jednota* (Union) in 1891, and began a rivalry that divided the Slovaks even more. The Lutherans, for instance, organized their own national fraternal called the Slovak Evangelical Union, headquartered in Pittsburgh, in 1892. Then, in 1896, militantly nationalistic and secularly oriented Slovaks established the Slovak Gymnastic Union Falcon (popularly called National Sokol) in New York City, while in 1905 Catholic dissidents broke away from it and, in Passaic, New Jersey, set up their own Slovak Catholic Sokol. By 1918 the Slovaks had established twelve large national fraternals. Each published its own newspaper and *Almanac*. Through these literary mediums members all across the country were kept in touch with each other; they voiced their concerns in letters to the editor; they were informed of the latest news; and they offered first-rate literature for both personal and community (such as plays) consumption. Furthermore, each national fraternal provided substantial insurance policies for members in affiliated lodges. Since the majority of Slovaks were very religious, 150,000 joined sectarian societies, while only 70,000 enrolled in secular ones by 1920.[10]

Once the national fraternals had been established, local lodges began to affiliate with them. In Bethlehem, for instance, the two men's Roman Catholic fraternals, mentioned above, joined the First Catholic Slovak Union as branches 156 and 345. Their female counterparts joined the First Catholic Slovak Ladies' Union, also founded by Stefan Furdek in Cleveland in 1892, as branches 74 and 89. The St. George's and Mary Magdalen lodges, on the other hand, affiliated with the National Slovak Society and the women's "Zivena" (Giver of Life) counterpart as branches 350 and 135. Similarly, the men's Lutheran Society of the Discovery of Christ Our Lord by the Wise Men, founded in 1906, and the women's Lutheran Holy Trinity Lodge, founded in 1909, affiliated with the Slovak Evangelical Union as branches 158 and 45 of each sex's counterpart. Meanwhile, the Greek Catholic men who organized the Society of Sts. Peter and Paul in 1906, and their wives who founded the St. Anne's Lodge, in 1907, affiliated with the Greek Catholic Union, headquartered in Wilkes-Barre, as branches 429 and 435 of their respective national organizations. Finally, a group of men established branch 93 of the National Sokols in Bethlehem in 1905, while their more devout neighbors organized the St. Anthony of Padua Society in 1910 and affiliated, as branch 78, with the Slovak Catholic Sokol in the same year.[11]

LODGE FUNCTIONS AND ACTIVITIES

One can infer from the examples given above that Slovak fraternals established in America served a social purpose. They did, indeed, serve as meeting places for people who spoke the same language, shared the same religion, came from the same region, aspired to the same status, or had a common political cause. In a land full of strangers these were important considerations.

After having established their lodges the members generally gathered monthly in one of the large neighborhood halls. Until the churches were built the societies met in one of the local saloons. Later they congregated in the church basements. In Bethlehem the National Sokols were the first to start a fund drive among their members and to erect a meeting hall in 1912. Catholic societies in the same town, meanwhile, sold shares to individuals and lodges and built a Slovak National Hall in 1914. In 1923, however, the Catholic Sokols bought out the other shareholders and rented the facilities to them. Those who did not get along with the Sokols continued to use the church basements.[12]

The monthly meetings of these lodges followed a fairly regular, and lively, pattern. In religious societies the president opened the gathering with a prayer while in secular ones he first admonished the "brothers" to behave themselves. The secretary then read the names of all the members in good standing while the treasurer collected the dues. Those who failed to attend usually sent their wives or children with their contributions, and this often delayed the proceedings because the women invariably found someone to scold while the children lost (or spent) some of the money. Once the wives and young ones left (or were thrown out by the sergeant-at-arms), the recording secretary would read the minutes of the previous meeting and call for their approval. This done, the president then asked the "visitors of the ill" to report on their rounds. Next the presiding officer called for the nomination of new members, who had to produce an initiation fee, ranging from $1 to $6, depending upon the lodge, and also a recommendation from a member in good standing. Upon acceptance or rejection of the newcomer, the president would then read any correspondence from the head office or from other lodges, and the members would act upon it. Quite often this involved an appeal for donations for needy members elsewhere. Individual lodges often responded generously to such requests, usually sending $2 to $5 and thus helping members in affiliated societies. Only during the Depression did they turn down such appeals. After this the financial secretary and the treasurer would give their reports, in the hope that their records would match. If they did not, a spirited discussion (and sometimes a brawl) would ensue until one or the other admitted an error, to be made up by him. Next they would discuss any unfinished business from the previous meeting, take up current matters of importance, entertain suggestions for the future, and close with a prayer (or a salute in secular societies).

INDIVIDUAL REWARDS

Beyond the social function, however, Slovak fraternals played even deeper roles, and these operated at the individual, group and community levels. The first and most obvious individual function consisted of providing accident, illness and burial insurance. When Slovak immigrants began to arrive and staff American coal mines, steel mills and oil refineries in the 1870s and 1880s, they found this country singularly devoid of any social services. Thus, if one had an accident, fell ill or died, little or no compensation was paid him or his family by either his employer or the government. Regular insurance policies were far too expensive, and, thus, the average immigrant was left to his own meager resources. As a result, when the workers in various factories began to organize into fraternals, they always set aside the largest part of their dues to compensate one another if tragedy struck. These fees initially consisted of 25¢ a month, and paid up to $5 a week in compensation in case of accident or illness until the treasury ran out. If one died, then usually each lodge member contributed $1 towards a proper funeral. After the lodges affiliated with national bodies the fees usually increased to 50¢ a month and benefits increased to regular $500 or $1,000 life insurance policies for both the husband and the wife. To prevent any false claims, and at the same time to show concern for the incapacitated, the lodges elected, for three-month terms, a "committee for the sick." These lodge brothers were charged with visiting each claimant, expressing their sympathy and verifying his problem. They then paid the claimant $2 a week in sick benefits. In this very practical and humane fashion, American Slovaks established their own, limited, social welfare system.[13]

In the same vein the lodges provided capital funds to deserving brothers. It was not at all unusual for a member to seek, and get, a personal or mortgage loan if he was considered a good risk. In 1902, for instance, one Bethlehem lodge granted a member a $1,400 mortgage loan. Similarly, in 1935, during the Depression, another lodge granted a "brother" a personal loan of $300. Dozens of individuals were helped in this way at the local level and thousands at the national. By lending at very low rates of interest these lodges helped Slovaks to build or buy their own homes which would have been out of reach at regular bank rates.[14]

Furthermore, the lodges offered to the ambitious Slovak a fairly good route to positions of leadership and financial rewards. Becoming an officer in a lodge meant that your colleagues recognized you as a leader and afforded you much esteem. In addition, if you became treasurer, you were able to handle large sums of money, and, if you handled it wisely, you might become rich. George Slafkoský's career in Bethlehem is a good example. He served as either president or treasurer of half a dozen societies for three decades, and, in addition to becoming a recognized spokesman for the community, he acquired so much wealth that he built and rented thirty houses. For these reasons, lodge offices were hotly contested in the early years and monthly attendance was very high.[15]

If he chose to do so, a lodge leader could use his office as a springboard for political aspirations. John Peters (originally Ján Petro) of Bethlehem, for example, relied on the power (through votes) of his past presidency of the St. Anthony of Padua Society to challenge and defeat the local Irish alderman in the 1923 elections.[16] Similarly, George J. Ruyak acquired a leadership reputation while he served as an overseer of the First Catholic Slovak Union from 1928 to 1935, and he used this reputation to win election of the presidency of the local Sts. Cyril and Methodius Society in Bethlehem. He then went on to become that city's first Slovak councilman in 1939. A crucial step, then, in a successful political career for a Slovak was to win an important office in the local lodge.[17]

GROUP FUNCTIONS

While the lodges helped people to fulfill certain of their political ambitions, they also served some very important group functions. Almost every single Slovak parish in America, whether Roman or Greek Catholic, Lutheran or Calvinist, was founded and supported by a lodge or lodges. In both Minneapolis and Bethlehem, for example, the local Sts. Cyril and Methodius societies founded the Roman Catholic parishes of the same name in 1891.[18] Similarly, the Holy Trinity Lodge in Cleveland founded its namesake Lutheran parish in 1892, as did the members of Bethlehem's Lutheran lodge, who created St. John's parish in 1911.[19] Finally, the Greek Catholic Society of Sts. Peter and Paul in Bethlehem organized the parish of the same name in 1917, as did branch 33 of the Slovak Calvin Presbyterian Union of Lakewood, Ohio, in 1921.[20] These lodges then raised money to construct a church building, either by dipping into their administrative funds or by taking up a collection or both, and they arranged for the appointment of a pastor and saw to it that he was financially supported, if they approved of him. Meanwhile, they contributed generously to the upkeep of the parish, usually helped in its decoration, especially in the purchase of very expensive stained glass windows, and generally worked for the good of the church.

Meanwhile, the lodges also took a hand in the spiritual welfare of their members. The Roman and Greek Catholic fraternals forced their members to adhere to the strict rules of the church. They insisted, for instance, that all "brothers" (or "sisters") fulfill their Easter Duty (confession and communion) each year or face a fine and, possibly, expulsion. Furthermore, most lodges fined their members for such spiritual transgressions as profanity, drunkenness and fighting, thereby exerting a great deal of social control that was meant to "civilize" them. In this way the lodges forced Slovaks in America to apply the kind of self-control that native American critics demanded, and this made the lodges unwitting agents of "Americanization."[21]

COMMUNITY ACTIVITIES

Finally, the lodges also fulfilled the very important functions of community centers. Almost every larger Slovak community in America has a local hall for this purpose. In Bethlehem, as we have seen above, both the Catholic and National Sokols have such a hall, and the other lodges use them for a multitude of purposes. Here the young people used to do calisthenics, they played basketball and volleyball and trained in gymnastics. Their elders, meanwhile, besides having used the facilities for their monthly lodge meetings, also frequented the downstairs bar for cool drinks and good fellowship. These lodge halls were rented by most of the fraternals for their frequent parties with the result that there was a major social event almost every week of the year. In addition, the receptions of most Slovak weddings were held here, as were the nonreligious parts of the lodges' annual communion breakfasts. In sum, then, the lodges were the linchpins that held the community together.

THE DECLINE OF LODGES

While lodge activities peaked in the 1920s—one could rightly call that decade the "golden age" of fraternals—the beginnings of their decline can also be traced from that era. In Bethlehem, for instance, while local leaders boasted of well-attended social events each week in the 1920s, the behavior of the youth caused them some concern. Reacting to nativist paranoia about the need for "Americanization," young men stopped wearing their fancy lodge uniforms to special occasions as they had in the past. This was the first symbolic step in the breakdown of ethnic solidarity.[22] In addition, the youth seemed much more interested in sports than in monthly lodge meetings and began to attend regularly only the yearly gatherings for the election of officers. Some fraternals, like the Sokols in Bethlehem, increased their sports program and managed to keep the interest of the youth. Others, like the lodges of the First Catholic Slovak Union, which did promote baseball teams in the late 1920s and early 1930s, ultimately failed in this endeavor because they had lost the initiative to the more aggressive Sokols. As a result, the Bethlehem lodges affiliated with the First Catholic Slovak Union remained staffed largely with older members of the second generation while the Sokols kept recruiting younger members of the second and even third generations. Eventually the Sokols of Bethlehem would leave the other lodges far behind in membership.[23]

Other lodges were hurt by changing political fortunes and the Depression. Those fraternals affiliated with the National Slovak Society and the Zivena in Bethlehem, for instance, suffered from a loss of their raison d'être and from their small size after World War 1. In a sense they were too successful. They led the nationalist drive to destroy Austria-Hungary during the war, and when Czechoslovakia emerged in 1918 many of their members were satisfied—so satisfied that they had virtually no sports program to attract the youth and their membership remained stationary. When the Depression broke out their small numbers, plus the advanced age of their members, worked against them in this time of financial crisis and sealed their doom. While a few stalwarts kept paying their dues even after World War 2, their numbers kept shrinking and both lodges have folded in the last decade.[24]

Fraternals that survived the Depression, meanwhile, faced new challenges after World War 2. The more affluent members of the second and third generations began to move to the suburbs and attended lodge meetings and Slovak halls even less frequently because of the distances involved. Television now filled many of the entertainment functions that lodges had provided before. At the same time, these suburbanites, in order to be able to pay off their mortgages, began to cash in their twenty-year insurance policies, which had largely been financed by their parents. And, with the growing amount of cheap American insurance and the thousands of professionals selling it, fraternal insurance lost its attractiveness. Finally, "boss politics," on which ethnic leadership had thrived in the past, declined precipitously after World War 2 and reduced the value of lodge offices. The cement that had bound Slovak communities together in the past began to come loose in the 1950s.

SLOVAK LODGES TODAY

The decline in the importance of fraternal-benefit societies had had a perceptible impact on Slovak communities in America. Since local lodge offices carry with them little value today, they are generally held or inherited by children of the former officers for no apparent reason other than family tradition. Indeed, leadership of a fraternal-benefit society today is an indication that one has not yet totally assimilated, that one is holding back and, perhaps, is not "successful" (in Anglo-American eyes). On the other hand, it also indicates a pride in the past that one is not willing to shake.[25]

Meanwhile, as all lodges decline in membership, Slovak women are coming to the fore. They have had their own organizations for almost as long as the men, and they are holding on longer for two reasons. First of all, they live longer than their men, and, secondly, they have always been the major culture carriers in Slovak communities. As a result, when one looks at a community such as Bethlehem, one immediately notices that women dominate most of the surviving lodges and functions. For this reason they do not feel any need for "women's lib" and do not support the movement. Whether their daughters will carry on in the same tradition remains to be seen.[26]

CONCLUSION

A study of Slovak fraternal-benefit societies, therefore, can reveal not only the inner workings of an ethnic community but may also serve as models for more recent arrivals to the United States. For, when Slovak immigrants came to this country in the 1880s, they managed to overcome not only their own divisions but also the extreme "rugged individualism" of America's capitalist society by organizing first into local, and, later, national bodies. While these societies reflected the religious, class and geographic elements that divided the Slovak people, they also gave to individual members a certain group cohesiveness that had temporarily been lost in the move to the New World. Furthermore, the lodges provided social services that neither capitalists nor governments were willing to give: basic insurance, low-interest loans, community centers, leadership education and moral authority. Through community action, therefore, American Slovaks overcame the problems associated with migration and urbanization.

PART THREE

THE POLITICAL AND IDEOLOGICAL BASES OF COLLECTIVISM

MICHAEL KARNI

FINNISH-AMERICAN COOPERATIVISM
The Radical Years, 1917-30

Between 1864 and 1920, over three hundred thousand Finns settled in America. They followed the footsteps of a few hundred of their countrymen who had come to New Sweden Colony on the Delaware in the 1630s. Unlike the Delaware Finns, who had long since disappeared into American culture, the new Finnish immigrants did not merge their identities with America quickly. Most of them came during a period of tremendous upheaval in Finland as Czarist Russia suffered through its last years. Many Finns, as members of a Grand Duchy of the Russian Empire, were drawn into revolutionary activities as early as the last decade of the nineteenth century. After the failure of the General Strike of 1905, hundreds of radicals went into exile to America. Once here, they and their followers clashed sharply with the much larger group of Finnish immigrants associated primarily with the Lutheran church. Both groups were beset by harsh working conditions in locations such as the Minnesota Iron Range and the Michigan Copper Range—and the attitudes of Americans toward them.

Instead of finding a land which "had shores sanded with gold," as an immigrant ballad expressed it, they found the streets of Minnesota mining towns covered with the red dust from iron ore. They also found a social atmosphere which was, at best, indifferent to their plight as unskilled strangers and, at worst, downright hostile to their presence. In fact, after deep involvement by Finnish radicals in the Mesabi Range strike of 1907, the federal government tried to deny all Finns citizenship on the grounds that they were "Mongols" and therefore ineligible for it.[1] Americans also soon stereotyped Finns as clannish, aggressive, and, because of their labor union activities in mines and lumber camps, as intractable workers and "radicals." Adding to their reputation as radicals was their establishment of numerous consumers' cooperatives in the western Great Lakes region beginning in 1903 and lasting until World War 2.

During the twenty years before the turn of the century, several agencies which could loosely be construed as "cooperative" were established by Finns in the United States. A Finnish mutual fire insurance company, for example, was formed in Calumet, Michigan, in 1878, and mutual benefit societies providing sickness, accident, and funeral benefits for members were established in Monesson, Pennsylvania, Ashtabula, Ohio, and Hancock, Michigan.[2] The venture by Matti Kurikka, Finnish utopian, on Malcolm's Island, British Columbia, the Imatra Society of Brooklyn (1890), and the numerous Finnish men's boardinghouses (or *poikatalot*), an institution without counterpart in Finland, also qualify as early attempts at cooperation among Finnish immigrants.

The decade 1890–1900 saw the establishment of Finnish-American mercantile companies operated on a stock company basis. Such stores existed in Crystal Falls, Michigan, and Worcester, Massachusetts, by 1891; in New York Mills, Minnesota, by 1894; and in Virginia, Minnesota, by 1900. While not truly consumers' cooperatives, these mercantile companies were, nevertheless, group-owned and designed to help members buy goods and services at reduced prices. They must be viewed as a kind of transitional institution between the simple mutual benefit society and a consumers' cooperative.

By the turn of the century, then, scattered attempts at economic cooperation had been attempted by the Finns in America with no tangible evidence to link the enterprises to Old World models. In fact, it was simultaneous to these attempts that the first Finnish cooperative society, the Pellervo, began to function in Finland. Finnish-Americans were probably more influenced by American models. Many Finns, for example, undoubtedly knew and used the services of the giant miners' cooperative, the Tamarack (Michigan) Cooperative Association, organized in 1890, and at one time the largest business-volume cooperative in the United States.[3] The Right Relationship League of the Grange, too, had established at least fifty cooperatives in Minnesota alone by the turn of the century. Thus, the Finns had many models on which to draw for their cooperatives.

While socialists came to dominate the early years of the Finnish consumers' cooperative movement, the first such store established by Finns had no political ideology and seems to have been established purely in response to exploitive local merchants in frontier Minnesota. In 1903, thirteen Finnish farm families in Menahga, Minnesota, formed a cooperative on the $170 they had pooled among themselves. Named Sampo, after the magic mill of plenty in the *Kalevala* which simultaneously produced grain, salt, and gold, the Menahga store was founded to ward off gouging storekeepers who, it seems, regularly cheated the farmers by paying less than originally agreed upon for farm produce. Often merchants would pay the farmers for their goods in "scrip," which was redeemable only in the merchant's store. In an isolated community a storekeeper could and often did charge excessively for his wares. The same pattern of rural exploitation led directly to the establishment of many stores, which often failed shortly after inception, in the backwoods of the western Great Lakes region. But by 1913 eleven such stores or buying clubs were flourishing in Minnesota, Michigan, and Wisconsin.[4] Most of these stores were nonpolitical in origin, the products of simple group effort to remedy a vexing economic problem.

Almost simultaneously with the development of these early cooperatives did the fledgling socialist movement see an advantage to be gained in cooperation. The socialists (and later the communists) were to provide the energy necessary to make the endeavor started in Menahga into the most remarkable and successful institution ever created by the Finns in America.

Cooperation was discussed at the first formal meeting of Finnish-American socialists held in Cleveland in 1904. The socialist newspaper *Työmies* (The Workingman), founded in 1903, also supported the establishment of cooperatives by pointing out that if the labor movement did not take advantage of the cooperative idea, the "enemy" might do so against the interests of the working class.[5] In Hibbing, Minnesota, where the socialists formally organized in 1906, the new Socialist Federation urged "socialists everywhere" to help found cooperative stores in their communities. The cooperative, however, was generally viewed by socialists not as an end in itself but rather as a temporary expedient in the class struggle. Cooperatives could provide good training in commerce and business for the future managers of the socialist commonwealth; they were not allowed to become substitutes for that commonwealth.[6]

This mild endorsement by the Finnish Socialist Federation and the Mesabi Range strike of 1907 caused a spurt of cooperative activity in Minnesota. A cooperative store sprang up in rented quarters on the main street of Eveleth, Minnesota, established by striking miners who could not get enough credit from local merchants to last through the strike. Similar ventures were started by striking miners in other range cities, such as Hibbing and Chisholm. One year later, "forty socialist miners" established the Elanto (Elements of Life) in Nashwauk, Minnesota. Elanto was first established as a boardinghouse where matters of mutual interest could be discussed and Finnish food obtained. Later it became a consumer's cooperative, known to every Finn on the Mesabi. In 1909, miners in Virginia, Minnesota, who had been denied credit during the 1907 strike, started a society. The 1913 Copper Strike in northern Michigan gave impetus to the movement around Hancock, Michigan, as did the Mesabi strike of 1916, which spawned several new societies.[7]

The single most important agency in promoting cooperativism among the Finns was *Työmies*. When the newspaper was moved from Hancock, Michigan, to Superior, Wisconsin, after the 1913 Copper Strike, it intensified its cooperative promotion. That year it began publishing a monthly periodical called *Pelto ja Koti* (Field and Home) which was devoted exclusively to promoting cooperativism and offering farm and home advice.[8] While the journal contained such features as a question-and-answer section on farming problems and sewing and cooking advice, and while it supported candidates like Allen K. Benson and George Kirkpatrick as the Socialist Party candidates for president and vice-president in 1916, it also devoted a good portion of each issue to cooperativism. Cooperative societies already in existence advertised in *Pelto ja Koti* and published their yearly financial statements and the minutes of their annual board meetings. The editors inserted articles describing cooperative movements in Europe and continually expounded the virtues of the Rochdale principles.

In August, 1917, *Pelto ja Koti* urged all cooperatives in Minnesota, Michigan, and Wisconsin to send delegates to Duluth to discuss the possible formation of a central wholesale. The article noted that the war had given speculators a chance to exploit producers and consumers because of wildly fluctuating prices. If even ten cooperatives could get together and buy goods in carload lots when prices were low, they could store the goods indefinitely and avoid increased costs when prices soared.[9] The September issue proudly announced the formation of the Central Cooperative Exchange *(Keskusosuuskunta)*, a nonprofit corporation with shares selling for $100 each. Some nineteen cooperatives had sent delegates to the organizational meeting. *Pelto ja Koti* was present, as were observers from the Waukegan, Illinois, Finnish cooperative association. The Exchange, which was to be located in Superior, Wisconsin—the geographical center of the western Great Lakes region—was to function as a purchasing agent for member societies as well as a marketing agency for farm produce. One of the main items of concern at the organizational meeting was the procurement of Scandinavian breadstuffs—hardtack, rusks, toasts, heavy ryes—made scarce by wartime conditions. The delegates also discussed the need for education and propaganda. *Pelto ja Koti* was designated the official newspaper, and an experienced cooperator, John Nummivnori, was named business manager. He was to have a desk in a corner of the *Työmies* building in Superior from which he was to begin making business contacts using the $15.50 raised by passing the hat at the organizational meeting.[10]

The Exchange's first years were difficult. One of its first purchases, a carload of potatoes, arrived frozen and useless. Plans for a bakery to provide Scandinavian breads had to be put off two years for lack of funds. Nevertheless, the enterprise showed a sales volume of $25,000 and earnings of $4,250 by February 1918. A year later, fifty-one cooperatives had bought over $129,000 in goods from the Exchange.[11] Soon the Exchange had its own warehouse and was marketing coffee under its own label. But financial problems beset the new organization during the early postwar years as inflation set in. The postwar period had seen a rapid growth in the number of cooperative societies, especially in rural areas. With the onset of inflation, many of them began to fail because of poor or, more charitably, amateur management. The Exchange sent teams of financial troubleshooters to failing societies and suggested ways to stay solvent. Their suggestions usually called for tightening up on credit, cutting down on overhead, and using better bookkeeping methods. These failures underscored the need for careful and uniform auditing. As a result, H. V. Nurmi, head of the Exchange's auditing department and later business manager, developed the "Nurmi system" of double-entry bookkeeping which, with a few modifications, was used in the stores until the early 1960s. The Exchange itself suffered losses during the postwar period also. It lost $3,000 on a carload of sugar when prices began to tumble.[12] And by 1931 sales had dropped from a high of $409,000 in 1920 to $312,000.

As the 1920s wore on, the Exchange began to suffer "image" problems. By now the words "cooperator," "communist," and "Finn" were practically synonymous. Suppliers in the Duluth-Superior area did not miss the fact that the Exchange and *Työmies* were closely connected. They were, therefore, often reluctant to sell to the Exchange. One such case involved the supplier of rolled oats who refused to do business with the Exchange on the grounds that he already had enough dealers for his product. The Exchange took the case to the Federal Trade Commission for a ruling. Even though the FTC ruled in favor of the Exchange, the supplier of rolled oats would not sell to the Finns. As a result of incidents such as this, the Exchange was forced to develop its own line of merchandise under its own label. The Exchange's label quickly became familiar in the tri-state area if for no other reason than that it bore the image of a red hammer and sickle nestled within the confines of a large yellow star. To loyal cooperators, the label was the proud declaration of their political principles. To outsiders, and especially to conservative Finns, the label was anathema.

Problems such as these forced the Finns to develop their own line of merchandise. One student of the movement claims that at this time the leaders of the Exchange did not view themselves as members of a true consumers' cooperative movement; that they were simply providing a service in the interest of class solidarity. Only when the cooperators were forced to become manufacturers did they begin to realize what consumers' cooperativism really meant: the total avoidance of the middleman first by manufacturing needed products, and, ultimately, control of the raw materials themselves through expansion of the movement. Ironically, then, the animosity generated by the Finnish radical cooperators' image to the outside world actually forced them to expand their movement.

Another problem facing the radical leaders of the Exchange was the controversy within some individual stores between radicals and conservatives over control, controversies which often went to the courts for settlement. Significant numbers of Finns were interested in the cooperative ideal but not the attendant political radicalism the leaders in Superior advocated. The records of the Exchange show that at least half a dozen such cases had to be settled in or out of court before 1929. Compounding these controversies over "image" was the inability of the Finnish cooperators to interest non-Finnish cooperatives in affiliating with the Exchange. The non-Finns seemed wary of the openly leftist attitude of the Finns, especially after their shift from socialism to communism following the Russian Revolution. Most notable was the large Scandinavian cooperative in Two Harbors, Minnesota. After the Exchange had been founded, the Two Harbors group willingly did business with it. But after the Exchange's communist reputation grew, the Two Harbors cooperators stopped buying and only resumed relations after the communists lost power in the movement in the 1930s.[13]

After the slump of the early 1920s, business began to improve greatly. By 1925 there were sixty-five member societies (including both buying clubs and consumers' stores) affiliated with the Exchange. Total membership in these societies amounted to 11,192. Sales for that year reached $835,532, and over ninety cooperatives had bought goods from the Exchange.[14] Two years later, seventy-six societies owned shares in the Exchange, and sales had gone well over the million-dollar mark. In the sixty societies classified as Regular Incorporated Member Societies (this classification excluded unincorporated buying clubs), there were 16,595 individual members. Of these sixty societies, thirty-one were in Minnesota (with 6,856 members), fourteen were in Wisconsin (with 2,942 members), and thirteen were in Michigan (with 3,528 members). Two societies were in other states. They had a combined membership of 3,169, in some forty-one of the sixty societies. The overwhelmingly Finnish character of the Exchange and its affiliates is reflected in the fact that fifty-four of the sixty societies were either exclusively Finnish or mixed with Finns predominating. Only two of the societies were purely "American." The final four were mixed with non-Finns predominating.[15] By the mid-1920s, the Finns had extended their ethnic organizational structure into the realm of successful economics. Not only could a Finn, if he wished, insulate himself from Americans by staying in his own social and political organizations, but he did not even have to shop at a non-Finnish store.

With success came pride and militancy. As the 1920s wore on, the management of the Exchange began to be more conscious of cooperative theory and philosophy because of its increasing number of contracts with the larger American cooperative movement. The Exchange was strongly represented in the Cooperative League of the United States of America (CLUSA), founded in 1916 by Dr. James Peter Warbasse, a philanthropist strongly committed to cooperativism but very much opposed to socialism or communism.[16] The Finns virtually controlled the Northern States Cooperative League (NSCL), which was headquartered in Minneapolis and had been founded in part by the Finns as an educational agency for the promotion of cooperativism. The Finns agreed with their American friends on all of the Rochdale principles of cooperation but one. These principles, established by the Rochdale weavers in 1844, called for

1. open and voluntary membership regardless of race, occupation, nationality, social class, religious creed, or political affiliation;

2. democratic control of cooperative organizations, i.e., one member, one vote and no proxies;

3. return of surplus earnings to shoppers;

4. cash trading only;

5. promotion of cooperative education;

6. political, religious, and racial neutrality.[17]

The Finns assiduously practiced the first five. Number six, however, was a different story.

In an article inserted into the 1926 *NSCL Yearbook,* George Halonen, education director of the Exchange, reinterpreted principle number six. The Rochdale weavers did not have the strength of a working-class movement behind them to help them fight capitalist exploitation by mill and factory owners. Things are different today because capitalism is centralized in the state, making the class struggle more difficult and requiring the combined efforts of all workers as a class. "The class struggle," Halonen concluded, "be it on the political or economic field, is a struggle toward which the workers cannot be 'neutral.'"[18] Eskel Ronn, the manager of the Exchange, in the same issue, put it more militantly than did Halonen: "To wrest [the] power of the state from the ruling class, and to prevent it from being used against them, the workers who are fighting exploitation through the cooperatives and the labor unions, must organize on another front also, namely the political front."[19]

Halonen and Ronn, of course were members of the Workers' Party and members of the Exchange's fraction committee, so such sentiments from them are not strange. But a measure of their leadership abilities in the Finnish community as a whole is that they could make such utterances and not alienate more of the thousands of non-radical Finns in the movement than they did. It must be remembered that at the time these statements appeared in print there were no more than 7,000 members in the Finnish Workers Federation, the organization allied to the Workers' Party, scattered throughout the whole country. Yet in a three-state area in the Midwest over 16,000 Finns belonged to the cooperative movement, despite the fact that its leaders were avowed communists. Men like Halonen and Ronn achieved their successes in crossing over ideological lines, however, by stressing the consumer aspect of cooperativism more than the political and by remaining tolerant of political differences of the people in the store societies.

In the meantime, another spirit was growing within the Finnish-American cooperative movement, a spirit inspired largely by one man who had been involved in Finnish and Finnish-American radicalism since the days of the General Strike in Finland in 1905. That man was V. Severi Alanne, perhaps the most able cooperator and theorist ever to be associated with the movement. He had come to believe that neutrality was crucial to the success of the cooperative movement so that it could become a movement of consumers rather than a movement of Finns or radicals or some other similar interest group. Alanne is an important figure in the story of Finnish-American radical adjustment to American values because he first pointed out to the Finns that to achieve any measure of success in the cooperative movement, to change American economic and social patterns, it was necessary first to break out of the insular Finnish ethnic world and form a coalition with like-minded Americans on the basis of consumerism. Alanne was a university-trained chemist who came to America as a socialist. He had been involved deeply in radical politics in Finland. In fact, he had even roomed with Lenin briefly and had been jailed for his activities in this country. While at *Työmies,* he wrote and published a Finnish-English dictionary which is still regarded here and in Finland as one of the best. At some time during his years at *Työmies* he came to see cooperativism as a movement more powerful in its own right than radical political action. More importantly, he wanted to see cooperativism play a greater role than merely as "a supply department for strike periods and an elementary school for revolution." He believed, rather, in "a sphere of activity which must be separated both from capitalism . . . and socialism," but which would build a new economic system based on democracy, economy, equity, unity, and liberty.[20]

In 1925, Alanne left the Exchange because of the restrictions he believed political affiliation placed on the growth of the Finnish movement and went to work at Franklin Cooperative Creamery in Minneapolis, where he continued to conduct the courses in cooperation and store management he had established in Superior and where he became executive secretary of the Northern States Cooperative League. While in Minneapolis, he also continued to persuade the Finnish movement to get away from politics. In an article in the 1928 *NSCL Yearbook,* he pointed to two factors that retarded cooperative growth. It must have been simple for the people at the Exchange to see that the article was aimed at them. The first obstacle, of course, was political affiliation. Political affiliation could only hurt cooperativism because if "cooperators . . . are ready to accept the intellectual hegemony of a certain political party . . . at least at times they are willing to take dictates in their cooperative work" from the party to which they belong. If cooperativism is to succeed, it must be built on the broadest possible working-class base—not merely on one segment of that base. Other retardants to growth, Alanne continued, are "language and racial difficulties." The Finnish movement, he said, has been too reluctant to accept non-Finns into its stores as anything but customers. Few non-Finns have become activists because the Finnish founders of the stores too jealously guard their control. Also, Finns have been reluctant to conduct their business meetings in English. Such practices only serve to drive away non-Finns and even second-generation Finns. If these practices continue, he concluded, the Finnish movement will never become "assimilated" by the larger American consumers' cooperative movement.[21] Alanne had begun to look beyond his "Finnishness"; he had come to believe in cooperativism as a movement of people—of consumers—not merely Finns. He, for one, had taken the first step toward breaking out of the traditionally isolated Finnish organizational structure. Alanne had thousands of supporters among the Finnish cooperators, who respected his intellectual gifts as well as the lifetime of public activism behind him.

The more radical leaders of the Exchange were well aware of his views and had been for many years. In 1927, when they could begin to perceive the real threat he presented to their hegemony, they branded him a "reactionary" for siding with moderates in both the NSCL and CLUSA.[22]

While the leaders of the Exchange did not believe in political neutrality as did Alanne, they were in accord with him completely on the Rochdale principle of education and publicity. The Exchange had had a director of education since 1920, and actually conducted its first course in accounting in 1918. Also in 1918 it offered a four-week Cooperative Training School attended by forty students. Alanne was later to expand the training school idea. When he began working for Franklin he wrote a basic text and lengthened the course to six weeks. As executive secretary of NSCL he had helped write correspondence texts for cooperative employees and managers.[23] Despite the Exchange's differences of opinion with Alanne, they continued to use his educational ideas.

In 1926, the Exchange first published the *Cooperative Pyramid Builder*. *Pelto ja Koti* had ceased publication in the early 1920s for financial reasons. Since then *Työmies* had carried cooperative news with a special weekly section devoted to it. It was decided, however, that an English-language organ was needed to reach Americans and young Finns born in America. Thus, in July of 1926, the *Builder* hit the newsstands describing itself as "an educational monthly—published in the interests of the consumers' cooperative movement." Published by *Työmies*, the *Builder* was a frank, provocative, and militant journal during the six years of its life in periodical form.

The education director of Cooperative Central Exchange, George Halonen, was an able propagandist. He could report, for example, that the Exchange had issued 76,000 leaflets on seven different topics in 1926. That same year, 8,000 circulars "dealing with educational questions were issued to education committees, employees and boards of directors" of the Exchange's affiliate societies.[24] Halonen's department even developed a kind of "guerrilla theater" to promote cooperative products and to educate in cooperative theory. Ivan Lanto, one of Halonen's assistants, for example, wrote a "musical comedy" called "A Gala Day in a Co-op Store," which was sent on tour to the rural areas in the tri-state region. All the players were employees of the Exchange. Modeled on vaudeville and musical comedy, the play featured the Red Star Chorus, a group of nine women in "flapper" dresses emblazoned with yellow hammers and sickles over the left breast. They danced and sang their way through such lyrics as: "You'll be a cooperator—sooner or later/Wake up from your slumber; join us in great number!" Skits set in a typical general store pushed Red Star coffee, macaroni, and rolled oats—and explained everything from the theory and principles of cooperativism to the question of employee loyalty and the values of standardization and centralized effort.[25] Lanto wrote at least two other plays. A one-acter, called "A Winning Way," was perhaps reminiscent of the 1907 Mesabi Strike or the

1913 Copper Strike. It urged the solidarity of the workers against citizens' alliances and corporations during a strike. Naturally, the play pointed to the valuable role coop stores could play during a strike when local merchants sided with the companies and denied credit to the strikers. A third play, "The Potato War," made the point that the best place to market potatoes was at a coop store.[26]

Thus, the Exchange by the end of the 1920s had a well-oiled propaganda machine run by capable and imaginative men. The wholesale had enjoyed remarkable success considering that it had grown from a $15.50 investment to an enterprise which did over $2 million per year in sales in little more than a decade. The future did indeed look bright in 1929 for the Exchange. Although it was led by communists, they had earned the respect of the heterogeneous rank and file for their dedication to the cooperative movement. In fact, their dedication and hard work were largely responsible for the fact that the cooperative movement, once regarded as a minor "auxiliary" to socialism and communism, was a viable and successful economic and cultural institution among Finnish Americans.

The chain of events that triggered the final struggle over the issue of political neutrality started far from Superior—in Moscow, in fact, when the Comintern veered sharply leftward in the late 1920s in preparation for the final collapse of capitalism, which was now in its so-called third period. The working class, the Comintern decreed, must ready itself to seize power when the moment of collapse came, and, to do so, mass organizations such as cooperative movements had to be purged of rightists and counterrevolutionaries. Cooperatives must become auxiliaries to the Communist Party.[27]

The first sign of trouble in Superior came by letter from New York, on July 25, 1929. On that day the Exchange fraction received word from William Z. Foster and Max Bedacht, leaders of the Workers' (Communist) Party, who demanded a "loan" of $5,000 from the Exchange to be paid immediately. The letter was quickly followed by others asking that more money be contributed to other communist activities.[28] A momentous decision was made by the fraction committee of the Exchange: they refused the demands and apparently kept them a secret from the non-communist cooperators for several months. The board minutes of the Exchange, at any rate, do not reveal that the matter was ever discussed officially until late October 1929. According to the by-laws of the Workers' (Communist) Party, this refusal was the same as open rebellion against party authority and was thus action which subjected fraction members to expulsion from the party. Halonen was quietly expelled, but no other action was taken. Instead Robert Minor, another Workers' Party official, appeared in Superior with a new demand: the Exchange should "drag off" 1 percent of its annual sales and contribute the money to the party on a regular basis. Again the fraction committee refused.

Apparently George Halonen and Eskel Ronn were offering the most resistance, for they, and especially Halonen, were singled out for bitter criticism by the party and by *Työmies,* which had now been mobilized to attack "the danger from the right." On October 30, 1929, the party demanded that Halonen be fired from his job. The Exchange's Board of Directors refused. The very next day *Työmies* began a series of harsh attacks on "renegade" cooperators in general and Halonen in particular which would last for the next several years. *Työmies's* attack signalled the beginning of a war, the first battle of which would climax the next spring at the annual meeting of the Exchange. It was a battle which would pit loyal communists against a significant number of communists and others who had decided to repudiate their party affiliation and try to rid the cooperative movement of communist influence.

After *Työmies's* opening salvo, both sides quickly adopted positions and held to them. The Exchange posed as the injured innocent, unable to understand why former friends of the cooperative movement, the communists, now seemed bent on ruling the movement or ruining it. The Exchange even left the door open for reconciliation by repeating that the cooperative movement could be a home for anyone who was against capitalist exploitation. But the movement itself must be neutral to all elements incorporated within it. Cooperativism could not favor one segment of the working class; it could not become an auxiliary to a political party.

The communists claimed that "rightists," "opportunists," and "party renegades" were trying to seize the cooperative movement and turn it into an enemy of the working class. They frequently raised the issue that party discipline had been violated, that the Exchange had failed to recognize party authority and had pursued its own selfish ends. They constantly accused Halonen and his followers of placing capitalistic gain before ideological considerations.

The conflict expressed itself in arenas other than the journalistic. Fist fights were reported occasionally, old friendships suddenly cooled, and some families split irrevocably over the issues. But perhaps the most dramatic episode was an apparent attempt by *Työmies* to burn an issue of the *Cooperative Pyramid Builder* after it was already printed, because it was thought to contain distorted reporting by cooperative editors on the controversy. About 1,500 copies were actually burned before the fracas was stopped. The incident persuaded the cooperators to start their own newspaper and publish it independently of *Työmies*—which they had relied on to publish all cooperative news in recent years. Shortly before the first of the year 1930, a new cooperative publication appeared under the name of *Keskusosuuskunnan Tiedonantaja* (The Central Cooperative Messenger). After a few issues it was renamed *Työväen Osuustoimintalehti* (Workers' Cooperative News).

Late in December 1929, Matti Tenhunen, one of the "renegades," and Henry Puro, leader of the communists, were called to Moscow to explain both sides of the controversy. While there Tenhunen changed his mind and became an ardent supporter of the party position. And, as if to exploit the advantage Tenhunen's defection seemed to symbolize, the Comintern and the Finnish Communist Party (in exile) unleashed a barrage of cablegrams containing instructions on how to fight the right danger in the cooperatives.[29] Thus, by the spring of 1930 the dispute had grown from a tiny local struggle to one of international proportions.

A decisive point in the continuing struggle came at the annual meeting of the Exchange in Superior in April 1930. After a hectic winter and spring, as both sides attempted to win the loyalty of the store society delegates, and after a feverish journalistic battle, the issue was at last brought to the meeting at Workers' Hall in Superior. Would the cooperative movement become an auxiliary to the international communist movement? Or would it continue to be a home for a variety of political philosophies whose adherents wanted to avoid being exploited by American merchants?

The test of strength revolved around Halonen's and Ronn's positions. If the communists could replace these two men, after demonstrating to the delegates that they were unfit for their jobs, they would win an important victory. So important was the battle that neither side let up on its campaign until the actual votes were taken. The Comintern and the Finnish Communist Party came to the support of the left even after the three-day meeting had actually begun. They both sent telegrams to be read to the delegates in which they strongly called for the removal of Halonen and his followers. The stage was set for a dramatic climax.

When the votes were counted, however, the only surprising turn of events was how soundly the communists had been defeated. Only 46 of the 233 delegates cast votes against the policies of the Exchange. The meeting then voted censure of *Työmies* and expelled a few societies, which were followed by several voluntary withdrawals. When it was over, sixteen societies had left the Exchange, taking about 2,000 members.

Tempers had not yet cooled when the next and final parliamentary confrontation took place. In October, 1930, the Seventh Congress of the Cooperative League of the United States of America was held in Superior. A group of communists attended the meeting and asked permission to address the delegates. Given such permission, they launched into a bitter attack on the Exchange and its leaders. After several bitter floor confrontations, and as Eskel Ronn was explaining to the national body what had transpired in the Finnish movement over the past six months, the communists stood up and walked out of the meeting en masse singing the *Internationale.* When V. S. Alanne edited the proceedings of the Seventh Congress of CLUSA for publication in the *Cooperative League Yearbook,* he reported of the leftist walkout: "Thus communism publicly and officially removed itself from the Cooperative League and the Congress was free to devote itself to cooperation."[30]

The only thing that can be said for sure is that after the struggle on the cooperative front was over, Finnish radicalism was not the same. The struggle signalled the beginning of the end of Finnish-American radicalism as an ethnic movement, a movement which had begun thirty years before as a reaction against American values and culture. After the struggle both sides were drawn into the mainstream of America, away from purely ethnic concerns.

The cooperators, for their part, quickly consolidated their victory. They soon changed the Exchange's name to Central Cooperative Wholesale; they changed the label on their merchandise to the familiar twin pines logo; and they went on a deliberate campaign to "wean cooperators away from communism;" as one veteran put it, by establishing auxiliary social organizations for couples, women, and children in exact duplicate of those of the communists. They also opened their doors to non-Finns. By the end of the 1930s, the number of non-Finns in the movement was approaching 30 percent, and even a Swede had served on the Board of Directors. All of this, coupled with the advent of the Depression, gave CCW a new respectability and phenomenal growth. By 1941, CCW claimed over 50,000 individual members in 126 affiliate societies with gross sales of over $4.7 million.[31]

With growth and change came a less militant philosophy of cooperativism. Gone were the ringing phrases of the class struggle and the militancy of the early years. What remained was a quiet compromise with the profit system. Oscar Cooley, editor of the *Builder,* expressed it in 1940 as follows:

In championing the free system, we cooperators shall find that we have a common objective with the profit system. But does that mean we shall defend the profit system? No. We shall, rather, defend the philosophy of life which has given rise to both profit seeking and cooperation. Freedom and democracy are the parents which have given birth to both profit business and cooperative business. We must defend the parents, not the child called profit.[32]

But while the cooperative movement—including all the old Finnish radicals in it—chose to make peace with the American system, such was not yet the case with the leftists who still rallied around *Työmies*. They established their own cooperative organization (called Farmers' and Workers' Cooperative Unity Alliance) whose philosophy was appropriately political. They continued to promote re-emigration to Soviet Karelia to participate in the Republic of Work. They threw themselves wholeheartedly into the hunger marches, unemployment councils, and farm holidays of the Depression years. They took part in the so-called Markham Uprising in rural St. Louis County, Minnesota, during the winter of 1932-33.[33] They supported the Republican side in the Spanish Civil War with both materials and men. They contributed ambulances and money, but, more tragically, several Finnish-American volunteers were killed in Spain, including the well-known Reino Tanttila. They worked hard during the CIO organizing drive in the steel industry of the late 1930s, a drive which brought several Finns to national leadership in both the labor movement and the Communist Party. Most notable, of course, was Gus Hall.

Though the leftists were not so quick to compromise with dominant traditional American values as were the cooperators, in one respect, at least, the results of the cooperative struggle were the same for the left. They moved out into the mainstream of American life, away from the exclusiveness of their ethnic group. The Finnish Workers' Federation merged with the International Workers' Order in the early 1940s. The struggle on the cooperative front did indeed mark an important point in the history of the Finns in the western Great Lakes region.

JOSEPH STIPANOVICH

COLLECTIVE ECONOMIC ACTIVITY AMONG SERB, CROAT, AND SLOVENE IMMIGRANTS IN THE UNITED STATES

Recent sociological studies indicate that immigrants from southern and eastern Europe and their descendants are disproportionately represented in the blue collar work force of the United States. These same studies indicate that these people are concentrated in the urban-industrial areas of the Midwest and Northeast, which themselves have disproportionately large concentrations of blue collar workers compared to other cities in the nation. Perry Weed, for example, indicates that the ratio of blue collar workers to all workers was one to three in 1960, but for Poles and Italians the ratio was one to two. In cities such as Chicago, Cleveland, Detroit, Pittsburgh, Gary, and Buffalo, these immigrants, as well as their children and grandchildren, work in relatively low-status, low-income jobs and attempt to cope with the strains and tensions of urban-industrial existence.[1]

The response of these people to the political, social, and economic upheavals of the 1960s and 1970s—the rise of the unmeltable ethnics, as Michael Novak described it—seemed to indicate to many social scientists that these people's occupational and geographical concentrations reflected a failure of the U.S. social and economic system to provide adequate opportunities for advancement. The ethnic political movement therefore was interpreted as their claim for a greater share of the economic "pie," in emulation of the claims of Blacks and affluent students who preceded them in political and social revolt. Weed argues that the ethnics became "increasingly positive about their own ancestral cultural traditions, confused toward American culture, and ... negative toward Anglo-Protestant dominance." The ethnics began to recognize shared grievances and, in order to obtain redress, organized politically by drawing together "both into their separate nationality groups and into the larger category of 'white ethnics.'"[2]

Undeniably the history of southern and eastern European immigrants and their descendants in the United States is for the most part the history of urban, industrial workers and their communities. Why this continues to be true, however, cannot be explained totally by the failure of the U.S. social and economic system to provide opportunities for advancement. Discrimination in housing, hiring, and the setting of wages did affect these immigrants adversely, but not to the degree that it affected Chinese, Japanese, and Black immigrants and migrants. And some groups, most notably the Jews and the Japanese, managed to achieve significant inter-generational mobility in the face of very severe discrimination. The pattern of ethnic social and economic development in U.S. history, as it is emerging from recent research and literature, suggests that the choices and activities of the immigrants themselves played primary roles in the process. It must be remembered also that these choices and activities were made and effected in the context of immigrant communities and not by uprooted individuals dazed by the collapse of a mythic *Gemeinschaft* and hell-bent to enrich themselves at any cost. The ethnic communities that became politically active in the late 1960s had long traditions of cultural diversity, distrust of the assimilative thrust of American culture, and long-term resentment at Anglo-Protestant domination. What is remarkable about the white ethnic movement of the past decade is not the result of new ethnic community feeling because that has been a constant feature of the immigrant communities, but rather that it became politically effective and meaningful on a national scale in a very short period of time. This inquiry shall attempt to make more understandable that movement, the realities of the urban-industrial world that helped spawn it, and the long-term importance of ethnic decision making in the determination of their affairs.

The hypothesis forwarded here is that lack of skills and technology and the resultant concentration of the immigrant workers in the bottom tier of the American occupational structure upon entry was the major obstacle to each group's mobility. The immigrants recognized the problem and attempted to deal with it by investing a large part of their savings in human development, that is, in the improvement and maintenance of the group's physical and mental health, in creating opportunities for skill-acquisition and general education, and in cultivating group identity and group goals through stimulation of individual and collective interest in group history, music, literature, and the other arts. The immigrants thought that such investment would enable them to break the bonds of their occupational homogeneity *while maintaining their cultural integrity* and enable them, in the long run, to overcome as *groups* artificial and institutional barriers to their occupational diversification and advancement. As the occupational distribution of the immigrants and their descendants would approach that of the indigenous population such collective economic activity would recede in importance and attract a diminishing share of immigrant savings. This would occur as a consequence of growing incomes, the greater accessibility of competing areas for investment, and specialization of the surviving collective enterprises in essential cultural activities. All other things being equal, a group or groups with a higher rate of investment in human development through group concerns should have approximated the occupational distribution of the indigenous population more rapidly than groups with lower rates of investment.

As shall be demonstrated with the Serb, Croat, and Slovene groups, not every immigrant group organized their collective economic activities in the same fashion or with the same result in spite of similarities of prior historical experience, cultural institutions, and language. While such collective organization seems to have been common to all groups of urban-industrial immigrants, the differences are of more than passing interest. Such differentiation affected the efficiency of the investment process and sometimes led to the diversion of savings away from those areas associated with human development in the host environment. An attempt will be made to demonstrate that such differences in organization and the ordering of different priorities can be explained in part by the physical characteristics of each immigrant group involved and in part by peculiarities in the history and culture of each group. The group's most important physical characteristics, as has been confirmed by research into the question, are the net size of the immigrant group, the pattern of geographic location of settlement and the density of same, the distribution of immigrants by industry (not to be confused with occupation), and the levels of skill and technology possessed at entrance.[3]

Unfortunately there are severe problems associated with the identification of the occupational distributions of immigrant groups at times beyond the entry phase. Immigration statistics provide, especially after 1890, a good deal of information about the skills that various nationality groups brought to the United States. The reports of the Senate investigation on the effects of immigration in 1907-10, the Dillingham Report, provide a great deal of information about the occupational diversity of immigrants in the peak period of immigration just before World War 1. No systematic and nationwide collection of data about the occupational distribution of immigrants and their descendants has been attempted since Dillingham, except for samples developed occasionally by the Bureau of the Census.[4] This paper, consequently, will attempt to describe and analyze the origins and progress of collective economic activity among the Serb, Croat, and Slovene immigrants during the entry phase and attempt to explain the different development of the activities of the three groups. A complete analysis of the relationship between collective immigrant economic activity and occupational advancement and individual mobility requires further research. Nonetheless, it does seem accurate to note that this particular area of inquiry has been overlooked by students of U.S. social history and certainly deserves attention.

THE SERB, CROAT, AND SLOVENE MIGRATIONS, 1890-1930

The description and analysis of the migration of Serbs, Croats, and Slovenes to the United States is contained in a large body of historical literature, and only a brief outline of the main features will be presented here.[5] The elements of these three groups who participated in the migration originated primarily in Austria-Hungary prior to 1914, although a large number of Serbs from Serbia and Montenegro also migrated. After World War I the majority of immigrants came from the Yugoslav state (named Yugoslavia in 1929), which was comprised of Croats, Serbs and Slovenes. Significant numbers also originated in rump Austria and in Italy.

The Slovenes began migrating to the United States in large numbers about 1890, and the foreign-born Slovene population reached its peak in 1915. The Croats began migrating around 1890 as well, but especially after 1893, and their foreign-born population in the United States also peaked in 1915. The Serb migration to the United States did not get underway until 1900 and the peak of Serb population was not reached until 1917. The Slovene foreign-born population was 30 percent larger than the Croats during the entire period, and the Croat population was 200 percent larger than the Serb group. The difference in size between the Slovene and Croat populations can probably be attributed to higher rates of repatriation in the period 1890-1910 on the part of Croats. The smallness of the Serb population relative to Croats and Slovenes is attributable to the later start of Serb migration, by ten to fifteen years, and very high rates of repatriation. The Croats and Slovenes also had more females in their migration stream than did the Serbs. Between 1899 and 1914, the Slovenes and Croats had a high male-female ratio of 864:100 in the 1902 flow, and a low of 244:100 in the 1911 movement. The Serbs and Bulgars, the latter another Yugoslav ethnic group whose male-female data are combined with that of the Serbs in U.S. migration statistics, had a high male-female ratio of 5000:100 in 1900, and a low of 446:100 in 1901. The ratio of males to females in the Slovene-Croat migration was consistently lower than that of Serbs and Bulgars between 1899 and 1930. The Serb-Bulgar ratio was lower in only two years, 1919 and 1930.

While more Slovene and Croat females were immigrating than were Serb and Bulgar females, more were also emigrating from the United States. The relationship between immigration and repatriation of males and females is clarified somewhat by the examination of census data. The male-female ratios for Slovenes, Croats, and Serbs were 212:100,

TABLE 8.1 Serb, Croat, and Slovene Populations in Major U.S. Urban Areas, 1930

City	Slovenes	Croats	Serbs
Cleveland	12,302	3,607	607
Chicago	3,603	8,288	1,568
Detroit	1,054	2,238	3,396
Milwaukee	2,767	1,668	217
Pittsburgh	661	2,830	742
New York	2,039	1,525	489
Los Angeles	1,660	923	382
Gary	118	1,242	1,109
San Francisco	1,483	476	297
Total	25,687	22,797	8,807

Source: Data were compiled by the author from the 1930 census, *General Characteristics of the Population*.

413:100, and 638:100, respectively, in 1910. In 1920 the Slovene ratio had declined to 171:100, the Croat ratio had dropped to 259:100, and the Serb ratio to 251:100. By 1930 the Slovene ratio had fallen to 153:100, that of the Croats to 184:100, and the Serbs to 233:100. The downward trend of the rates reflects a movement toward equilibrium within the immigrant communities. The Slovene lead over the other two groups in this respect reflects the longer duration of their migration. The Croat lead over the Serbs reflects their relatively longer participation relative to that group. The dramatic decline in the Serb ratio of males to females, from 638:100 in 1910 to 233:100 in 1930, reflects the short duration of the Serb migration before it was interrupted by World War 1, U.S. immigration restriction in 1924, and the development of new opportunities for potential migrants in Yugoslavia and Latin America after 1920.

The Serbs, Croats, and Slovenes were seeking industrial employment in the United States, and their search took them to large urban, industrial places, primarily in the Midwest and the Northeast. Cleveland, Chicago, Pittsburgh, and Detroit were the major areas of concentration,

TABLE 8.2 Estimates of Distribution of Serb, Croat, and Slovene Immigrant Workers, by Industry, 1914

Immigrant by Industry	Percentage of Group	Number
Slovenes		
Coal mining, bituminous	40	30,000
Iron and steel	35	26,250
Meat processing	8	6,000
Metals, nonferrous (all phases)	5	3,750
Other	12	9,000
Total	100	75,000
Croats		
Iron and steel	42	63,000
Coal mining, bituminous	35	52,500
Meat processing	15	22,500
Metals, nonferrous (all phases)	4	6,000
Other	3	4,500
Total	100	148,500
Serbs		
Iron and steel	70	29,400
Meat industry	18	7,560
Coal mining, bituminous	5	2,100
Metals, nonferrous (all phases)	5	2,250
Other	2	900
Total	100	42,210

Sources: Data were compiled from the U.S. Census, 1900 and 1910; the reports of the Dillingham Commission, 1907-20; and Lewis Corey's *Meat and Man* (New York: Viking Press, 1950).

with Cleveland having the largest Slovene concentration, Chicago the largest Croat population, and Detroit the largest Serb population (see table 8.1). These groups also had major concentrations in other large cities, such as New York, Milwaukee, Los Angeles, and San Francisco, and in smaller industrial cities, such as Kansas City, St. Louis, Youngstown, Gary, and Alequippa. While most of the workers of all three groups were unskilled laborers, approximately 86 percent of the total, their distribution by industry varied from one group to another. The Slovenes were well represented in coal mining, meat processing, iron and steel production, together accounting for 83 percent of the total Slovene work force, but with 17 percent distributed over several other industries. In comparison, three industries—iron and steel, meat, and coal mining—accounted for 93 percent of the Croat work force, with 7 percent distributed over all other industries. One industry, iron and steel, accounted for 70 percent of the Serb workers, and if meat, coal, and metals are added, 98 percent of the Serb workers are accounted for (see table 8.2). These differences reflect the Slovenes' longer exposure to the U.S. labor market and their better information concerning available industrial employment relative to Croats but more so to Serbs. The Croats' experience relative to the Slovenes reflects their higher rates of repatriation, which drained off experienced and informed workers, and their shorter period of time in the U.S. labor market. The Serb pattern reflects their relatively late arrival and the opportunities available to them at that time.

Combined, these different characteristics of each of the three groups indicates significant differences in the timing and the motivation for migration. The combination of large numbers of women and the lower rate of repatriation, compared to those of the Serbs and Croats, indicates the more permanent nature of the Slovene migration. The greater industrial and geographic diversity of the Slovenes, especially the former, reflects their earlier commitment to the new environment relative to Croats and Serbs. This is further reflected by the large population of Slovenes compared to Serbs and Croats in the United States, even though their population in Europe was only one-seventh that of the Serbs and one-fourth that of the Croats. It is safe to conclude that the majority of Slovenes came to the United States in this period with a desire to commit themselves to the new world. On the other hand, the majority of the Serbs came for short-term reasons, especially the accumulation of savings for investment in the old country, and so did not have large numbers of females in their ranks, had high rates of repatriation, and took advantage of other opportunities when they presented themselves. The Croat migration falls between the Slovene and Serb migrations in these regards.

THE ORIGINS OF COLLECTIVE ECONOMIC ACTIVITY

The permanence of settlement greatly affects the intensity and rate of development of collective economic activities among immigrant groups. Migrants with short-term goals and interests did not need and did not organize enterprises which facilitated their long-term adaptation to the host environment. Such organization would proceed only as growing numbers of migrants made long-term commitments to the new environment. Long-term committed immigrants, on the other hand, would initiate such organization as rapidly as their skills, resources, and numbers would allow.

The Slovenes were the first chronologically of the three groups under consideration to initiate collective economic activity. However, the pattern of development for such enterprises was generally the same for all three groups. The uniformity of this pattern seems explicable in that each of the three groups was responding to fundamental features of the new environment, such as high accident rates for unskilled industrial labor with a high incidence of deaths and disabling injuries resulting from them. The pattern can be seen to develop in three stages. First, in response to such events local groups of immigrants, finding kin resources lacking, would organize funeral and survivors' assistance funds. Second, these local groups, usually bound together by kinship, village, and regional loyalties, as well as need, would establish contact with other such groups in other areas through the immigrant press, through exchanges of information among kinspeople, through contacts between members of the immigrant clergy, and through exchanges between various immigrant intellectuals. Attempts to coordinate activities through formal institutional forms resulted from such contacts. Third, as the numbers of participants grew, the geographical area expanded, and the volume of funds increased, formal organizations were created and established through existing legal mechanisms. While this overall pattern was the same for all three groups there were significant differences in the timing for moving from one stage to another for each group. The Slovenes reached stage three by 1894 (see table 8.3). The Croats did not reach stage three until 1897 and the Serbs until 1927. The Croats and the Serbs remained in stage two for a longer time than did the Slovenes. The explanation for these differences seems to be tied to the Slovenes' rapid progress, a rapidity best explained by their earlier commitment to the new environment, their higher skill levels at entry, and the successful organizational activities of the Slovene Roman Catholic clergy in the immigrant communities.[6]

The U.S. legal system had long experience with fraternal insurance organizations by the end of the nineteenth century, and the efforts of the Serb, Croat, and Slovene immigrants to establish such bodies were bound by law. The basic form of such organizations was not determined by the Slovene, Croat, Serb, or other immigrants at this time who attempted to establish them. The National Fraternal Congress, which had been created by preexisting societies in the 1880s, drafted uniform legislation for enactment by the states in 1891-92, and some thirty states adopted such laws within two years. This legislation varied somewhat from state to state, but all had eight common features. The societies could not be joint stock companies; they had to be organized and maintained solely for the mutual benefit of the members and their designated beneficiaries; they could not be conducted solely for profit; they had to employ a lodge system, which implied local autonomy and insured local participation; they had to employ ritualistic forms for the conduct of business; they had to have representative means for self-governing; they had to include death benefits among the total range of benefits offered to members; and the beneficiaries had to fall within a clearly defined, restricted group. The National Fraternal Congress also was instrumental in developing actuarial methods and materials, especially mortality tables, which could insure the efficient operation of the organizations from an economic standpoint.[7]

While the forms of the immigrant organizations were prescribed by law, the content, purpose, and spirit were developed by the immigrants themselves. In the preambles, constitutions, and by-laws of their first economic organizations, the immigrants stressed spiritual and cultural tasks as well as material ones. The development of the arts, the development of morals and community integrity, the education of young and old in the knowledge of the new country as well as the old, and the support of other immigrant organizations and projects were aims stressed by all of the organizations. The lodge system reinforced community ties and kinship networks especially, as did the ritual forms which were essential for lodge work as well as the national organization. The immigrants were also able to require certain norms of behavior for their members through their organizational by-laws. The different norms expected by different groups is clearly reflected in the rules and sanctions of each organization. The research of Margaret Galey into this area is enlightening in this regard.

Her work reflects how different groups of immigrants utilized the structure of fraternal organizations and adapted their own sanctions to maintain the values of the group. She shows how the Croats, for example, made members ineligible for benefits by reason of obesity, for violation of the rule of secrecy concerning organizational business, for slander or libel of other members, and for divorce, whereas the Serbs considered none of these basis for expulsion or the withholding of benefits. Both Serbs and Croats considered adultery, drug use, venereal disease, felony conviction, and murder for profit as grounds for expulsion. Galey writes that "sanctions may be said to have reinforced the notion that cash payments and socio-cultural benefits were not simply to be provided to those of similar ethnic background, but only to those whose behavior was congruent with expectations of association members."[8] The monitoring of the immigrants' behavior by their organizations in the United States was an extension of the monitoring that was carried on by the church, family, and village in the old country. To participate in community affairs the individual had to respect community values.

CONSOLIDATION AND GROWTH OF COLLECTIVE ECONOMIC ACTIVITIES

The Serbs, Croats, and Slovenes established their collective organizations, but a striking development began to set the Slovenes apart from the other two groups. The Slovenes, unlike the Serbs or Croats, established several national organizations which were competitive and among which no single organization predominated (again, see table 8.3). The lack of organizational diversity among the Serbs is understandable because of their small numbers relative to the Croats and Slovenes. The Croats present a more difficult problem, however, because there were as many Croat immigrants in the period as Slovene immigrants. The physical characteristics of the Croat migration and the economic needs of the immigrants alone do not explain this difference in organizational response to conditions in the new environment. The differences stem from group cultural developments and history prior to emigration.

It is significant that the Slovenes, alone of the three groups, had extensive experience with collective economic organization prior to 1890 and the initiation of large-scale emigration. The Slovenes had achieved a high degree of national and social consciousness, had reduced but not done away with the importance of familial and regional loyalties in the maintenance of their communities, and had established their immigrant communities and organizations in an atmosphere of broad rather than constricted ideological concern. In their European homeland they had established secular economic collectivities as well as religious-nationalist ones; in the United States they did the same. The Croats and Serbs of Austria-Hungary did not accomplish this until after large-scale emigration had begun. The Slovenes had developed a peasant political movement by 1890, a social democratic movement by the early 1890s, a very successful agricultural cooperative movement by 1900, and a national banking movement to develop national resources by 1919. The Croats and Serbs of Austria-Hungary, on the other hand, were unable to develop peasant political movements until after World War 1 and were unable to develop a successful national cooperative movement. The Serbs of Serbia and Montenegro, especially the former, were much more successful in this regard, but these areas had relatively low rates of emigration and high rates of repatriation. Nationalistic politics of an anti-German and anti-Magyar nature among Serbs and Croats in Croatia, Bosnia, and Dalmatia culminating in the revolutionary movements which led to Sarajevo and the assassinations there in 1914 consumed more organizational efforts than did basic economic work. Nationalistic politics were brought to the United States by these immigrants and had a great influence in organizational decisions—greater than did economic matters. Consequently, the Serbs and Croats created monolithic organizations which attempted to contain all diversity in the group, while the Slovenes created ideologically motivated organizations which would operate within the bounds of the ethnic group.

The diversity of collective organizations among the Slovenes enabled them to mobilize a greater percentage of their immigrant population than was true for the Serbs or Croats. The individual Serb or Croat who became disgruntled with the dominant organization had only two viable alternatives: to participate in a miniscule fringe group or not to participate in the group's collective activity at all. The individual Slovene, on the other hand, could choose from among eight major organizations, by 1915 at least, and could participate in several simultaneously without violating any ideological considerations. The differences between the Slovené organizations were real, however. The Slovene National Benefit Society was social democratic in philosophy in the tradition of the Second Socialist International and sought to improve the lot of Slovene workers in the United States and organize them for social democratic action. The Slovene Progressive Benefit Society also was oriented toward workers' political and economic activities but was motivated more by liberal humanism than the Marxist revisionism of the Slovene social democrats. Nationalistic clericalism was the hallmark of the Carniolan-Slovene Catholic Union, while interethnic clericalism sparked the Jugo-Slav Catholic Union. It is important to note that the social democratic and liberal workers' organizations were as successful and sometimes more successful than the bourgeois-nationalist Slovene organizations in attracting members and in accumulating capital. The Slovene experience clearly demonstrates the compatibility of collective political ideology with collective social and economic activity in a democratic, culturally plural, free market environment.

The Slovenes succeeded in mobilizing more of the group's assets as well as more members than did the Serbs or Croats. By 1930 the Slovenes had $74.16 in assets per organizational member and had more members than did the Serbs and Croats combined (see table 8.3). In the same year the Croats had $58.91 in assets per organizational member while the Serbs had $48.12 in assets per member. Organizational diversity does not explain these figures. The diversion of immigrant savings from the host environment to the place of origin completes the picture. Statistics on immigrant remittances are not complete, but estimates developed from a variety of sources can give some idea of the magnitude of the flow.[9] Between 1890 and 1940, Serb, Croat, and Slovene immigrants remitted at least $30 million to Europe. This Figure covers only those movements of money

TABLE 8.3   Serb, Croat, and Slovene Collective (Mutual Benefit) Economic Activities in the United States, 1930

Organizations	Date organized	Membership	Insurance in force ($)	Assets ($)	Number of locals
Croats					
Croat Fraternal Union	1897a	92,458	64,747,067	5,481,676	940
Croat Catholic Union	1922	4,758	2,689,774	203,621	46
Others	–	1,942	1,322,000	156,548	23
Total		99,158	68,658,841	5,841,845	1,009
Slovenes					
Carniolan-Slovene Catholic Union	1894	34,491	23,365,253	2,659,574	188
Jugo-Slav Catholic Union	1898	21,116	13,043,094	1,499,742	187
Slovene National Benefit Society	1904	63,448	41,766,825	4,764,187	653
Slovene-Croat Alliance	1903	1,974	1,273,480	231,385	25
Western Slavonic Alliance	1908	3,298	1,876,442	141,708	39
Slovene Progressive Benefit Society	1909	11,158	6,208,924	697,941	200
Slovene Workers' Alliance	1910	9,739	5,979,009	827,383	52
Slovene Assistance Society	1915	2,093	831,334	66,937	17
Others	–	2,556	1,594,900	226,218	17
Total		149,873	95,939,261	11,115,075	1,378
Serbs					
Serb National Federation	1927b	21,885	14,608,265	1,054,772	360
Others	–	951	556,000	44,099	15
Total		22,835	15,164,265	1,098,871	375

[a]Constituent bodies date back to 1894.
[b]Constituent bodies date back to 1901.

Sources: Data were compiled from Dinko Tomasic, "Americans from Yugoslavia," mimeographed, Immigration History Research Center, University of Minnesota, and from newspapers and fraternal publications located in the Yugoslav collection at IHRC.

recorded by international postal money orders purchased and bank draughts, and does not include cash mailed unsecured and cash carried by returning immigrants. Of this total figure, the Croats remitted an estimated $180 million, the Serbs $40 million, and the Slovenes $80 million for the rates of annual remittance. From these data and from data concerning repatriation it can be seen that the Croats diverted a higher percentage of their savings to the homeland than did the Slovenes but a lower percentage than the Serbs. Thus, the Slovenes endowed their immigrant communities with more wealth for investment in human development both absolutely and relatively when compared with the Serbs and Croats.

From data on the accumulation of capital in the economic organizations and from data on remittances it appears that the rates of saving for Serbs, Croats, and Slovenes were nearly the same. The assets per member of the immigrant group organizations in 1930 plus the average per capita remittance for each group between 1910 and 1930 equalled $86.36 for the Slovenes, $85.94 for the Croats, and $63.45 for the Serbs. The lower figure for the Serbs reflects the large drop in their population in the United States after 1920 and their probable preference for carrying cash on return rather than trusting to bank draughts and money orders. From these figures it appears that the Slovenes were investing 79 percent of their savings in their communities in the United States and 21 percent in their homeland. The Croats were investing 41 percent of their savings in the United States and 59 percent in the old country, and the Serbs were investing 29 percent of their savings in the United States and 71 percent in Europe. It is conjectured here that this pattern of savings and investment would be reflected in complete occupational data for the Serb, Croat, and Slovene immigrants in that such data would reveal the Slovenes approximating the national occupational distribution more rapidly than the Croats and Serbs, and the Croats approximating the national pattern more rapidly than the Serbs. While these groups would have higher rates of approximation compared with each other, all would be slower than northern and western European groups (e.g., Scandinavians, Germans, English, Dutch, Scots), of immigrants and native-born Anglo-Protestants to the extent that they were discriminated against in the labor market and that they used their investment in the United States for the maintenance and growth of their separate cultures. Such investment would be of no value in the Anglo-dominated marketplace, which placed value only on cultural activities of the dominant group, and such investment could even draw negative effects through outright political, social, cultural, and economic pressure (e.g., nativistic attacks and institutionalized "Americanization" programs).

It is no accident that the remittance of savings to the homeland is similar to the pattern of repatriation for the three groups. The remittances, as best as can be determined, were used primarily for the purchase of land by the returning migrants. Some part of the remittances, especially after the end of unrestricted immigration in 1924, was used for the raising of standards of consumption for family and village in the old country, but the majority of the funds, at least 80 percent before 1927, was used for purchase of land. The temporary migrants also left some of their savings in the United States as they contributed equally to the collective organizations while they were here in order to protect their investments and the investments of family and friends in themselves which they and their backers stood to lose in the event of their death or the receipt of disabling injury. These temporary migrants were at great risk in terms of accident and death on the job and off because of their lack of interest in English and indirectly in safety, their willingness to reduce consumption to a bare survival level and hence increase the possibility of disease, and their willingness to work in the most dangerous occupations in order to remain employed continuously in the short run. The concentration of all three groups in coal mining and the iron and steel industry, deadly work for the unskilled worker between 1890 and 1930, alone established high risk, but the injection of these temporary migrants increased that risk significantly for the Croats and especially for the Serbs. These factors also explain the lower total savings and investment figures for the Serbs.

DIVERSIFICATION OF COLLECTIVE ECONOMIC ENTERPRISES

The fraternal benefit societies were the most important collective economic enterprises among the Serb, Croat, and Slovene immigrants, but as time passed they proved unable to meet all the needs the immigrant communities felt. Foremost among these needs was housing. Indigenous U.S. financial institutions were unwilling and often, because of profit considerations and low South Slav incomes, unable to provide investment in South Slav housing. The Serb, Croat, and Slovene immigrant communities responded to this by establishing savings and loan associations in the early 1920s. In the four major urban areas of these three groups' settlement—Pittsburgh, Chicago, Cleveland, and Detroit—they established thirteen savings and loan associations with combined assets in 1930 of $8,828,717.50. Eight were Croatian with $4,142,597.16 in assets, four were Slovenian with $4,576,120.34 in assets, and one was Serbian with $110,000 in assets.[10] Such organizations enabled the Serbs, Croats, and Slovenes to develop their urban communities in neighborhoods composed of single-family dwellings. By the late 1920s the fraternal organizations also began providing mortgage money for their membership as the savings and loan associations could not meet the entire demand. Mainstream U.S. economic institutions do not appear to have played a significant role in the financing of South Slav housing until after 1950.

During the same period of time the Slovenes, Croats, and Serbs made massive investments in education primarily through their community churches. Complete statistics for all three groups are not available, but some data exist for the Slovenes.[11] In 1928 there were thirty-five whole and fifteen mixed Slovene Roman Catholic parishes in the United States. Sixteen of the former and five of the latter had elementary schools with a total number of pupils of 7,831 and an average of 372 pupils per school. The average value of each school building was $11,500, with total investment exceeding $250,000. These schools operated at a per capita level of expenditure that was one-third as high as the national per capita average for public school expenditure primarily because of the low incomes of the nuns and priests and a few lay teachers who provided the personnel for these schools. The Slovenes were able to control the education of their offspring, they were able to educate them less expensively than through public education, and by retaining ethnic homogeneity in their neighborhoods were able to keep their taxes for education lower than they would have been by reducing demand for public schooling. And all three groups were very much interested in controlling the education of their children. While they were concerned that their children should acquire the skills they needed to make their way in the American labor market, they were more interested in education serving to reinforce the cultural values that were reflected in the immigrant family, immigrant community, and immigrant culture and which the immigrants saw as the greatest—and most important—legacy.

The Slovenes, Croats, and Serbs also made expenditures for the care of orphaned children and the aged in the 1920s. Such expenditures were made by the fraternal organizations and by the church organizations. By 1930 the Slovenes had two orphanages and two homes for the aged, while both the Serbs and Croats had one of each. The "homes" for the aged immigrants were not of the nursing variety but were usually communally organized with an emphasis upon the continued participation of the aged and their continued pursuit of productive and meaningful lives. They were primarily aimed at those migrants who had no kin or whose kin were unable or unwilling to support them in their old age.

While the 1920s saw the Slovene, Serb, and Croat enterprises concentrating their efforts in the housing market, all entered upon vigorous programs to develop the arts among the immigrant populations. National mail order libraries were organized, travelling chorus and orchestras created, travelling repertory companies organized to present classic and original dramas in immigrant communities, and scholarships provided for exceptional students to pursue their studies in the U.S. system of higher education. As a result of these and a great many other programs, of the relatively small contributions per immigrant, and of the dedication of a small group of immigrant scholars and intellectuals and artists, the foundation was laid for the long-run development of Serb, Croat, and Slovene immigrant high and popular culture in the United States.[12]

CONCLUSION

The ability of the Serb, Croat, and Slovene immigrant groups to overcome their occupational confinement at the bottom of the American occupational structure depended, in the long run, upon their willingness to pay the costs of acquiring marketable skills and technology and usable knowledge of the new environment. In economic terms, it is clear that, of the three groups under consideration, the Slovenes were the most capable of meeting these costs. Their advantage stemmed from their talents for organization, their willingness to accept ideological diversity within their community, and their adaptability to changing conditions. The Croats and Serbs were less able to meet these costs because of their higher rates of repatriation, their higher remittance rates, and their monolithic approach to organization. The Croat and, to an even greater extent, the Serb immigrants sacrificed the maximization of their economic interests here in order to assist kin, communities, and nation, or *narod*, in the old world. The collective economic enterprises of these immigrant groups reflect not only their economic goals but also the group's aspirations as well as the cultural values that shaped them and infused them with meaning.

Close examination of the Slovene activities, however, indicates that their investment in the U.S. environment was designed to lead to social mobility not directly but indirectly. For example, the immediate goals of the Slovenes were to maintain and reinforce kin ties to provide adequate housing—the physical basis of their communities in the city—and to instill in their offspring the values that had guided their thoughts and actions. If social and economic mobility were compatible with this process of transfer and with the values themselves, so much the better. This is clearly reflected in the Slovene view of education. The primary goal of the Slovene educational system was, to use E. F. Schumacher's phrase, "to clarify central convictions" and not merely to provide marketable training. It was important that the children learn human values, the history of the community, and that which their parents held sacred, be it in the guise of Roman Catholic Slovene tenets or Slovene social democracy. The Slovene emphasis on housing finance reinforces this view as does their concern for the aged, infirmed, and orphaned, and their careful cultivation of their history, arts, and literature.

In this light, the continued concentration of these immigrants' descendants in industrial occupations in urban areas becomes more explicable. In one way or another, through remittances to the old country or through economically irrational uses of assets in the United States, Serb, Croat, and Slovene immigrants consistently placed human over purely material priorities. Thus, the rational pursuit of individual self-interest alone is not a good guide to understanding the three groups' activities. Such pursuit was carried on, but for most of these immigrants it was carried on within the parameters of their own values and historical view of themselves, their forebears, and their descendants. Such values and the people who nourish them have survived and, occasionally, even prospered in the United States as a result of the collective efforts of the first immigrants to establish the means to do so and to impress upon their successors the importance of those means and the ends behind them.

Given this view of southern and eastern European immigrant economic behavior, as represented by the Serbs, Croats, and Slovenes, and its primary results—the maintenance of immigrant culture on the one hand and the disproportionate concentration of their descendants in blue collar work in the blighted urban-industrial areas of the Midwest and Northeast on the other—the white ethnic political movement of the 1960s and 1970s becomes more understandable. The ethnics mobilized politically, not to demand a greater share of the economic "pie," but in order to conserve and protect the communities for which they and their forebears had sacrificed so much economically in order to preserve. It is ironic and bitterly painful to ethnics that the U.S. social and economic system, in which they accepted low status and low income voluntarily, could eventually come to threaten the communities and ways of life they had sacrificed so much to build and to maintain. It is even more ironic that the U.S. system of market capitalism could think of snuffing out sub-communities devoted to the concepts of acceptance of limits, social interdependence, quality of life rather than quantity of goods, and social awareness at a time when such attributes logically would seem to be at a premium. The ethnics' plight and the course of their history is mute testimony to the great chasm that separates the promise of the ideal of "life, liberty, and the pursuit of happiness" and the grim realities of the U.S. social and economic system.

DENNIS CLARK

THE EXPANSION OF THE PUBLIC SECTOR AND IRISH ECONOMIC DEVELOPMENT

In a period when Americans are seeking more intently than ever before to understand the causes of neighborhood growth and decline, exploration of the complexities of our urban traditions may provide us with some further insights into how ethnic communities managed to grow and prosper. We know embarrassingly little about the social development of neighborhoods in contrast to what we do not know. This ignorance is nowhere better illustrated than in the area of urban development, where ethnic traditions and business activity intermingle. Knowledge of the specific development roles of the Irish, Jews, Italians, and Germans, as well as the economically emergent Blacks and Puerto Ricans, might provide us with a better comprehension of the dynamics that have had a strong impact upon our urban expansion. Yet, the extent to which our cities have been structured socially and institutionally by the interplay of ethnic traditions within them has only been broadly sketched in the past. One of our most able historians of business has noted, "Many important social areas have never been examined by historians."[1] This is still true, in spite of the fact that the history of each of our major cities represents a densely interwoven process of urban growth which blends ethnic, business and political themes.

The purpose of this chapter is to present information about a key tradition of urban enterprise strongly influenced by the ethnic affiliation and identity of men engaged in it. The information deals largely with

---

This is a slightly revised version of an article which appeared in *Ethnicity* (June 1978), under the title "Ethnic Enterprise and Urban Development."

businesses in Philadelphia, a city which provides a rich context for business and ethnic interaction. The enterprises chosen for examination are in the field of general construction contracting. This field tends to be dispersed, flexible, and economically eccentric. The enterprises in the field are not, of course, distinctly ethnic in themselves. General contracting shares the large scale and concentration of activity common to many urban pursuits. The field, did, however, become the vehicle for ethnic business aspirations and development as successive ethnic groups sought livelihoods and fulfillment within it, and it was the Irish who paved the way for this tradition in the nineteenth century in such cities as Philadelphia.

Economic development in Irish neighborhoods represents a revealing example of urban self-help in America. The repeated influxes of Irish into American society placed in urban communities a continuing reservoir of economically disadvantaged people. The fact that this reservoir turned over its membership in response to opportunities for advancement and further migration made the squalor characteristic of Irish slum neighborhoods no less regrettable. The quality of life within working-class settlements was, as Engels pointed out with respect to the Irish in Manchester, England, a logical and inevitable product of industrial life.[2]

At the neighborhood level, however, Irish small village craft and business traditions did provide a basis or impetus for petty enterprise. After a period of initial immigrant adjustment, all kinds of small businesses were conducted in Irish neighborhoods in the nineteenth century. As Irish political power began to emerge, some businesses became oriented toward the growing public sector expenditures and contracts produced by the demand for increased social services. Irish neighborhood development, then, represents a unique combination of public and private economic development.[3]

As the Irish invested their labor and talents in specific areas of activity, they drew with them, in a natural fashion, family members, associates, and clients. Eventually they became identified with certain enterprises, reinforcing this identification with an ethnic prominence that served to augment their business and community status.

The contractor-boss is one of the central figures in the history of the American city. The builder-developer with strong political ties and influence is a familiar figure. There is a considerable literature delineating the political features of the "boss," whose influence is variously interpreted as nefarious or socially beneficial depending upon which historian or political scientist one reads. The ethnic identification of these figures has begun to be reconsidered without the bias often found in earlier interpretations.[4] The contractor as a builder and as an agent of urban expansion and development, as distinguished from the contractor as political boss, has rarely been examined in his role as a businessman, particularly as an ethnic business type.

The Irish immigration of the 1820s and 1830s involved the immigrants with the building of internal public sector improvements, such as roads and canals. How large this laboring influx was is problematical because of the primitive state of early statistics, but contemporaries found Irish workers widely distributed. The massive influx of the 1840s and 1850s coincided with city growth and industrial development. From 1845 to 1860 about 1,800,000 Irish people entered the country and became the chief resource of unskilled labor in all the major cities. In the post-Civil War years the continued expansion and growth of cities drew a steady stream of immigrant Irish, as Brinley Thomas has demonstrated. This Irish labor supply was central to the urban development process in both the private and public sectors.

An examination of the occupational statistics concerning immigrants compiled by Edward P. Hutchinson shows a notable concentration of Irishmen as builders and contractors. According to the 1870 and 1880 U.S. Census figures summarized by Hutchinson, the Irish led all other immigrants in this occupational category. By 1890 the Irish had twice the proportion of builders and contractors other immigrant groups had.[5] This concentration was not accidental. Rather, it was a function of the social position of the Irish in nineteenth-century America. Among the immigrant groups in the last century, the Irish were the most urban in their demographic distribution. The vast influx of refugees from the catastrophe of the Irish potato famine in the 1840s coincided with a period of rapid industrialization and urban expansion in the Eastern cities. Because the Irish, coming from a society that was singularly rural, initially entered the United States largely without skills relevant to the new industrial technology, they entered the work force as unskilled labor, and such labor was in great demand for the construction of canals, railroads, and cities.

For many men anxious to improve themselves, an opportune route out of the unskilled labor pool was to become a small-scale building contractor. It was not too far from the truth to say that any man with his own shovel and wheelbarrow could style himself a "contractor." Such a pursuit required little initial capital, but aggressiveness and strong backs were important, and these the Irish had. They also had easy access to fellow countrymen who, after a preliminary adjustment to city life, had developed skills in stonecutting, bricklaying, iron work, and most of the trades associated with building. Because of ethnic and religious discrimination in public schools, the overwhelmingly Catholic Irish felt impelled to construct a whole network of churches, schools, and welfare institutions in the major cities. This they did with alacrity, and the building work for these institutions provided a continuing source of construction operations for the Irish contractors.

In Philadelphia between 1830 and 1860, for instance, the Catholics, largely Irish, built twenty-three churches. Each usually had a school. Rectories and convents followed.[6] The churches were very often not simple American gothic; they were massive European gothic, enormous, elaborate, and in many ways a contractor's dream for the employment of labor and sustained activity. This church work provided an alternative to general contract and community-building work. It was a large-scale ethnic business, both rewarding and prestigious. From neighborhood wheelbarrow work a contractor with a tie to Catholic building activity could emerge as a local economic competitor in the broader urban construction field.

An illustration of the evolution of the Irish construction magnate can be found in Philadelphia, a city whose rich colonial past has overshadowed its interesting history during the period of industrialization and urban expansion. When the Irish first arrived in Philadelphia in great numbers in the wave of immigration following the potato famine of 1846-47, the city was in a period of extensive growth.[7] In 1854 the consolidation of the outlying areas in the County of Philadelphia expanded the legally defined city greatly. The development of street railways opened up the newly annexed hinterlands to workers and the middle class alike. As early as 1852 Irish contractors were monopolizing most of the public construction work in the Port Richmond district.[8] In 1853 builder Thomas Dugan was selling three-story houses in the Kensington area for $1200 each.[9] In 1856 James Tagert advertised in the Philadelphia *Evening Bulletin*, "There is not a man in the consolidated City of Philadelphia but can avail himself of a home if he desires."[10] Tagert, born in County Tyrone, was president of the Farmers and Mechanics Bank and a promoter of various building activities.

Financing for home-building operations did not come easily. In the mid-nineteenth century most banks were wary of lending mortgage money to ordinary working people. This produced in Philadelphia an extraordinary proliferation of a local business invention, the building and loan association. These popular societies grew up rapidly in the 1840s and 1850s. They were nonprofit savings organizations specifically designed to make capital available for the construction and purchase of homes.[11] In a city where brick row housing could be constructed economically, their utility was patent. The Irish immigrants organized dozens of these societies. One man, Bernard Rafferty, was secretary of thirty-five such societies in the 1870s and 1880s.[12] With this mechanism of capitalization behind them, the home-building contractors of the city worked to extend the row house residential pattern that became the most prominent physical feature of the Philadelphia landscape.

Home building, however, had its limitations. Its market uncertainties were proverbial. Railroad and public works construction offered a large-scale area for more lucrative operation. Tipperary-born Thomas Costigan did much local railroad work, as did William J. Nead and Francis McManus.[13] The large pool of Irish pick and shovel laborers in the city provided practically the only resource needed for a smart contractor to organize an excavating crew to perform the enormously arduous work of digging cuts, grades, and tunnels for the railroads.

The business of Patrick McManus indicates the kinds of jobs the contractor could become involved in. McManus was born in Pottsville, Pennsylvania, of Irish parents in 1847. His first major job was the building of stockyards for the city of Philadelphia. He laid special tracks to serve the grounds of the great Centenniel Exposition in 1876 in Fairmount Park. Later he and his partner, James B. Reilly, built stone bridges over the Schuylkill River and constructed track beds and stations for the railroads, including the Reading Company's line to Atlantic City, New Jersey.[14]

In a city noted for the ubiquity of its brick construction, some contractors specialized exclusively in this work. Michael Magee and Company built huge brick structures in the closing decades of the nineteenth century. These buildings, often covering a whole city block and ranging up to eight stories in height, included the Disston saw factories, the Bromley textile mills, the J. A. Dougherty distilleries, and the elegant Lorraine Hotel. Magee varied such work with the steady construction of Catholic hospitals and institutions.[15]

In a period when business and politics were closely allied, the contractors were engaged frequently in public works. Edward J. Lafferty from South Philadelphia helped to build the city's famous water works. Martin Maloney, who started as a simple mechanic, invented a gas burner for street lamps. He went into business laying gas utility lines and helped organize the United Gas Improvement Company in the city.[16] The continuing expansion, renovation, and rebuilding of urban facilities offered such men repeated opportunities. Corruption, fraud, and shady practices were common enough. Seymour Mandelbaum has maintained that the only ways that the burgeoning cities could be controlled politically and ordered physically was by resorting to massive payoff schemes.[17] Philadelphia's politics became a national byword for corruption, and the contractors were in the middle of it. Although the dollar costs of gouging the public can be estimated in some instances, the social costs of not expanding and building the city in a time of great population growth and immigration can only be conjectured. Whatever the malpractices involved, many of the contractors did produce. They built, and the city is still full of their works, aging but utilitarian, a century after their erection.

By 1900, 63 percent of the building firms in the nation were located in 200 cities, and urban construction was 90 percent of the national total.[18] What had transpired since the 1840s was an unprecedented urban development, and the Irish contractors had ridden the wave of this growth. Asa Briggs in *Victorian Cities* pointed out the primary role played by the provision of sanitation, utilities, and public works construction, in urban development. Irish contractors made a heavy contribution in those areas. They were one of the "new categories of talent and connection" that city expansion called forth.[19] Starting in the ditches as excavators, they had gained command of a business medium that was flexible enough to meet the needs of the fast-breaking urban building segment of the economy. Construction activity has historically been a speculative and economically eccentric field, more sensitive to cycles of boom and bust than most areas of the economy. This has led to a saying in the field that a construction man must of necessity be a gambler. A sudden contraction of credit, a hard rock strata struck in excavation, or a laborers' strike could jeopardize not only a single project, but a whole business. Competition in a field where heavy capitalization was not required for entry was always keen. The contractor could attempt to stabilize his work by obtaining jobs through political preference, but the high risk element remained.

The interaction of general contracting and politics suited the Irish admirably. Their early prominence in politics was consolidated until by the late nineteenth century they held strategic positions in both the Democratic and Republican parties in Philadelphia. As the new immigration from southern and eastern Europe developed, they took up the role of political intermediaries, and this role has been one of the distinctive features of the political history of the Irish in the cities.[20] In contracting, also, they were intermediaries as well as principals. In hiring labor, presiding over subcontractors, architects, engineers, union bosses, and clients, they demonstrated the same facility for maneuver and mobilization that they displayed in politics.

An example of the interaction of business and politics can be seen in the career of James P. "Sunny Jim" McNichol, the first Irish Catholic to become a top Republican potentate in the Philadelphia firmament. McNichol, born in the tough Tenth Ward, formed a building firm with his brother as a young man. Between 1893 and 1895 his business forged ahead, doing six million dollars worth of work in those years.[21] From 1898 to 1902 McNichol served on the Select Council of the city, and then in the State

Senate. In 1907, after a controversy involving municipal contract work, he said, "Never again under any circumstances will I go after municipal contracts." Business sense, however, overcame political irritation. In 1908 McNichol was completing the subway excavation from City Hall into South Philadelphia, building the million dollar Torresdale water filtration plant, performing extensive sewer and utility pipe-laying work, handling asphalt and granite block paving contracts, and conducting a half million dollar garbage disposal business through his Penn Reduction Company.[22] A total of more than two and a half million dollars in contracts was thus handled by McNichol in one year. During his career McNichol built the subway tunnel for the Market Street line, the imposing Benjamin Franklin Parkway, which is still one of the most appealing features of the city, and the eight-mile Roosevelt Boulevard, which opened the broad fields of the northeast section of the city to the automobile traffic and residential development of the twentieth century. In terms of urban construction, few men in the last hundred years have changed Philadelphia's physical aspect and orientation more extensively than "Sunny Jim" McNichol.

Not all of the contractors, of course, ascended to such power. Many were content to make a good living and try to keep ahead in the rough contest of competitive bidding and control of costs. Such a man was David J. Duffin, who arrived in the city from County Antrim in the north of Ireland with the strong arms of a stonecutter. He began as an excavator with a horse and wagon, then with his sons went into home building and roadwork. After almost going broke excavating the foundations for Philadelphia's Convention Hall because of a hidden rock formation, the firm of Duffin and Sons prospered in building Catholic churches. The desire of the Irish Catholics for huge churches, schools, and institutions stimulated a huge network of parish building. With his own quarry supplying stone, Duffin worked on thirty separate parish complexes, raising walls and steeples for the "lace curtain" Irish in various parts of the city.[23]

Perhaps the most attractive of all the city's contractors was John B. Kelly, one of a family with talent to spare. One of Kelly's brothers was a Pulitzer Prize playwright, one was a noted entertainer, and Kelly's daughter, Grace, was a movie star. In the case of John B. Kelly's rise from bricklayer's apprentice to ownership of the largest brickwork company in America, a somewhat more glamorous tinge is added to the contractor image. One of ten children of an immigrant from County Mayo, John B. Kelly was raised in the Falls of the Schuylkill area of the city. After service in World War I, he made a spectacular record as an oarsman, winning 125 races and endearing himself to Irishmen everywhere by beating the British sculling champion in the Olympic Games of 1920. John B. worked as a bricklayer, foreman, and superintendent for his contractor brother, Patrick, then set up his own company. The business grew until "Kelly for Brickwork" became a byword in Philadelphia. In 1933 he entered politics as a Democrat supporting the New Deal of Franklin D. Roosevelt. "Until I saw a bread line for the first time, I stayed out of politics," Kelly said. In 1935 he ran for mayor of Philadelphia, losing a close election that his adherents and many others considered stolen by the fraudulent vote tallies of his embattled Republican opponents. [24] Kelly remained a prominent figure in the city's business and political life. His rise in politics symbolized a change in the political life of the city. James Reichley, analyst of reform politics in Philadelphia, credits Kelly with bringing about the first true opposition party in the city since the Civil War. [25]

A keen competitor of Kelly's for contracting work was Matthew H. McCloskey, whose activities took the contractor-politico evolution one step further onto the national stage. McCloskey, one of eight children of a father from Dungiven, County Derry, went into business for himself when he was only eighteen. His first large job was a construction of a wartime building at the Philadelphia Navy Yard in 1917. It was a job that typified the hard-driving McCloskey style. His men built 160,000 square feet of construction in sixty days. Reverses hit the young builder hard in 1923, however, and he barely escaped bankruptcy. He had lost money trying to complete a barracks at the U.S. Military Academy at West Point, New York. Recovering, McCloskey built more schools in the city than any other single contractor, a fact not without significance with respect to political considerations. He built the Philadelphia Convention Hall and government buildings in the state capital of Harrisburg. For six decades Matthew McCloskey pursued his business, compounding his reputation as an intense competitor and a shrewd calculator of contract costs. One of his most notable successes was a twenty-five million dollar project with the Pennsylvania Railroad for the Penn Center Transportation facilities, keystone of the downtown renovation that transformed the center city business district of Philadelphia in the 1960s.

In 1932 McCloskey went into politics after discussions with James Farley, Franklin D. Roosevelt's able party chieftain. From 1955 to 1962 he was national finance chairman of the Democratic Party, a position that he handled with mastery. McCloskey's association with President John F. Kennedy was especially warm. In 1962 he was appointed U.S. Ambassador to Ireland, a post that accorded with his interest and affections.

Perhaps the largest contractor of all in this tradition is John McShain. Son of a County Derry carpenter, McShain built an immense construction business. His ability to figure huge contracts tightly became legendary. Beginning in Philadelphia he built the Board of Education Building in 1930, then the Municipal Court Building, as well as many schools and churches. He served on the city's Board of Zoning Adjustments from 1936 until 1952, a significant position for business and governmental ties. In Philadelphia he constructed the Veterans Hospital, the Naval Hospital, and worked on the Philadelphia International Airport and various college and university building programs. He also became a director of several banks and a transportation company. The scope of McShain's work extended far beyond the city, however. His contracts included work on the forty million dollar Clinical Research Building of the National Institute of Health, the General Accounting Office, the National Airport, the Jefferson Memorial, the State Department Building, and restoration of the White House, all in the nation's capitol. It is calculated that his firm has completed over one billion dollars in government contract work. Largest of all his projects was the Pentagon Building in Washington, an eighty million dollar construction. [26]

McShain's political allegiances are not as clear as those of John B. Kelly or Matthew McCloskey. He has worked with administrations of both political parties. As a contractor with a national enterprise, he has apparently avoided close identification with either party. The scale of the McShain work on government contracts is manifest testimony to his business and political acumen. His Irish ties have remained. A keen horse fancier, he acquired an 8,500-acre estate in Killarney, where his racing thoroughbreds are stabled.

There are numerous other examples of the Irish contractor tradition in Philadelphia, including Austin Meehan, long a power in the Republican machine that fought the reform movement of the Democrats in the post-World War II period. [27] Other examples would not add substantially to the characteristics displayed by Kelly, McCloskey, and McShain. Their careers represent the penetration of an American business medium by the sons of immigrants and a latter-day enactment of the Horatio Alger cycle. These men were gifted with strong initiative. They were men of practical education. Kelly stated, "Most of my education was in night schools, at the YMCA classes and at Spring Garden Institute." [28] Matthew McCloskey attended Banks Business College in 1908 and studied at Drexel Institute of Technology for three years before entering business at eighteen. McShain attended La Salle High School, St. Joseph's Prep School, and Georgetown University for one year. None of the three married into old line Philadelphia families, and, despite their wealth, they do not appear in the Social Register. [29] Their common business attributes are a powerful drive for success and a ruggedness of character that withstands well the rigors of economic and political competition.

Upon analysis, the contracting enterprises described above reveal a pattern that is in accord with the general business history of urban building activities. The contractors' ethnic origins and connections did not exempt their firms from the broad trends at work in their field. The early Irish contractors, such as Thomas Costigan, Edward Laffety, and Patrick McManus, were part of the Gilded Age. Their enterprises were individually led businesses depending upon strong personal contacts and leadership. Their familiarity with the Irish laboring gangs and the reliability of their word went far toward drawing together the skills and resources they needed.

The businesses of "Sunny Jim" McNichol and Michael Magee represent a more formalized, institutional stage of contracting. Technological changes in building practices, such as the use of steel frames, elevators, and the advent of electrical equipment, made construction much more technical and complex. Building regulations by municipalities raised new legal and technical problems. These trends of the late nineteenth century led to new practices in planning and managing work which, while not so rigorous as the human engineering schemes of George Frederick Taylor, was still a step toward regularizing large-scale construction activity. The great factories built by Michael Magee and the subway work of James McNichol had to be governed according to a new rationale. Both contractors developed horizontal business ties which assured them of supplies and services. Magee had his own brickyards and McNichol aligned a wide diversity of productive holdings. These business represented a stage of contracting that was fully incorporated, technologically adaptive, and moving toward further diversification.

The businesses of John B. Kelly, Matthew McCloskey, and John McShain exemplify a third stage of contracting development. These men built enterprises that became enormous in scope, ranging far beyond the local area. They became fully diversified, with holdings in real estate and a great diversity of production and service fields. The complexity of contracting and these other business operations had become so great by the mid-twentieth century that systems management skills became mandatory. What resulted were great contracting systems backed by the consolidations of capital and resources that enhanced their power tremendously.

If the timing of the Irish influx coincided with a wave of city building, the character of the immigrants themselves contributed to their business rise as contractors. Their group ties and competitive spirit served them well as they worked to make a reality the pompous prophecy of that nineteenth-century Philadelphia rhetorician Russell Conwell, who declaimed "and never in the history of the world did a poor man without capital have such an opportunity to get rich quickly and honestly as he has now in our city."[30] The Irish contractor with political potential appeared in almost every major urban area. "Honey Fitz" Fitzgerald, grandfather of President John F. Kennedy, represents the type in Boston evolution. In New York the contractors graduated to heady and diversified wealth by the 1870s. In the new cities along the Mississippi and in the West, they came with railroads and helped the cities grow. All the way to San Francisco, where magnate Patrick Calhoun matched wealth with mining millionaires, the Irish builders testified to their enterprise. [31]

The recent findings reported by Clark illustrate clearly the relationship between political power and Irish economic development. [32] His data document more generally the case studies characteristic of the Irish developers in the city of Philadelphia. He finds that urban areas with numerous Irish residents manifest higher fiscal expenditures than other cities, especially in the police and fire departments. Most importantly, the Irish budgetary pattern holds across three data sets spanning a time frame between 1880 to 1968. Clark contends that patronage was the socioeconomic force that provided the dynamic for the Irish style of neighborhood and community development:

The Irish had access to many resources which assisted their political activity: their number, their English language, and social solidarity reinforced by the Church and the Democratic Party. The Irish ethnic of non-ideological particularism helped too—it emerged from practicing Catholicism, trust and personal loyalty, sociability, localism, and social conservatism. The Irish ethnic in turn legitimated and reinforced the spirit of patronage politics: a style of leadership distinguished by its use of separable goods, resources allocable to distinct individuals and social sectors. The basic resources exchanged in patronage politics are favors, votes, and government jobs. Such resources helped the Irish succeed dramatically as political candidates. Favors dispensed by political campaigners "got out the vote." Campaigners were supported by government jobs, which Irish officials increased. This in turn raised municipal expenditures.[33]

Thus, while the Philadelphia pattern may have some unique characteristics, there is ample evidence describing a distinctive Irish style in the area of community and neighborhood development in other urban areas.

The history of American city growth has been studied mostly in terms of technological growth and architectural innovations. [34] As the essays in this volume suggest, only recently have we added social and political dimensions to urban study relatively free of past prejudices and historiographical limitations. The connection between community and neighborhood development in cities and the ethnic needs, career drives, and business tendencies of various minorities still needs much exploration if we are to understand the complex forces behind our extraordinary city settlement and development patterns.

PART FOUR

COLLECTIVISM AND ASSIMILATION
The Transition to Orthodox Capitalism

MARK ROSENTRAUB

DELBERT TAEBEL

JEWISH ENTERPRISE IN TRANSITION
From Collective Self-Help to Orthodox Capitalism

Students of ethnic enterprise have attempted to understand the forces influencing the distribution of immigrants in economic systems. Much of this work has led to the development of theories which attempt to identify the causal elements affecting distribution. The "disadvantage theory" focuses upon the problems aliens encounter in a foreign country. [1] Discrimination, cultural differences, and exclusion from traditional business opportunities each provide incentives for close association and cohesion on the part of conationals or coreligionists. This close association frequently manifests itself in the area of commerce, resulting in a concentration of particular minorities in particular sectors of the economy. Bonacich suggests "host hostility" can be particularly effective in contributing to concentrations of minorities in distinct commercial and occupational categories of an economy. [2] Other students of ethnic enterprise have identified cultural variables influencing immigrant business development. [3] This view suggests foreigners possess certain skills which are valued in the alien economy. Earlier in this volume, Light has shown how both the disadvantage and cultural theories can be applied to explain the business and commercial activities of Asian-Americans.

The implicit value in examining ethnic group economic behavior and developing accurate theories of minority enterprise lies in the development of policies and programs capable of assisting groups that have not

---

We wish to express our appreciation to Professor Scott Cummings for his patient reviews of this article and the many criticisms offered. Some were accepted, and we alone are responsible for those we were too foolhardy to incorporate. This project also benefited from the financial support of the Organized Research Fund of the University of Texas at Arlington.

been successful in an economic system. In all societies in which some ethnic groups have been economically successful, others have failed to move, in large numbers, from the lower class. In the United States, the Jews, the Chinese, Mormons, and Irish Catholics have been far more successful than Blacks, Puerto Ricans, Chicanos, and Irish Protestants. Bonacich has provided examples of poverty and prosperity in yet other societies.

Much of the research endeavoring to explain ethnic enterprise has concentrated on the actions or activities of groups attempting to improve themselves. In this sense the research focuses upon developmental variables inducing ethnic group cohesion, concentration, and ultimately commercial activities.[4] The research discussed in this chapter will offer a somewhat different perspective on ethnic economic behavior. This essay will discuss the changes in the behavior of group members when economic prosperity has been achieved. Research of this nature can provide answers to the question of whether or not the collective orientations among an initially poor ethnic group become a permanent fixture in its approach to economic life or whether the spirit of collective enterprise becomes altered and attenuated when economic success is realized. In this regard the research reported here is not interested in validating either the disadvantage or cultural theory but in producing information on the extent to which collective approaches to business development are either intensified or weakened when a group moves from poverty to prosperity.

Jewish enterprise in American cities rests upon collective commercial principles. This history of Jewish-American enterprise is largely a success story, an economic transformation from poverty to prosperity. The Jews who arrived in this country during the years of substantial immigration were extremely poor. Yet, today, the notion that Jews have "made it" in America is widely accepted. [5] Howe, for instance, notes, "By the fifties a substantial Jewish working class could still be found in New York City, but, within the Jewish community as a whole, the proletariat segment kept shrinking in both absolute size and relative weight."[6] Levy and Kramer's demographic analysis of Jews in the 1960s indicate "Jewish-Americans live in unparalleled prosperity.... [They] are solidly middle class; and many more are upper middle-class and even wealthier.... The number of Jews in white-collar jobs is two or three times the national average."[7] And Banfield, in *The Unheavenly City*, points to Jews as one of the most successful ethnic groups in American society.[8] Some Jews, of course, have not achieved prosperity in the United States. There are still several pockets of Jewish poverty in the old ghettos dominated by other ethnic groups.

The existence of some level of Jewish poverty notwithstanding, the economic and social advancement of Jews is frequently identified as an ideal-typical illustration of the relationship between collective self-help and upward social mobility. Most students of Jewish life and culture agree that economic self-help institutions, rather than individualistic striving or educational attainment, played a significant role in the advancement of Jewish immigrants. Such a relationship is, of course, hard to quantify; yet the circumstantial evidence is substantial. Before 1920, more than 650 organizations created by Jews existed to help other Jews deal with the problems of American urban life. [9] These organizations dealt with the problems common to the urban poor of any time period: family and social pathologies, illiteracy, language barriers, and low incomes. Jewish settlements in U.S. cities were plagued by all these maladies. "Diabetes, associated with perpetual nervous strain, was common. Suicide, rarely recorded among the small-town Jews of Eastern Europe, also found its victims in the tenements of New York. Despair, poverty, and the fears generated in the imagination led some immigrants to take their own lives."[10] Jewish prostitution was common at the turn of the twentieth century. Fraud, too, was prevalent, and by the 1920s Jews were involved in organized gambling.[11] Between 1900 and 1920 family desertion by Jewish males was so common that the Jewish daily paper, *The Forward* ran a "Gallery of Missing Husbands."

The self-help organizations created by Jews also had to deal with problems of literacy. While those immigrants who arrived after 1905 tended to be better educated than the earlier arrivals, ignorance and language barriers still existed for thousands. The public schools of Eastern cities were not only ill-equipped to deal with the multitude of immigrants, but they gave evidence of anti-immigrant and anti-Jewish attitudes in the periods of heaviest Jewish immigration.[12]

Jews, then, faced many of the same urban problems other immigrant groups would or had encountered. But, with a service infrastructure composed of more than 650 organizations, they moved forward in American society. It seems obvious that at least some of the prosperity achieved by Jewish-Americans is related to the number of self-help organizations developed in the late nineteenth and early twentieth centuries.

The theme of this volume is that under certain circumstances various immigrant groups respond in a collective fashion to economic conditions. Although classical theories of capitalist development emphasize individualistic values of capital accumulation, many minorities cultivated collective values and created economic institutions premised upon these values. Jews, like other urban minorities, also responded in a collective fashion. The interest here is in determining whether these collective activities have continued in the age of Jewish prosperity. First, a brief review of Jewish economic life is presented, in which we will illustrate the collective premises upon which Jewish economic institutions were based. The second section examines the contemporary economic and commercial activities of prosperous Jews and develops our thesis that contemporary Jews have severed their collective economic traditions. The final section explains why Jewish enterprise may have moved from early collectivism to orthodox capitalism.

JEWISH ENTERPISE AND COLLECTIVE SELF-HELP: THE EARLY TWENTIETH CENTURY

Slightly less than 33 million people immigrated to the United States between 1820 and 1920. The yearly rate of immigration, however, varied considerably. In the forty-year period of substantial Jewish migration, 1880-1920, 23,430,000 immigrants came to the United States. Jews represented less than 10 percent of this group.[13]

Limited sources of information reduce the ability to describe completely the characteristics of the Jews that did come, but historians have produced some descriptive data sets.[19] First, unlike some immigrant groups, the Jewish migration was family-oriented and committed to life in America. In the first ten years of the century, 56.6 percent of the immigrants were male; 43.4 percent female. Nearly 25 percent of all immigrants were children. Records also indicate only 5 percent of Jewish immigrants ever returned to Europe. This compares to a return rate of 33 percent for other groups. Second, the Jews who came to America were slightly more skilled and less dependent on farming for income than other groups. Many Jewish families had been forced off the farms in Europe and Russia before 1875 and were somewhat familiar with urban life. Third, the Jews that migrated around 1920 were better educated and more skilled than those arriving in the late nineteenth and early twentieth century.

Those Jews arriving at the turn of the century and immediately after encountered an economy attempting to absorb millions of new workers and provide services for these new urban residents. Neither goal was achieved with great success. In the years after the Civil War, the demand by railroads and other industries for cheap labor created a favorable economic climate for immigrant employment opportunities. "American business interests sent special agents to Europe in order to attract immigrants."[14] The economic environment, however, changed radically for immigrants at the turn of the century. Economic declines in the 1880s and 1890s intensified competition for low-paying jobs. Anti-immigrant feelings and protests were spawned in several cities. The fear of more immigrants entering an already crowded marketplace and an extremely tight housing situation during the 1890s prompted even liberal unions to discuss anti-immigration legislation and policies.

Living conditions were also extremely poor in crowded tenements. "In the other twelve [flats] each room had its own family living and sleeping there. . . . In one bed we counted six persons." Code enforcement was virtually unknown. "There had not been water in the tenements for a month."[15] Sanitation services were no better. A March 1893 story in the *New York Times* reported mud and garbage was so deep in certain areas that spring would give "most of the streets in this city the appearance of a veritable mud river."[16] Schools were also poorly organized at the turn of the century.

> If we take 60 as the largest number of pupils that one teacher can instruct with any degree of effectiveness and the largest number that may occupy an ordinary class-room without danger to health, it appears that in October last there were 377 classes in which the conditions of effective teaching and hygienic precaution did not exist. . . . . Of these classes, 231 had registers between 60 and 70; 65 classes had registers between 70 and 80; 22 classes had registers between 80 and 90; 18 classes had registers between 90 and 100; 2 classes had registers between 100 and 110; 16 classes had registers between 120 and 130; 4 classes had registers between 130 and 140; 2 classes had registers between 140 and 150; while one class reached the enormous total of 158.[17]

These harsh economic realities, in terms of jobs and living conditions, compounded by a language barrier for most immigrants, confronted the vast majority of Jews who came to the United States. As discussed earlier, the difficulties of urban life in the United States brought to the Jewish families the social ills commonly associated with crowded conditions, poverty, and unemployment.

Several traits of Jewish culture as well as the unique features of Jewish history provided the social and psychological bases of collectivism in the economic arena. Paramount among these factors may have been the dietary requirements of Jewish life. Specialized butchers able to provide immigrant Jews with kosher meat were required, as were bakeries that could produce c̶ Additionally, several religious holidays required special foods. The combination of those needs served to create demands from the food industry which only Jews could satisfy. The small businesses created in response to this demand also provided several immigrant Jews with jobs. However, the numerous butcher shops and bakeries were not the major elements of collectivism that dominated Jewish enterprise in the early twentieth century.

In the turmoil and poverty that was the immigrants' world between

1880 and 1920, several important Jewish agencies developed and attempted to find jobs and housing and provide services for the immigrants. Some of these agencies became so powerful that Washington, D.C. offices were opened to lobby for protection of immigrants, expanded immigration quotas, and support of Jewish programs and against feelings of nativism. Like Oriental economic behavior, then, Jewish business activities are consistent with both the disadvantage and cultural explanations of ethnic enterprises.

The financial and organizational support for some of these activities came from German-Jewish families who had emigrated to the New York area early in the nineteenth century. Some of these families had become quite prosperous, and in their efforts to establish themselves in American society they "were embarassed by the gruff, uncouth, saggy-bearded, conspicuously un-Americanized, newcomers. These people, the Germans [Jews] felt, were loud, pushy, aggressive....The German Jews even coined a word for their coreligionists, a word based on the fact that many Russian names end in 'ki.' The word was kikes."[18] Fear of being grouped with the newcomers by other New Yorkers encouraged some German-Jews to organize employment and referral services to help Americanize Eastern European and Russian Jews, the immigrants, themselves. And, as these agencies developed and became among the most powerful within the Jewish community, relationships with German-Jews became more productive.

The combined efforts of German, Eastern European, and Russian Jews to develop organizations to help immigrants and themselves led to the creation of numerous types of associations. In order to describe these institutions, a typology of seven kinds of collective economic institutions was created: immigrant-supporting, religious, charities and collectives, financial services, unions, educational and cultural, and health.

Two organizations were formed to help immigrants deal with the confusion of urban life in the United States. The first, the Hebrew Emigrant Aid Society (HEAS) was short lived. Founded in 1881, "the HEAS was utterly unprepared for the flood of immigration . . . (and) in October, 1882 some four hundred immigrants housed by HEAS . . . rioted, charging, *The New York Times* reported, that they were being brutally treated by HEAS officials who fed them decayed food and beat both men and women with the least provacation."[19] In 1882, the HEAS was dissolved.

In 1892 the Hebrew Immigrant Aid Society (HIAS) was founded. This society was far more effectively organized and eventually had offices in Washington, D.C., numerous port cities in America, and even sent agents to foreign ports to assist in negotiating passage for immigrants. From Washington, D.C., HIAS became an effective lobby for immigrants and provided a valuable training ground for immigrant leaders to learn the politics of Washington and Congress.

HIAS officials at immigration points distributed information about America and helped arrange housing for the newcomers. Once admitted to the United States, HIAS employment offices attempted to place immigrants in a suitable position. Records for 1912 indicate 150,000 people contacted HIAS offices; 14,992 were new immigrants. More than 4,000 children attended Saturday classes and 3,000 people were housed at HIAS facilities.

It is impossible to enumerate all the synagogues established between 1885 and 1920. "As early as 1892 a contemporary directory listed 136 religious societies on the lower east side" of Manhattan.[20] Almost every small community had several synagogues, including, in later years, orthodox, conservative, and reformed congregations. More important than the exact number of synagogues organized is the realization that each facility provided immigrants with a sense of community, an opportunity to belong to a congregation, and a focus for education and charities. *"Zedukah,"* the Hebrew word denoting the act of charity, became an important part of synagogue's functions. Money could thus be collected and distributed through the religious structure of Jewish life.

Separate from the charitable functions of the synagogues, Moses Rischin estimates 534 different Jewish benevolent societies existed in 1914.[21] These groups not only delivered services to paying members but provided numerous benefits, including insurance, burial plots, summer camps and programs for children, day-care service when schools were not in session, inexpensive summer resorts for poor Jewish families, and organized charity functions. Various educational programs were also established, including special programs for the elderly.

Credit unions, trade associations, and banks were formed in the early twentieth century. These institutions provided invaluable experience for immigrants who would become very successful in these fields. The initial experiences with banks, however, was not particularly successful. Three major banks collapsed in 1914; with their failures $3,102,000 was lost by Jewish immigrants, and rioting followed these failures.[22] But the extent of these losses was evidence of the growing economic strength of the Jewish community. Despite low wages, accumulation of capital was taking place. Shifting to more conventional banks, this wealth would continue to grow after the default of the "Jewish" banks.

Credit unions and trade associations were formed in the late 1890s and early 1900s. Many of these were weak and collapsed during periods of recession and depression. They did, however, provide invaluable experience for later efforts that would be more successful.

Unions dominated by Jewish members emerged in both the public and private sector, where Jews received employment opportunities in large numbers. Development in the public sector would not occur until after World War II and the rise of public employee unions. The International Ladies Garment Workers Union (ILGWU) was the first of the major Jewish unions. Founded in 1900, it called a major strike in 1909 with 20,000 workers, "about two-thirds of them Jewish," leaving their jobs. [23] A series of meetings for workers was held, and when the long strike was over, 10,000 new workers had joined the ILGWU. A strike by cloakmakers later that year was supported by 18,000 workers against Jewish employers. The settlement of that strike established Jewish workers' unions as a force for representing the immigrants' economic needs. Although many more strikes and labor actions would follow the events of 1909 and 1910, the initial strikes established workers' unions for Jews.

Despite an obvious need for improved schools, Jewish educational services for Jews started slowly. Poor immigrants had little money for private schools, and many needed wages from their children to survive. By 1915, however, several schools had been formed by religious groups. What was to become Yeshiva University was created before 1910. Within the Jewish community, however, there was disagreement about joining secular education with religious studies. Tainting religious training with American studies became an ideological issue. This controversy retarded the development of Jewish schools. But gradual acceptance of the need for both religious and secular training and increasing Jewish wealth led to the development of several yeshivas, academies, and Hebrew schools by 1920. While some of these schools did charge tuition, many used community donations to offset the costs of education.

To provide some limited form of health care for the immigrants, hospitals were started by some Eastern Europeans at the turn of the century. Both Israel Hospital, the Jewish Maternity Hospital, and the Lakeview Home for Unmarried Mothers each provided services to the poor.

These brief descriptions of a variety of organizations and a pattern of life among Jews at the turn of the century demonstrate the existence of an extensive network of organizations designed to promote the economic welfare of Jews. Almost all aspects of an individual's life—from education and training to housing and employment referral to health care—could have been affected by one of the several hundred organizations created. Those Jewish organizations, then, represent an almost unprecedented dedication to assisting other Jews. Most sought to help Jews function in the capitalist system that existed in the early twentieth century. A few were more politicized, and emphasized socialist policies. But all were dedicated to assist fellow Jews advance in the American economy. Most importantly, the response to industrial America was collective in nature. The welfare of the group took precedence over individual gain and self-interest.

JEWISH ENTERPRISE IN TRANSITION: ORTHODOX CAPITALISM IN THE 1970s

As the initial immigrants became more successful in American life, as a result of both self-help programs and individual sacrifice, the Jewish community began to move away from its old centers. Initially the changes involved new fields of employment. These changes were followed by geographic movements: first, to the suburbs surrounding the old centers and then to other sections of the country. While New York City is still the cultural center for American Jews, substantial and important Jewish communities have developed in Chicago, Cleveland, Baltimore, and Milwaukee. The growth of California after 1945 and Texas after 1960 has also meant political and economic gains for the Jewish communities in the Los Angeles, Houston, and Dallas areas. These Jews who moved away from the older cultural centers or grew up in the post-self-help age of American Jewry, after 1925, carried with them a rich heritage of self-help which had assisted them in reaching new levels of economic success in American society. There were, then, two transitional phases in the immigrant Jewish community. There was a geographic decentralization from the familiar nodes of Jewish life. This change was coupled with the movement of large numbers of Jews out of the lowest income groups. Our contention is that these basic transformations have significantly altered the way in which contemporary Jews carry out commercial activities in the American economy. While contemporary Jewish prosperity rests upon a collective foundation, prosperity has eroded collective values and insititutions.

In order to illustrate the impact of these transitions on contemporary Jewish enterprise, a questionnaire was mailed to 1,810 Jewish households in the Dallas-Fort Worth metropolitan area. These families can be considered representative of Jews who have completed the geographic and economic transitions just described. Not only is the Dallas-Fort Worth Jewish community geographically isolated from the center of Jewish life, New York City, but it is a wealthy community. Annual family income for almost 50 percent of the respondents was $35,000 or more. Less than 10 percent of families had annual incomes below $15,000. Additionally, this group had also moved into various sectors of the economy. More than 95 percent of the males (each household supplied information on males and females) held white collar jobs. The 548 returned instruments, 30.2 percent, represent responses of Jews who have made the transition from poor immigrant to middle-class Americans. It is a group extremely interested in business and commerce but not along lines in any way consistent with collective values or ethnic self-help. The economic and business orientations of Jews in Dallas and Fort Worth are more representative of orthodox capitalist behavior.

Similar to the immigrants from Europe and Asia a half century or more before, the Jews in the Dallas-Fort Worth metropolitan area came to Texas for economic opportunities. More than half the respondents listed "economic opportunity," and another 29.6 percent listed "prospects for a job" as the prime reason for relocating in Texas. Only family associations, similar to the patterns observed among Eastern European Jews, and the climate in Texas accounted for more than 20 percent of the main reasons for relocation. Friends and education each accounted for less than 10 percent of the reasons given for moving to Texas.

Almost one-quarter, 24.7 percent, of the respondents were born in Texas. The vast majority, 62.8 percent, were born in other states. Given the recent growth of Texas, this is not surprising. It is interesting to note that, while 21.4 percent were born in New York, 16 percent were born in Illinois, Ohio, and Pennsylvania. Slightly more than one-fifth of the respondents can be considered second-generation Texans, while 18.6 percent are third-generation Texans. Only 4 percent of the sample were fourth-generation residents, while 54.6 percent of the respondents were the individuals in their family who had moved to Texas.

Even though the majority of the Jews living in the Dallas-Fort Worth metropolitan area came from other parts of the United States, their average length of residence was 20.6 years. This suggests a certain degree of stability and permanence in the lives of Jews residing in Texas. Only one-fourth of the respondents have lived in Texas less than four years. Another indication of stability in the Jews of the Dallas-Fort Worth area is the incidence of home ownership. More than four-fifths, 85.4 percent own their own home. This figure for home ownership is considerably larger than those reported for Jews in other American cities. Professor Cummings, in his introductory essay, noted 51 percent of Jews in the Northeast sample owned their home. The larger figure in Texas is probably a partial result of housing market differences. However, part of the variation may also be related to basic transformations which have taken place in the Jews' traditional role as a sojourning merchant.

Occupational status was also quite high; 95 percent of the men held white collar jobs. More than 75 percent of the male members of each household had attended college, and 45 percent had attended graduate or professional schools. For the female members of the household, educational levels were almost as high; 67.8 percent had attended college and 31 percent had attended graduate or professional schools. In terms of employment and educational status, the Jews in the survey conform to the accepted notions about American Jews. In terms of income, occupational status, and education, the households surveyed have "made it" in American society.

The Decline of Cultural Ties and Associational Networks. As has been suggested, part of the stimulus for the collectivist activities of Jews was the elements of Jewish culture that required interaction with other Jews. These occurred in the marketplace, butchers and bakeries, and at the synagogue. In the prosperous life achieved by Jews in Dallas-Fort Worth, however, cultural ties have apparently weakened. Kosher food products do not appear to be a major concern to Jews in the Dallas-Fort Worth area. No survey question was asked concerning kosher food since there is only one butcher in the entire region who sells kosher meat. As there may be as many as 50,000 Jews in the area, the single outlet for meat is significant since Jewish communities in New York, Chicago, and Los Angeles are known to have several in each community. There is apparently less demand in North Texas for kosher products.

The religious ties of this group are also weakening. Only 11.2 percent are members of orthodox (traditional) congregations; 47.0 percent prefer the less ritualist, reformed congregations, and 61.2 percent report they attend synagogues less than once a month. While almost three-quarters attend services on the high holidays, more than half, 52.1 percent, reported the synagogue is not important as part of their social life.

There is also a mixed social pattern for these Jews. When entertaining in their home, 45.7 percent indicate their guests are both Jewish and non-Jewish, and 11.8 pecent indicate their guests are mostly non-Jewish. When socializing outside their house, only 39.1 percent report mostly Jewish associations.

To assess more fully the declining cultural ties among Jews making the economic transition described earlier, an analysis of cultural preferences was made according to selected characteristics: birthplace, income, and generation in Texas. It could be expected, for instance, that individuals born in New York City, an area with strong associations between Jews, might place more emphasis on relationships with Jews than respondents born elsewhere. Similarly, newer residents of Texas might not have the same interest in developing relationships with the Jewish community as more established Texas residents. The data did not strongly support any of these expectations.

There was a slightly higher preference for orthodox congregations among Texas and foreign-born Jews; New York Jews had a lower preference (significant at .05 level), for the more traditional service. This variable also illustrated differences for attending high holiday services, but, again, New York-born Jews were the least interested in attending; foreign and Texas-born the most interested. As might be expected, these respondents living in Texas for longer periods of time were more interested in attending high holiday services than newcomers. Texas and foreign-born Jews also placed more emphasis on the synagogue for their social life than did others.

These data, then, indicate for all Jews sampled, the cultural ties would appear to be less strong than those evident in earlier periods. If we assume that cultural ties producing high levels of association were an important element causing a collective response in the economic arena, then it is quite clear that these ties are declining in significance. This, then, is the first observation possible for the Jews who have changed from the immigrants to the "at home" middle class. If cultural ties are important to collectivist actions, then a weakening in collective orientations could be expected.

Cultural ties can also be developed through membership in Jewish organization. Indeed, it may have been the plethora of organizations in the 1900s that provided the foundation for collectivist activities. At the zenith of Jewish collectivism, more than six hundred different organizations existed to assist Jews. Consequently, the participation of immigrants in these organizations was high since most were wholly operated by Jews. The participation rate of Jews in social organizations has also continued at a high rate. Several studies indicate the relatively high participation rates in social, economic and political organizations by Jews when compared with other groups.[24]

In terms of describing orientations toward associational membership among Jews in the Dallas-Fort Worth metropolitan area, however, the data also indicate a decline in collective values and principles. Each household was asked not only to enumerate the organizations its members joined, but the roles they played. Two different categories of organizations were specified: Jewish-affiliated and secular.

A high level of participation is evident for both kinds of organizations. Only 30 respondents, 5.6 percent, indicated no member of the household participating in a Jewish organization. A substantially larger group of 155, or 29.2 percent, was not active in secular organizations. Respondents also participated to a large extent in leadership roles: 45.2 percent held officer positions in Jewish organizations and 20.7 percent held leadership roles in secular institutions.

The data also indicate a significant difference in participation rates by Jews in the two categories of organizations. There is a substantial level of participation by Jews in secular organizations, but Jews are far more likely to hold positions of authority in Jewish organizations. This finding, by itself, may not mean a declining attitude in values towards collective activities. The Jews participating in secular organizations could still represent Jewish interests and assist other Jews through their organizational associations. Nonetheless, there is evidence suggesting a move away from organizations involving Jewish interests to those favoring issues related to the general

TABLE 10.1 Organizational Memberships

Organization	Percent Sample Members	Percent Sample Officers	Rank
Jewish	94.4	45.2	—
American Jewish Committee	18.2	4.3	11
B'nai B'rith	77.5	29.7	2
Community centers	60.9	15.9	3
Council of Jewish Women	42.5	19.3	6
Hadassah	49.8	14.6	4
Hillel	16.3	16.3	12
ORT	18.9	3.8	10
Synagogue	82.8	25.6	1
Secular	96.1	49.7	—
Arts Council	16.0	1.0	13
Chamber of Commerce	27.9	3.9	7
Charities	24.7	8.0	8
Community theatre	15.4	4.5	14
Consumer cooperative	1.9	1.7	17
Unions industrial	1.2	.6	16
Unions—trade	3.2	0	15
United Way	23.9	3.9	9
Other	45.3	5.4	5

Source: Compiled by the authors.

community. This movement, however, has not resulted in widespread Jewish participation in leadership positions in secular organizations.

There is a considerable level of clustering of participation in four Jewish organizations: B'nai B'rith, community centers, synagogues, and Hadassah. More than four-fifths of the sample, 82.8 percent, were members of a synagogue, and 77.5 percent were members of B'nai B'rith. The various community centers (60.9 percent) and Hadassah (49.8 percent) were the next most popular organizations. The individual secular institution with

TABLE 10.2 Participation in Jewish and Secular Organizations

	Jewish Organizations	Secular Organizations
	Overall Participation	
	Mean Score	Mean Score
Birthplace		
Texas	6.23*	2.5*
U.S.	5.09	1.86
N.Y.C.	5.02	1.65
Foreign	5.52	1.91
Generations in Texas		
First	5.07*	1.68*
Second	5.29	1.97
Third	6.27	2.78
Fourth	6.42	2.71
Income		
Below $15,000	3.55*	1.00*
$15-20,000	4.17	1.31
$20-25,000	4.82	1.78
$25-35,000	5.89	2.80
$35,000 or more	6.13	2.26
	Leadership Positions Held	
Birthplace		
Texas	1.37*	.53
U.S.	.97	.36
N.Y.C.	.89	.29
Foreign	1.07	.33
Generations in Texas		
First	.96*	.32
Second	1.02	.40
Third	1.30	.55
Fourth	1.24	.33
Income		
Below $15,000	.57*	1.06*
$15-20,000	.85	1.19
$20-25,000	.99	1.63
$25-35,000	1.15	2.56
$35,000 or more	1.22	2.06

TABLE 10.2 (continued)

	Jewish Organizations	Secular Organizations
	Number of Memberships Held	
Birthplace	Mean Score	Mean Score
Texas	3.98*	2.26*
U.S.	3.52	1.75
N.Y.C.	3.5	1.53
Foreign	3.83	1.86
Generations in Texas		
First	3.49*	1.61*
Second	3.69	1.81
Third	4.01	2.41
Fourth	4.05	2.71
Income		
Below $15,000	2.57*	1.06*
$15–20,000	2.75	1.19
$20–25,000	3.21	1.63
$25–35,000	3.89	2.56
$35,000 or more	4.13	2.06

*Denotes significant differences beyond .05 level (F-ratio)
Source: Compiled by the authors.

the largest number of Jews in membership were the Chambers of Commerce. Jews were hardly involved with unions or cooperatives. The "other" category for secular groups had the most number of Jewish participants.

To assess more fully the participation of Jews in various secular and Jewish organizations we also analyzed participation according to selected characteristics: birthplace, income, and generation. It could be expected, for instance, that Jews from New York City, an area rich in organizations, would be eager to participate in organizations. This eagerness could exceed the interest of Jews from other areas. Wealthier residents could also be expected to have more time and resources to devote to both Jewish and secular organizations. Those Texans who have lived in the state for three or four generations could also be expected to participate in civic, social, and religious organizations more so than newcomers to the region. New migrants, less sure of their long-run stake in Texas affairs, might be less willing to participate extensively in various organizations. Should there be differences in participation patterns, these differences would indicate which segments of the Jewish community are making the transition from collectivist activities to more traditional forms of capitalist behavior. Texas-born Jews are more involved with both Jewish and secular organizations than New York Jews or migrants from other states or foreign countries. To determine organizational participation, a four point scale was constructed for each household: a 3 was coded if a member was an officer, a 2 if the respondent indicated a family member was on the board of directors, a 1 for membership in an organization, and a 0 if no one was involved in an organization. The combined mean score for Texas-born Jews participating in Jewish organizations was 6.23; the mean for the New York Jews was 5.09. Only foreign-born Jews scored less than New Yorkers. For secular organizations, the same pattern was evident.

Tables 10.2 and 10.3 summarize the result and significance levels for eighteen different tests of participation. Thirteen of the results are significant within conventional norms. Texas-born Jews are more active and hold positions of leadership more often than any other of Jews, and, the longer in Texas, the more active the household. The only change in this observation occurs with regard to the third and fourth generations. In some cases, third-generation Texans were slightly more active than fourth-generation Texans. Yet, in all instances, fourth-generation Texans were more active than first and second-generation families in the Dallas-Fort Worth area. Wealthier families also appear to be more active in Jewish and secular organizations. In those instances where the differences were not significant, it is still interesting to note that the patterns held.

In terms of participation, then, one finds an apparently high level of Jewish involvement with secular organizations even though participation is still concentrated in Jewish organizations. When the characteristics of the Jews were analyzed, important differences were observed. Those Jews who had been born in Texas were most active. In most instances, Jews from New York City were the least active. In all instances, New York Jews were less active than Jews born in Texas. Participation was also related to income and length of residency in the state. Those Jews who were second and third-generation Texans were more active than first-generation Texans. Wealthier Jews participated more so than those with less wealth.

For the question of economic transition, the data indicate the Jews who are the most recent immigrants to Texas have the least interest in building associations with Jewish organizations. This was particularly true for those Jews born in the New York City area. Wealthier residents are still concerned with Jewish organizations, but this does not reduce the general trend toward less concentrations of association with Jewish organizations. This outcome combined with the observations dealing with cultural ties leads one to infer that Jews in this sample have made a transition from collective self-help programs to orthodox capitalism.

The Erosion of Collective Self-Help. The concept of collectivist action as used in this volume deals with economic activities that maximize the interest of an ethnic group and the individual members of the group. Achieving both goals simultaneously, however, poses problems. For self-help programs, the interest of the ethnic group must be maximized first. Once group needs are met, individuals can then attempt to maximize their own positions. This might mean, for instance, that if greater individual profit can be realized by trading with a non-Jew, group norms and the ethic of group interest may prevent extra-community commercial transactions.

This sort of behavior differs from orthodox capitalism. Under that framework, an individual would attempt to maximize his position first and then, if possible, improve the well-being of co-religionists. If Jews have made a transition from collectivist actions towards orthodox capitalism, one should expect actions concentrating on improving an individual's economic position.

In terms of participating in collective self-help programs, which maximize group interest, individuals can transact business with group members through formalized institutions or individualized exchanges. A Jew interested in collective programs could, for instance, donate to Jewish charities. This would be an example of self-help in an organizational context. The act of a Jew purchasing goods or services from another Jew is also an example of self-help designed to maximize group interest. In this instance, however, the medium for self-help is individualized and, although possibly normative in the sense of a religious obligation, involves no formal organization.

The participation of Jews in numerous secular and Jewish organizations indicates the existence of an extremely developed infrastructure capable of assisting Jews in the Dallas-Fort Worth metropolitan area. To examine the extent to which collective self-help is actually an important goal of this organizational participation we posed several questions to the sample. Some dealt with assistance received from organizations when the respondent immigrated to Texas; others examined attitudes towards charitable contributions. The point of these questions was to determine if the transition from low to middle income brought with it a declining reliance on organization assistance when relocation occurs.

Each of the organizations established by Jews in the Dallas-Fort Worth area has the capability of assisting relocating families in finding housing, jobs, and schools and in meeting other needs. Each respondent was asked to identify, from a list, those organizations which had provided relocation assistance when the respondent's family came to Texas. An overwhelming majority of 436, or 82.0 percent, received no help from any organization. Only 15.5 percent received aid from one or two sources. The most significant agents in delivering help to newcomers were the various synagogues. Of the ninety-eight households receiving help, seventy-one noted it came from the various synagogues. The numerous community centers, the

B'nai B'rith, and Hadassah were the next most frequently mentioned organizations, 7.9 percent, 3.7 percent, and 2.6 percent respectively. The only other organizations mentioned were National Council of Jewish Women (.9 percent), and Hillel (.4 percent).

What is of some interest is the fact that foreign-born Jewish immigrants coming to Texas were the only ones who sought and received help. Jews immigrating from other states, on the other hand, tended neither to seek nor to receive help from any of the organizations. In other words, the principal "clients" of self-help were foreign-born or first-generation American-Jews—a parallel, to some extent, of the New York City experience. The attitude among second-generation Jews who had moved to Texas seemed to be "we're on our own." Such an attitude can be considered more fitting a philosophy of individualistic capitalism than the collectivist ideas evident earlier in the twentieth century. For the immigrants of the 1900s, HIAS and HEAS were usually the first and most important stops.

Jews have a long history of contributing to charities. The sample from the Dallas-Fort Worth area was no exception. However, only 3.2 percent indicated they contributed solely to Jewish charities. Almost one-third, 27.2 percent, indicated they made donations regardless of affiliations. The vast majority contributed to both Jewish and non-Jewish organizations, (69.7 percent). This suggests another weakening of the cultural ties between poor and wealthy Jews.

No statistically significant differences in charitable donations could be found related to the income, birthplace, migration time, or generation. The insignificance of income in explaining contributions ($F = 2.008$, significance .09) may be evidence of the cultural norm of *zedukah* important in Jewish life. However, this norm has shifted to a more secular stance reducing cultural obligations to other Jews.

In addition to self-help programs through organizations, there are numerous ways Jews can help or aid other Jews economically. These involve individual spending patterns, hiring, and selling decisions made through voluntary exchanges. Specifically, Jews can make a concerted effort to purchase goods or services sold by other Jews. Further, Jews who own their own businesses can hire other Jews. To analyze the feeling of the sample toward self-help in their personal economic transactions, a series of questions was directed toward Jews who owned their own businesses and another group of questions was asked of the entire sample.

A total of 249 respondents, 46.6 percent, owned their own businesses. Only 2.0 percent felt it was "very important" to recruit Jews for positions within their firm, and 9.6 percent indicated it was "somewhat important." The vast majority, 214, or 85.9 percent, felt it was "not important" to emphasize employment of Jews in their firms. This represents an important element in the transition of middle and upper-income Jews. The practices so important in collective efforts are now "not important."

The importance of hiring Jews did not vary according to the number of generations a respondent had been in Texas or the year the family migrated to Texas. Hiring of Jews was most important to first-generation Texans, but the differences were not statistically significant. There were, however, statistically significant differences related to the birthplace and income of the respondents. Foreign-born Jews placed greater emphasis on hiring Jews than did other groupings. New York Jews ranked third, placing only slightly more emphasis on hiring Jews than native Texans. Those Jews earning less than $15,000 and between $25,000 and $45,000 placed the highest emphasis on hiring Jews; those earning between $20,000 and $25,000 placed the next highest emphasis. Although the observed differences were significant, the relationship was not linear.

Another mechanism for improving the economic position of a group and its members is to keep businesses in the hands of other group members if a transfer of ownership becomes necessary. This issue has been addressed not only earlier in this volume but also elsewhere. To analyze the attitudes of the sample in retaining businesses as Jewish-owned operations, several questions were directed toward those respondents who owned a business.

Slightly more than a fifth, 22.1 percent, of the businesses owned by the sample were purchased. Of these 55 businesses, 39 or 70 percent were purchased from other Jews. In addition, 141 or 56.6 percent of the Jews owning a business have a partner, 53.9 percent of whom are Jewish. Despite this high level of interaction with Jews in business, only 17 or 6.8 percent of all owners felt it would be important to sell to a Jew. The overwhelming majority, 237 or 93.2 percent felt it was unimportant to sell to a Jew if a transfer was necessary.

Looking at all owners of business, there were no statistically significant differences related to birthplace, income, or generation of respondents in the desire to sell their business to Jews. We also examined the attitudes of those Jews who had purchased their businesses from Jews. Those Jews consistently indicated a stronger desire to sell to Jews than those who had not purchased their business from a Jew. The largest differences were for those Jews who represented first, third and fourth-generation Texans, and whether the respondent was born in Texas. Jews born in New York who had purchased businesses from Jews did not care if their business was sold to Jews.

Jews can also help each other if they make a conscious effort to trade with Jewish merchants, make purchases from Jewish-owned business, or use Jewish professionals for specialized services. Only 15.0 percent of the sample indicated they made a special effort to patronize Jewish businesses or services. The majority of the sample, 52.2 percent, made no special effort to identify Jewish businesses, and 31.8 percent indicated they purchase from Jews if the facilities are conveniently located.

There were no significant differences in attitudes regarding consumption related to any demographic characteristics of the sample. Only the analysis of differences related to income approached conventionally accepted significance levels (.08). The relationship was not linear but indicated a peaked preference for consumption from Jewish businesses by households with incomes between $20,000 and $25,000.

In terms of the five measures of self-help used in this study—immigrant-supporting institutions, charities, employment, selling of businesses, and consumption—self-help is not important to the Jews sampled. To each question posed, the sample responded with answers indicating individual maximization took precedence over group benefits. Consumption from Jewish businesses is done if convenient, and it is neither important to hire Jews or sell a business to a Jew. From the perspective of the group, capital accumulation is now an individual responsibility. Growth of the group is a function of the growth of individuals rather than any concerted effort to improve the economic standing of Jews.

There were some differences in the responses related to birthplace or whether the individual had purchased a business from a Jew. Over time, however, these categories of Jews are shrinking. As a result, collective efforts for economic self-help do not appear to be an important goal for the Jews in our sample.

JEWISH ENTERPRISE IN TRANSITION

Studying self-help among Jews is important because it produces information and insights into the experience of an ethnic group that has achieved general prosperity in American society. An analysis of the Jewish transition from poverty to prosperity can illuminate the question of whether self-help orientations among ethnic groups became a permanent fixture in a group's approach to economic life or become altered or attenuated. Specifically, do ethnic groups that achieve prosperity cease to rely on collective economic efforts to better their lot?

The results of this study, interpreted in light of Jewish self-help during the period of massive immigration and poverty, indicate North Texas Jews in the 1970s, more wealthy and better educated than Jewish immigrants to the United States seventy-five years ago, have little interest in collective programs and institutions. Jews in Texas still join Jewish organizations and participate in Jewish affairs. However, they appear to behave so as to maximize individual gains rather than collective or group goals. If the group benefits when an individual's position is maximized, all the better. But individual maximization appears to be the first priority.

Findings of this nature inevitably raise at least two questions. First, is this phenomenon characteristic of Jews elsewhere in the United States? Second, if these trends are evident nationwide, what does it suggest for students of ethnic enterprise?

Many scholars have studied Jews who have been able to leave the ghettos of New York, Chicago, and Baltimore and have moved to the suburbs or other areas. A general observation drawn from these studies is that individuals undergo a transformation that involves a rejection of the reminders of old patterns of behavior but not a total rejection of heritage ethnicity. "Whatever spoke to traditional ideologies in Yiddish secular life, was left behind . . . most immigrant institutions held little appeal for the new suburbanites, they were at once too keen in memory and too inharmonious with present desires."[25]

The rejection of institutions and organizations that help the poor has not meant disassociation from Jewish identity. The fact that Jews have achieved prosperity has not eroded the realization that they still exist in an alien culture and are still perceived as Jews. This realization has led to the development of other modes of participation in Jewish affairs. Past studies have noted these new areas of involvement tend to be the synagogues and the community centers. Not that the suburban or relocated Jews are any more religious than their counterparts in the old ghettos; rather, the synagogue has become a social, educational, and cultural center led by rabbis versed in popular literature, Israeli politics and affairs, current movies, and the scriptures. Specifically, contemporary Jewish institutions appear less concerned with purely economic affairs.

These observations generally describe the Jews in suburbia and in the Dallas-Fort Worth area. While the Dallas-Fort Worth area is further from the center of American Jewry, our research sample can be considered similar to the Jews who have moved to the suburbs in other areas of the country. Their behavior, in some instances, fits the descriptions of suburban Jews in the northeast and northcentral United States who have rejected the organizations that represented self-help programs for poor immigrants though not participation in Jewish organizations. Their economic status, combined with the social status of American Jews, yields a freedom from the kinds of organizations so important to Jews at the turn of the century. They have, in a sense, adopted traditional forms of capitalist behavior.

The institutions and associations that improved life for immigrant Jews were reminders of life styles wealthier and better-educated Jews wanted to forget. A symbolic aspect of having achieved prosperity is the decision not to join the organizations that assisted the poorer, less-Americanized Jews. These attitudes, apparently widespread, bear some resemblance to the ideas and notions of German Jews in the early 1900s. The German Jews were the ones who had "made it" by 1900. However, the sheer number of immigrants required their participation in self-help programs. If the Eastern European and Russian Jews were not aided, then American society might lump the German Jews with their more numerous but poorer, less educated coreligionists.

The need for participating in programs that help poor or immigrant Jews is less apparent to the Jews of the 1970s. The numbers are now on the side of the middle class. They are more numerous than the poor, less-educated Jews still in the old ghettos. Interestingly enough, where the German Jews who made it by 1900 suffered from their identification with the poorer immigrants, it is now the poor Jews who suffer from the stereotyping of American Jews. The quest for respectability, once exhibited by early German Jews, may now have negative consequences for those Jews remaining in poverty. Whereas the stereotype in the 1900s was of the Jewish immigrant laborer, today's stereotype is of the well-educated Jewish professional.

One mitigating factor, then, in explaining self-help programs and their impetus may be related to the quest for middle-class respectability and the vast number of members of an ethnic group still residing in poverty. If the Jewish middle class feels it can blend into American society—but the Jewish poor are too numerous and visible reminders to American society of a life style for the group that the middle class would prefer rejecting—self-help programs are likely to be very popular. For the German Jews of 1900, the wave of immigrants may have represented a threat in terms of how American society would relate to the Jewish middle class. The fear of being classified as a "greenhorn" may have encouraged some middle-class Jews to help their coreligionists.

A second factor accounting for the growth of self-help programs was obviously the real needs of the majority of a group's members. The Jews of the early twentieth century, needed jobs, education, and training. Collective action was most efficient in meeting these needs. But for many Jews in the 1970s, these needs are not as pressing and can be satisfied by individual action. Certain employment sectors are now dominated by Jews. Therefore, collective action is not needed; individuals can secure jobs and education without group assistance.

If the middle class is more numerous than the lower class, its interest in self-help programs may diminish. First, the members of the middle class may not need self-help programs for their own advancement or the enhancement of their image in American society. Second, without the tacit involvement of the middle class, there may not be sufficient initial leadership to establish a base for self-help programs. This is not to suggest that the lower class cannot operate self-help programs. Rather it is a recognition that the tacit cooperation of the middle class may be required for the successful initiation of self-help programs.

The Haggadah, the traditional Passover prayer book, contains a description of children attending the celebration of Passover. One child, the wise son, asks, "What are these testimonies, statutes, and judgments which the Eternal commanded you?" The wicked child, however, asks, "What do you mean by this service? By the word 'you' is clear he doth not include himself and thus hath withdrawn himself from the community. . . ."

Jews, now prosperous and well educated, may be like the wise and wicked children at the celebration of Passover. Economic threats to the prosperous community raises the old memorial of collective action, and a unified *political* response is made. But when the economic needs of the under class are presented in terms of needed jobs and opportunities, the response of the middle class may be like the wicked child at Passover; "What do you mean self-help? We belong to the synagogue and community center." The transition to orthodox capitalism and self-interest is complete.

These reactions are not only reflected in the survey data and results of other studies of suburban Jews but also exemplified in the reaction of the Jewish community to the two most recent threats to the economic security of large numbers of middle-class Jews: the decentralization of public schools and scatter-site public housing. An experiment in school governance become a focal point for confrontation between Jews and Blacks in New York City. Community control advocates favoring citizen control over schools in Black neighborhoods were pitted against the largely Jewish United Federation of Teachers which feared that Jewish teachers would be dismissed by Black community boards. The Jewish community supported the teachers and Mayor John V. Lindsay, portrayed as a community control advocate, was bitterly assailed in Jewish areas where two short years before he had been enthusiastically supported in his election.[26]

A short time later, the Lindsay Administration attempted to extend its scatter-site housing program to the middle-class Jewish neighborhood of Forest Hills. This attempt was perceived as an assault on the economic position of Jews, and Mayor Lindsay was again attacked by Jewish leaders in all parts of New York City and several other communities in the United

States. This support for the Jewish middle class by the Jewish middle class over possible threats to job and housing opportunities indicates that collective self-help can be mobilized on specific issues, even though attitudes towards general self-help may have diminished. In these cases, political action for the middle class by the middle class involving the new nodes of activity, the synagogues and community centers, was still a potent force. Collective action, however, was supportive of the status quo, an attempt to preserve and protect resources secured through earlier efforts and activities.

The problem with forgetting or rejecting the old traditions might mean that the group may not have the knowledge or necessary infrastructure to recreate the self-help programs should vested economic interest become jeopardized. Yet, participation of Jews in Jewish organizations makes this outcome unlikely. However, the collective self-help programs that do exist will probably be conservative in nature as well. In this sense the transition is also complete. Supporting Israel and protecting the life style of middle-class Jews are likely to be the points around which economic or political self-help will be organized. Efforts to help new immigrants, migrants, and the poor are more likely to be relegated to positions of less importance.

The case study analysis suggests to students of ethnic enterprise the likelihood that self-help programs, originally initiated to help poor immigrants and a large lower class, may eventually shift their focus to the concern of the middle class. However, when the shift occurs, it may be total in the sense that those group members who have not moved ahead on the economic ladder may simply be left behind. In the case of Jews, our opinion is that transition from collective self-help to orthodox capitalist behavior is virtually complete. The irony suggested is that while collectivism is premised upon egalitarian principles, its successful application contains the seeds of its own demise.

NOTES

1. COLLECTIVISM

1. Florence Kelly, "The Sweating System," in Ann Cook, Marilyn Gittell and Herb Mack *City Life, 1865 - 1900: Views on Urban America,* (New York: Praeger, 1973), p. 215.
2. Max Weber, *The Protestant Ethic and the Spirit of Capitalism* (New York: Charles Scribner's Sons, 1958).
3. C. Wright Mills, "The Professional Ideology of the Social Pathologists," *American Journal of Sociology,* 49, No. 2 (September 1943).
4. David M. Gordon, *Problems in Political Economy* (Lexington, Mass.: D. C. Heath, 1972); see also Gordon's *Theories of Poverty and Underemployment* (Lexington, Mass.: D. C. Heath, 1972).
5. William Ryan, *Blaming the Victim* (New York: Vintage Books, 1971), p. 7.
6. Gordon, *Problems in Political Economy,* p. 60.
7. Campbell McConnell, *Economics: Principles, Problems and Policies,* (New York: McGraw-Hill, 1972), p. 18.
8. Robert Park, *Race and Culture* (New York: The Free Press, 1950); Robert Park and Ernest Burgess, *Introduction to the Science of Sociology* (Chicago: University of Chicago Press, 1921).
9. Edna Bonacich, "A Theory of Ethnic Antagonism," *American Sociological Review,* 37 (October 1972) pp. 547-59.
10. John Higham, *Strangers in the Land* (New York: Atheneum, 1963), p. 45.
11. William Yancey, Eugene Erickson, and Richard Juliani, "Emergent Ethnicity: A Review and Reformulation," *American Sociological Review,* 41 (June 1976): p. 393.
12. John Fitch, *The Steelworkers* (New York: Arno Press, 1969) Caroline Golab, "The Immigrant and the City; Poles, Italians, and Jews in Philadelphia, 1870-1920," *The Peoples of Philadelphia* ed. Allen Davis and Mark Haller (Philadelphia: Temple University Press, 1973), pp. 203-30; Victor Greene, *Slavic Community on Strike* (Notre Dame, Ind., University of Notre Dame Press, 1968): *Immigration and Urbanization: The Slovak Experience: 1870-1918,* Mark Stolarik, Ph.D. diss. University of Minnesota, 1972.
13. Terry Clark, "The Irish Ethic and The Spirit of Patronage," *Ethnicity* 2, (Winter 1975), 305-59; Edwin Fenton, *Immigrants and Unions, A Case Study:*

Italians and American Labor (Cambridge, Harvard University Press, 1962) Irving Howe, *World Of Our Fathers,* (New York: Simon and Schuster, 1976); Moses Rischin, *The Promised City.* (New York: Harper & Row, 1973); William Shannon, *The American Irish* (New York: MacMillan, 1973).

14. Andrew Greeley, *Ethnicity in the United States.* (New York: John Wiley and Sons, 1974).
15. Angus Campbell and Howard Schuman, "Racial Attitudes in Fifteen American Cities," in *Supplementary Studies for the National Advisory Commission on Civil Disorders* (Washington, D.C.: Government Printing Office, 1968).
16. Religio-ethnic identification was measured by an item asking: "Which country did most of your ancestors come from?" Eastern Europe includes Hungary, Russia, Armenia, Estonia, Latvia, and Lithuania.
17. Gus Tyler, *The Labor Revolution* (New York: Viking Press, 1966), p. 32.
18. Golab, "Immigrant and City"; Greene, *Slavic Community on Strike,* Stolarik, *Immigration and Urbanization.*
19. Humbert Nelli, *The Italians in Chicago,* (New York: Oxford University Press, 1970).
20. Clark, "Irish Ethic." Shannon, *American Irish.*
21. Charles Anderson, *White Protestant Americans,* (Englewood Cliffs, N.J., Prentice Hall, 1970).
22. Howe, *World of Our Fathers.* Rischin, *Promised City.*
23. Ivan Light, *Ethnic Enterprise in America* (Berkeley: University of California Press, 1972).
24. Nels Ackerson and Lawrence Sharf "Community Development Corporations: Operations and Financing," *Harvard Law Review,* (May 1972), pp. 1559-1671; Charles Hampden-Turner, *From Poverty to Dignity* (New York: Doubleday, 1974); Report of the Twentieth Century Fund Task Force on Community Development Corporations, *CDCs: New Hope for the Inner City* (New York: The Twentieth Century Fund, 1971).
25. R. S. Ahlbrandt and P. C. Brophy, *An Evaluation of Pittsburgh's Neighborhood Housing Services Program* (Washington, D.C.: U.S. Department of Housing and Urban Development, 1975); R. S. Ahlbrandt and P. C. Brophy, "Neighborhood Housing Services: A Unique Formula Proves Itself in Turning Around Declining Neighborhoods," *Journal of Housing* (January 1976) pp. 36-39.
26. Harry Edward Berndt, *New Rulers in the Ghetto* (Westport, Ct.: Greenwood Press, 1977); Jerome Pratter and P. F. Mittelstadt, "St. Louis Inner-City Neighborhood Reclaiming Itself Through Community Development Corporation," *Journal of Housing* (October 1973). 484-90.
27. Eleanor L. Brilliant, *The Urban Development Corporation* (Lexington, Mass: D. C. Heath, 1975).
28. *Preservation Programs of the Federal Government in the Area of Housing and Community Development,* Staff report to the Sub-committee on Historic Preservation and Coinage and the Committee on Banking, Currency and Housing (Washington, D.C.: Government Printing Office, 1976).
29. William Witte, "Community Development's Third Year: A Report on Trends and Finds of NAHRO'S CD Monitoring Project," *Journal of Housing* (February 1978).
30. Berndt, *New Rulers in the Ghetto;* see also the special issue, "Community Economic Development," *Law and Contemporary Problems* 36, (Winter 1971), No. 1.

2. ASIAN ENTERPRISE IN AMERICA

1. Ivan Light, *Ethnic Enterprise in America* (Berkeley: University of California Press, 1972), pp. 10-18; see also Amsun Associates, "Excerpts From Socio-Economic Analysis of Asian-American Business Patterns," Mimeographed (Prepared for Office of Minority Business Enterprise, U.S. Department of Commerce, 1976), pp. 2, 9.

2. See, for example, Cyril S. Belshaw, "The Cultural Milieu of the Entrepreneur: A Critical Essay." *Explorations in Entrepreneurial History* 7 (1955); 146-63.
3. Peter Maris and Anthony Somerset, *The African Entrepreneur* (New York: Africana, 1971), p. 237.
4. Fredrik Barth, ed., *The Role of the Entrepreneur in Social Change in Northern Norway* (Bergen: Norwegian Universities Press, 1963), p. 9.
5. Light, *Ethnic Enterprise*.
6. Edna Bonacich, "A Theory of Middleman Minorities," *American Sociological Review* 38 (1973); 583-94.
7. John Waterbury, *North For The Trade,* (Berkeley: University of California Press, 1972), pp. 199-200.
8. Light, *Ethnic Enterprise;* John Modell, *The Economics and Politics of Racial Accommodation; The Japanese of Los Angeles, 1900-1942* (Urbana: University of Illinois Press, 1977), esp. pp. 90-93.
9. Robert N. Ray, "A Report on Self-Employed Americans in 1973," *Monthly Labor Review* 98 (1975), 49-54.
10. *The Korea Times* (Los Angeles), October 16, 1976; but cf. Rev. Matthew Y. Ahn, "Koreans in Los Angeles Area," mimeographed, (Los Angeles: Korean Community Services, 1975), p. 17.
11. U.S. Department of Health, Education, and Welfare, "Korean Field Study," mimeographed (Los Angeles, May 6, 1974).
12. L. Clay Terry, and Valiant R. Stull, "An Independent Study of the Los Angeles Korean Community and Its People" (Paper submitted to Faculty of Ethnic Studies Department, University of Southern California, July 1975), p. 5.
13. Edna Bonacich, Ivan Light, and Charles Wong, "Small Business among Koreans in Los Angeles," pp. 437-49, in *Counterpoint: Perspectives on Asian America,* ed. Emma Gee, (Los Angeles: Asian American Studies Center, University of California, 1976); *idem,* "Koreans in Business," *Society* 14 (1977); pp. 54-59; Kil-Narn Roh, "Korean Community Business Survey;" (Paper presented to *Korea Times* Symposium on Community Business, April 1, 1977); David Kim and Charles Choy Wong, "Business Development in Koreatown, Los Angeles," pp. 229-45, in *The Korea Diaspora,* ed. H. Kim, (Santa Barbara: ABC Clio, 1977).
14. *The Korean Business Directory of Southern California* (Los Angeles: Keys Printing Company, 1975); U.S. Department of Commerce, Bureau of the Census, *County Business Patterns, 1973, California, CBP-73-6,* (Washington, D.C.: Government Printing Office, 1975), pp. 62 ff.
15. Department of Health, Education, and Welfare, "Korean Field Study," p. 21.
16. H. Kim "Ethnic Enterprises among Korean Immigrants in America," in Kim, ed. *Korean Diaspora,* p. 97.
17. Terry and Stull, "Los Angeles Korean Community," p. 20.
18. Kwan-Chi Oh, "The Economics of Kye: An Informal Association of Individuals for Savings and Loans in Korea" (Ph.D. diss., Vanderbilt University, 1972), p. 12.
19. Gerard F. Kennedy, "The Korean Fiscal Kye (Rotating Credit Association): An Urban Accommodation in a Modernizing Society," (Ph.D. diss., University of Hawaii, 197
20. Oh of Kye," p. 25.
21. Kennedy, "Korean Fiscal Kye," p. 27.
22. Ibid., pp. 112-13; Light, *Ethnic Enterprise,* pp. 58-61.
23. *The Korea Times,* March 14, 1977, p. 1.
24. Oh, "Economics of Kye," p. 30.
25. Kim, ed., *Korean Diaspora,* p. 99.
26. Kim and Wong, "Business Development in Koreatown," p. 240.
27. Terry and Stull, "Los Angeles Korean Community," p. 35.
28. *New Korea,* March 20, 1975.
29. Terry and Stull, "Los Angeles Korean Community," p. 43.

30. Light, *Ethnic Enterprise*, p. 90.
31. Bonacich, "Middleman Minorities," p. 584.
32. Cornelius Osgood, *The Koreans and Their Culture* (New York: Ronald Press, 1951), p. 337.
33. Stanford M. Lyman, *The Asian in North America*, (Santa Barbara: ABC-Clio, 1977), pp. 119-30.
34. Michael Hechter, *Internal Colonialism; The Celtic Fringe in British National Development, 1536-1966* (Berkeley: University of California Press, 1975).
35. Edna Bonacich and Ivan Light, "American Capitalism and Korean Immigrant Small Business" (Paper presented to 1978 meeting of the International Sociological Association, Uppsala, Sweden).

3. CLAN STRUCTURE AND ECONOMIC ACTIVITY

1. C. Wright Mills, *White Collar* (New York: Oxford University Press, 1951), pp. 3-12.
2. Joseph A. Schumpeter, *The Theory of Economic Development* (Cambridge: Harvard University Press, 1934), pp. 59-68.
3. Bert F. Hoselitz and Wilbert E. Moore, eds., *Industrialization and Society* (Paris: UNESCO-MUTON, 1968); Peter Kilby, ed., *Entrepreneurship and Economic Development* (New York: Free Press, 1971); Milton Singer, *Entrepreneurship and Modernization of Occupational Cultures in South Asia* (Durham, N.C.: Duke University Press, 1973).
4. Arthur J. Vidich and Joseph Bensman, *Small Town in Mass Society* (Princeton: Princeton University Press, 1968), p. 323.
5. Edna Bonacich, "A Theory of Middleman Minorities," *American Sociological Review* 38 (October 1973); p. 586.
6. Ivan H. Light, *Ethnic Enterprise in America* (Berkeley: University of California Press, 1972), pp. 62-100.
7. Theodore Saloutos, *The Greeks in the United States* (Cambridge: Harvard University Press, 1964), pp. 44ff.; Evan Vlachos, "Historical Trends in Greek Migration to the United States" (Paper read at the 1976 Annual Meeting of the Modern Greek Studies Association), p. 7.
8. Vlachos, "Historical Trends," pp. 6-15.
9. Saloutos, *Greeks in the United States*, pp. 45-70, 258-80.
10. Ibid., pp. 265-67; Robert James Theodoratus, "A Greek Community in America: Tacoma Washington" (Sacramento: Sacramento Anthropological Society, 1971), p. 15; Federal Writers' Project, "The Greeks of New Haven," mimeographed (New Haven, 1937).
11. E. P. Hutchinson, *Immigrants and their Children: 1850-1950* (New York: Wiley, 1956), pp. 335-49; U.S., Bureau of the Census, *National Origin and Language,* Census of Population, 1970; Special Reports (Washington, D.C.: Government Printing Office, 1973), p. 140.
12. Lawrence A. Lovell-Troy, "Ethnic Occupational Structures: Greeks in the Pizza Business," *Ethnicity*, forthcoming.
13. John K. Campbell, "The Kindred in a Greek Mountain Community," pp. 73-96 in *Mediterranean Countrymen,* ed. Julian Pitt-Rivers (Paris: Mouton, 1963); Ernestine Friedl, *Vasalika: A Village in Modern Greece* (New York: Holt, Rinehart and Winston, 1962); Peter Loizos, *The Greek Gift: Politics in a Cypriot Village* (New York: St. Martin's Press, 1975); Scott G. McNall, *The Greek Peasant* (Washington, D.C.: American Sociological Association, 1974).
14. David S. North, *Immigrants and the American Labor Market* (Washington, D.C.: Manpower Research Monograph No. 31, U.S. Department of Labor, 1974), pp. 30-31, 61.
15. The generalizations presented are based on my relatively small, and not randomly selected, sample. I do not mean by my use of the term that I am generalizing from those interviewed to the total population of Greeks in Connecticut, much

less to those in the United States, or to other ethnic groups. I offer these generalizations only as general trends that were discovered from my respondents in eastern Connecticut. They are intended more as summaries of findings and as hypotheses for further research than as generalizations from a sample to a population.
16. Light, *Ethnic Enterprise,* pp. 62-100.

4. MORMON RESISTANCE AND ACCOMMODATION

1. The inherent liberalism of Mormon metaphysics and theology is examined in my article "Mormonism—A Nineteenth-Century Heresy," *The Journal of Religious Thought* 26 (Autumn-Winter 1969): 44-55; Sterling M. McMurrin, *The Philosophical Foundations of Mormon Theology* (Salt Lake City: University of Utah Press, 1959); and *The Theological Foundations of the Mormon Religion* (Salt Lake City: University of Utah Press, 1965).
2. Quoted in Davis Bitton and Gordon Irving, "The Continental Inheritance," in *The Peoples of Utah,* ed. Helen Papanikolas (Salt Lake City: Utah State Historical Society, 1976), p. 221.
3. Fawn Brodie, *No Man Knows My History* (New York: Alfred A. Knopf, 1945).
4. *The Doctrine and Covenants of the Church of Jesus Christ of Latter-day Saints* (Salt Lake City: Church of Jesus Christ of Latter-day Saints, 1958), section 42. This volume contains revelations received for direction of the church. Hereafter this volume will be referred to as the D & C, with subsequent notations indicating the section and verses.
5. D & C 42.
6. "The Equality and Oneness of the Saints," *The Seer* 2 (July 1854); My citation is from a privately published copy of two of Pratt's more influential essays, *The New Jerusalem* and *The Equality and Oneness of the Saints* (Salt Lake City: Parker P. Robinson, n.d.), p. 58.
7. Arrington, et al., *Building The City of God,* p. 23. See also Brodie, *No Man Knows,* pp. 112-13.
8. Mormon city planning, including this conception of Joseph Smith, is reproduced and discussed in Lowry Nelson, *The Mormon Village: A Pattern and Technique of Land Settlement* (Salt Lake City: University of Utah Press, 1952).
9. The most blatant example is from conservative Republican J. Reuben Clark, Jr., *The United Order and Law of Consecration as Set Out in the Revelations of the Lord* (Salt Lake City: Church of Jesus Christ of Latter-day Saints, 1945).
10. Hamilton Gardner, "Communism among the Mormons," *Quarterly Journal of Economics* 37 (November 1922): 150.
11. Leonard J. Arrington, et al., *Building the City of God* (Salt Lake City: Desert Book, 1976).
12. *Missouri Intelligencer and Boon's Lick Advertiser* (Colombia) August 10, 1833. This is reprinted in an excellent collection of primary sources covering the Mormon experience from its origins through the first half of this century, *Among the Mormons,* ed. William Mulder and A. Russell Mortensen (Lincoln: University of Nebraska Press, 1973), p. 78.
13. B. Pixley, "New Jerusalem: Letter from Independence," in ibid., pp. 72-75.
14. Ibid., pp. 78-79.
15. Ibid., p. 69.
16. Thomas F. O'Dea, *The Mormons* (Chicago: University of Chicago Press, 1957), pp. 42-49.
17. Robert B. Flanders, *Nauvoo: Kingdom on the Mississippi* (Urbana: University of Illinois Press, 1965), p. 5.
18. Ibid., pp. 306-41.
19. Quoted in B. H. Roberts, *A Comprehensive History of the Church of Jesus Christ of Latter-day Saints: Century I,* vols. (Salt Lake City: Deseret News Press, 1930), 3: 269.

20. Quoted in Leonard J. Arrington, *The Great Basin Kingdom* (Lincoln: University of Nebraska Press, 1966), pp. 51-53.
21. Arrington, *Great Basin Kingdom*, p. 88.
22. William Mulder, "Scandinavian Saga," in Papanikolas, ed. *The Peoples of Utah*, (Salt Lake City: Utah State Historical Society, 1976), p. 145.
23. Gustive O. Larson, "The Story of the Perpetual Emigration Fund," *Mississippi Valley Historical Review* 18 (September 1931); 184-94.
24. Quoted in F. S. Buchanan, "Imperial Zion: The British Occupation of Utah," in ed., Papanikolas, *The Peoples of Utah*, (Salt Lake City: Utah State Historical Society, 1976), pp. 68-69.
25. Mulder, "Scandinavian Saga", pp. 151-52.
26. "Bound for the Great Salt Lake," in Mulder and Mortensen, eds., *Among the Mormons*, pp. 334-44.
27. Arrington, *Great Basin Kingdom*, p. 137.
28. Ibid., p. 174.
29. Ibid., p. 97.
30. Arrington, *Great Basin Kingdom*, p. 338.
31. See Arrington, *Great Basin Kingdom;* Klaus Hansen, *Quest for Empire* (Lincoln: University of Nebraska Press, 1974); and Gustive O. Larson, *The "Americanization" of Utah for Statehood* (San Marino, Calif.: The Huntington Library, 1971).
32. Arrington, *Great Basin Kingdom*, p. 361.
33. Ibid., p. 360.
34. Ibid., p. 371.
35. Richard Ely, "Economic Aspects of Mormonism," *Harper's Monthly Magazine* 106 (April 1903); 671.
36. He declared; "Now I hoped and prayed and I voted and did all I could in the hope that the good people of this city would vote it dry so that we would not be compelled to allow a saloon or bar to be operated in the Hotel Utah. If you had voted it dry we would not have had any bar there." Quoted in Erikson, *Mormon Group Life*, pp. 71-72.
37. "Change Comes to Zion's Empire," *Business Week* (November 23, 1957); 108.
38. Arrington, *Great Basin Kingdom*, p. 409.
39. Glenn M. Vernon, *Sociology of Mormonism: A Preliminary Analysis* (Salt Lake City: privately published, 1975), p. 13.
40. Neil Morgan, "Utah: How Much Money Hath the Mormon Church? " *Esquire* (August 1962); 86-91.
41. Bill Beecham and David Briscoe, "Mormon Money and How It's Made," *Utah Holiday* (March 22, 1976). For additional works dealing with the recent economic activities of the Mormons, see Samuel W. Taylor, *Rocky Mountain Empire: The Latter-day Saints Today* (New York: Macmillan, 1978), pp. 132-44; and Jeffery Kaye, "An Invisible Empire: Mormon Money in California," *New West* (May 8, 1978); 36-40.
42. Kaye, "Invisible Empire," p. 36.
43. Quoted in Leonard J. Arrington, "Taxable Income in Utah, 1862-1872," *Utah Historical Quarterly* 24 (January 1956); 46.
44. See, for instance, Ezra Taft Benson, "Standup for Freedom" (Address to the Utah Forum for the American Idea, Salt Lake City, Utah, February 11, 1966); Ernest L. Wilkinson, "The Changing Nature of American Government from a Constitutional Republic to a Welfare State" (Address to Brigham Young University, April 21, 1966); Daniel L. Ludlow, "Our Divine Destiny: A Third Dimensional View," *Speeches of the Year* (Salt Lake City: Brigham Young University Press, 1970), pp. 5-7.
45. Quoted in J. Kenneth Davies, "The Mormon Church: Its Middle-class Propensities," *Review of Religious Research* 4 (Winter 1963); 84-95.
46. See Wallace Turner, *The Mormon Establishment* (Boston: Houghton Mifflin, 1966), pp. 291-94.

47. Davies, "The Mormon Church."
48. Vernon, *Sociology of Mormonism*, p. 136.
49. Ibid.
50. Jack Carlson, "Income and Membership Projections for the Church through the Year 2000," *Dialogue* 4 (Spring 1969); 135.
51. E. L. Thorndike, *Science* 92 (1940); 137.
52. E. L. Thorndike, "The Origin of Superior Men," *Scientific Monthly* 56 (May 1943); 424-32.
53. Kenneth R. Hardy, "Social Origins of American Scientists and Scholars," *Science* 185 (August 1974); 497-506.
54. Edwin S. Guastad, "America's Institutions of Faith," in *The Religious Situation 1968,* ed. Donald Cutler (Boston: Beacon Press, 1968), pp. 851-53.
55. See Marc Rose, "The Mormons March Off Relief," *Reader's Digest* (June 1937); 43-44; "Titles and Security" *Time* (August 1, 1938); 26.
56. Frank Jonas, "Utah: Sagebrush Democracy," in *Rocky Mountain Politics,* ed. Thomas Donnelly (Albuquerque: University of New Mexico Press, 1940), p. 48.
57. Thomas F. O'Dea and Evan Z. Vogt, "A Comparative Study of the Role of Values in Social Action in Two Southwestern Communities," *American Sociological Review* 28 (December 1953), 645-54.
58. Mark P. Leone, "The Economic Basis of the Evolution of Mormon Religion," in *Religious Movements in Contemporary America,* ed. Irving Zaretsky and Mark Leone (Princeton: Princeton University Press, 1974), pp. 722-66.

5. THE PROFITS OF NONPROFIT CAPITALISM

1. The quotations are from *Naród Polski* (The Polish Nation), March 27, 1901, *Chicago Foreign Language Press Survey* (hereafter cited as *CFLPS*), reel 49, section IB3c; and *Dziennik Zwiazkowy* (Alliance Daily), March 30, 1917, *CFLPS,* reel 49, section IB3c. Also see *Dziennik Zwiazkowy,* May 27, 1917, *CFLPS,* reel 49, section ID1b.
2. Quoted in Stanislaus A. Blejwas, "The Origins and Practice of 'Organic Work' in Poland: 1795-1863," *The Polish Review* 15 no. 4 (1970); 23. Also see Stanislaus A. Blejwas, "Organic Work and the Polish Question: The Historiography" (Paper delivered at the Second Congress of Polish American Scholars and Scientists at Columbia University, April 23, 1971); Stefan Kieniewicz, *Historia Polski* (History of Poland) (Warsaw: Polish Academy of Sciences, Institute of History, 1970), vol. 3, pt. 1, pp. 247-57, 434-54; Adam Bromke, *Poland's Politics: Idealism vs. Realism* (Cambridge; Harvard University Press, 1967), chap. 1.
3. Celina Bobińska and Andrzej Pilch, eds., *Employment-Seeking Emigrations of the Poles World-Wide XIX and XXC* trans. Danuta E. Zukowska (Kraków: Jagiellonian University, 1975); Wladyslaw Rusinski, "The Role of the Peasantry of Poznan (Wielkoposka) in the Formation of the Non-agricultural Labor Market," *East European Quarterly* 3; no. 4 (1969); 509-24.
4. Helena Znaniecki Lopata, "Polish Immigration to the United States of America: Problems of Estimation and Parameters," *The Polish Review* 21; no. 4 (1976); 85-107.
5. Jiri Kolaja, review of Joel Raba, *Robotnicyślascy, 1850-1870, Praca i byt* (Silesian Workers, 1850--1870; Their Working and Living Conditions) (London: Odnova, 1969), in *The Polish Review* 15; no. 4 (1970); 117-18.
6. Andrzej Brozek, *Slazacy w Teksasie* (Silesians in Texas) (Warsaw: State Scientific, 1972), pp. 5-38; T. Lindsay Baker, "The Early Years of Rev. Wincenty Barzyński," *Polish American Studies* 32; no. 1 (Spring 1975); 29-52; Helen Busyn, "The Political Career of Peter Kiolbassa," *Polish American Studies* 7; no. 1-2 (1950); 8-22; Helen Busyn, "Peter Kiolbassa--Maker of Polish America," 8; no. 3-4 (1951); 65-84.

7. *Dziennik Chicagoski* (Chicago Daily News), June 11, 1891, *CFLPS*, reel 54, section IIC. Stanislaw Osada, *Historya Zwiazku Narodowego Polskiego* History of the Polish National Alliance) (Chicago: Polish National Alliance, 1905), pp. 35–66; Karol Wachtl, *Z.P.R.K. Dzieje Zjednoczenia Polskiego Rzym.-Kat. w Ameryce* (PRCU History of the Polish Roman-Catholic Union in America) (Chicago: n.p., 1913), p. 55; Joseph Parot, "The American Faith and the Persistence of Chicago Polonia, 1870-1920", (Ph.D. diss., Northern Illinois University, 1971), pp. 10–27. Also see the following works which survey the history of Polish fraternalism in the United States: Waclaw Kruszka, *Historya Polska w Ameryce* (History of Poland in America), 13 vols. (Milwaukee: Kuryer Press, 1905–08), 3: 139–48, 4: 3–82; Thomas and Znaniecki, *The Polish Peasant*, 2: 1575–1644; Helena Znaniecki Lopata, "The Function of Voluntary Associations in an Ethnic Community: 'Polonia'" (Ph.D. diss., University of Chicago, 1954); Joseph Wytrwal, "The Role of Two American Polish Nationality Organizations in the Acculturation of Poles in America" (Ph.D. diss., University of Michigan, 1958).

8. Osada, *Historya Zwiazku,* pp. 97–183; *Ksiega Protokólow Posiedzeń Sejmów Zwiazku Narodowego Polskiego w Stanach Zjednoczonych* (Book of Proceedings of the Sessions of the Diets of the Polish National Alliance in the United States), manuscript copy for the years 1881-95 in the Library of the Polish National Alliance in Chicago.

9. *Constitution of the Polish National Union of North America* (New York: n.p., 1882), pamphlet in the University of Notre Dame Archives, pp. 2–21.

10. Ibid., pp. 22-28; Osada, *Historya Zwiazku,* pp. 196–98, 205-09, 213-327; Edward A. Chmielewski, "Minneapolis' Polish Fraternals," *Polish American Studies* 19, no. 2 (1962); 91–99; *Historja Unji Polskiej w Stanach Zjednoczonych Polnocnej Ameryki* (History of the Polish Union in the United States of North America) (Wilkes Barre, Pa.: Polish Union in the United States, 1940), pp. 48–49.

11. Osada, *Historya Zwiazku,* pp. 277-327; Józef Miaso, *The History of the Education of Polish Immigrants in the United States,* trans. Ludwik Krzyzanowski (New York: Kosciuszko Foundation, 1977), pp. 60–96; Adam Olszewski and Stanislaw Osada, *Historia Zwiazku Narodowego Polskiego* (History of the Polish National Alliance), 6 vols. (Chicago: Polish National Alliance, 1957), 3: 369-72, 386, 389–91, 4: 109, 111-12, 172-73; *Sprawozdania na sejm Zwiazku Narodowego Polskiego w Philadelphia, Pa. 1924* (Reports to the Diet of the Polish National Alliance in Philadelphia, Pa. 1924) (Chicago: PNA, 1924), p. 39; *Sprawozdania na sejm XXVII Zwiazku Nar. Polskiego w Baltimore, Md. 1935* (Reports to the 27th Diet of the Polish National Alliance in Baltimore, Md. 1935) (Chicago: PNA, 1935).

Dziennik Zwiazkowy: December 19, 28, 29, 1911, August 18, 1914, April 3, 1917, February 14, 1918, *CFLPS*, reel 49, section ID1a; July 31, 1912, *CFLPS*, reel 50, section ID2a; April 8, September 2, 1910, November 15, 1911, *CFLPS*, reel 51, section IH; December 5, 1910, January 11, 1928, *CFLPS*, IIC. *CFLPS*, reel 49, sections ID2a (2) and ID2a (3) indicate considerable support from the fraternals for craft unions and mixed support for industrial unions. Also see Sister M. Remigia, "The Polish Immigrant in Detroit to 1914," *Polish American Studies* 2; no. 1-2 (1945); 7-8.

12. Osada, *Historya Zwiazku,* pp. 268–413; Stefan Lenartowicz, ed., *Zlota Ksiega Zjednoczenia Polsko Narodowego w Brooklynie, U.S.A. 1903-1953* (Golden Anniversary Book of the Polish National Alliance in Brooklyn, U.S.A. 1903–1953) (New York: PNA of Brooklyn, 1953), pp. 116–202. Three more federations rounded out the list of smaller secular fraternals: the White Eagle Association in Minneapolis, the Federation Life Insurance in Milwaukee, the Polish Alliance of America in Plymouth, Pa. See, for example, Angela T. Pienkos, *A Brief History of Federation Life Insurance of America, 1913-1976* (Milwaukee: Federation Life Insurance, 1976).

13. Wachtl, *Z.P.R.K.,* pp. 63-64, 74, 76, 82-88, 92-93, 95-97, 112; Lopata,

"The Function of Voluntary Associations," pp. 243, 292-93; *Dziennik Chicagoski*, August 18, 23-25, 1894, February 7, 1895, May 23, August 18, 1896, June 18, 1897, *CFLPS*, reel 54, section IIC.

14. *Dziennik Chicagoski*, April 28, June 18, 1897, *CFLPS*, reel 54, section IIC; *Naród Polski*, July 3, 1901, *CFLPS*, reel 54, section IID2; *Dziennik Zwiazkowy*, September 29, December 7, 1910, *CFLPS*, reel 54, IIC; ibid., December 8, 1910, *CFLPS*, reel 54, section IID2; *Dziennik Zjednoczenia* (Union Daily), June 2, 1926, *CFLPS*, reel 54, section IID2; *Constitution and Laws . . . of the Polish National Alliance . . . 1909* (Chicago: PNA, 1911), uncatalogued material at the Immigration History Research Center of the University of Minnesota; *Konstytucya Zjednoczenia Polskiego Rzymsko-Katolickiego w Ameryce* (Constitution of the Polish Roman Catholic Union in America) (1913), uncatalogued material at the Polish Museum of America, Chicago. The staffs of the Immigration History Research Center and of the Polish Museum, Rev. Donald Bilinski, OFM, Curator, were unfailingly helpful in securing access to these and other materials in their collections. Also see Osada, *Historya Zwiazku*, pp. 423-621; Wachtl, *Z.P.R.K.*, 98-100, 104, 116, 126-27, 131-32, 149-51; Lopata, "The Function of Voluntary Associations," p. 247; Olszewski and Osada, *Historia Zwiazku*, 2: 1-2, 38, 42, 44, 46, 54-60, 82, 87, 256-57, 263-64, 287-88, 4: 39.

15. Wachtl, *Z.P.R.K.*, pp. 114, 128, 132, 136, 152, 336, 342,; Jadwiga Karlowiczowa, *Historia Zwiazku Polek w Ameryce* (History of the Polish Women's Alliance in America) (Chicago: PWA, 1938), pp. 25-26, 53-54; Lopata, "The Function of Voluntary Associations," pp. 243-44, 276-77, 288, 298; Olszewski and Osada, *Historia Zwiazku*, 2: 37, 3: 345.

16. *Dziennik Chicagoski*, February 21, 1894, *CFLPS*, reel 54, section IIC; Wachtl, *Z.P.R.K.*, p. 64; Karlowiczowa, *Historia*, p. 113; *Historja Unji*, p. 54; Lenartowicz, *Zlota Ksiega*, pp. 82-94, 174-202; Lopata, "The Function of Voluntary Associations," pp. 243, 277-78, 288; Olszewski and Osada, *Historia Zwiazku*, 2: 87, 3: 280.

17. *Pamietnik Zlotego Jubileuszu Polsko Narodowej Spójni 1908-1958* (Golden Jubilee Souvenir Book of the Polish National Union 1908-1958) (Scranton, Pa., Polish National Union, 1958), pp. 36-37, 41-54.

18. Olszewski and Osada, *Historia Zwiazku*, 2: 99, Arthur Waldo, *Sokolstwo przednia straz narodu. Dzieje idei i organizacji w Ameryce* (The Sokol Movement as the Advance Guard of the Nation. The History of the Idea and Organization in America), 4 vols. (Pittsburgh: Polish Falcons of America, 1953-74), pp. 36-37, 41-54, carries the story of the Falcons through 1918.

19. *Naród Polski*, January 15, 1913, *CFLPS*, reel 49, section IB3c; Wachtl, *Z.P.R.K.*, p. 125; Olszewski and Osada, *Historia Zwiazku*, 3: 317, 373-374; Lopata, "The Function of Voluntary Associations," p. 245.

20. Wachtl, *Z.P.R.K.*, pp. 84, 86-87, 92, 94, 96, 111, 113, 116, 119-21, 123, 125, 130, 134, 146, 158; Karlowiczowa, *Historia*, pp. 35, 37, 42, 46, 50, 72, 77, 81, 85, 96, 106, 113, 118, 121, 142, 155-57; Olszewski and Osada, *Historia Zwiazku*, 2: 11; Helena Znaniecki Lopata, *Polish Americans. Status Competition in an Ethnic Community* (Englewood Cliffs, N.J.: Prentice-Hall, 1976), p. 150; *Sprawozdania na Sejm XXV Zwiazku Narodowego Polskiego w Chicago Ill. 1927* (Chicago: PNA, 1927), pp. 32, 79; *Sprawozdania na Sejm XXVII Zwiazku Nar. Polskiego w Baltimore, Md. 1935*, pp. 75, 99-100.

21. *Dziennik Chicagoski*, May 4, 1892, *CFLPS*, reel 54, section IIC; *Dziennik Zwiazkowy*, December 22, 1910, *CFLPS*, reel 54, section IIC; Olszewski and Osada, *Historia Zwiazku*, 2: 39-40.

22. Stanley R. Pliska: "Polish Independence and the Polish Americans," (Ph.D. diss., Teachers College, Columbia University, 1955); "The Polish American Army, 1917-1921," *The Polish Review* 10 (Summer 1965); 46-59; "The Polish American Community and the Rebirth of Poland," *Polish American Studies* 26 (1969); 41-60.

23. Paul H. Douglas, *The Theory of Wages* (1934; rpt. New York: Kelley and Millman, 1957), p. 182; Obrebski, "The Changing Peasantry," p. 56; Zbigniew

Landau, "Poland and America: The Economic Connection 1918-1939," *Polish American Studies* 32; no. 2 (Autumn 1975); 50; Joseph Parot, "Ethnic versus Black Metropolis: The Origins of Polish-Black Housing Tensions in Chicago," *Polish American Studies* 29; no. 1-2 (1972); 22-25; Miaso, *History of the Education of Polish Immigrants*, pp. 47-52; Karlowiczowa, *Historia*, p. 25.

24. Charles Frank Emmons, "Economic and Political Leadership in Chicago's Polonia: Some Sources of Ethnic Persistence and Mobility," (Ph.D. diss., University of Illinois at Chicago Circle, 1971), p. 52.

25. *Dziennik Zwazkowy*, December 14-15, 20-22, 1910, *CFLPS*, reel 54, section IIC; ibid., September 26, 1916, *CFLPS*, reel 54, section IIC; Olszewski and Osada, *Historia Zwiazku*, 2: 33, 44, 74-75, 88; ibid., 3: 21-22; *Sprawozdania na Sejm XXVII Zwiazku Nar. Polskiego w Baltimore, Md. 1935*, pp. 99-100; *Sprawozdania na Sejm XXIX Z.N.P. w Boston 1943* (Chicago: PNA, 1943), pp. 87, 119-20; *Sprawozdania na Sejm XXX Zwiazku Narod. Polskiego w Cleveland, Ohio 1947* (Chicago: PNA, 1947), pp. 3-5 98; *Glos Polek*, October 10, 1935; *Pamietnik . . . Spójni*, p. 37.

26. Olszewski and Osada, *Historia Zwiazku*, 4: 154-98, 464-67, 480-85, 518-19, 527, 583; Lopata, "The Function of Voluntary Associations," pp. 286, 288, 293-94; Lopata, *Polish Americans*, pp. 150-51; *Statistics of Fraternal Benefit Societies* (1895-).

6. A PLACE FOR EVERYONE

1. Timothy Smith, "New Approaches to the History of Immigration in Twentieth-Century America," *American Historical Review* 71: no. 4 (July 1966); 1265.

2. William P. Dillingham, Chairman, *Reports of the Immigration Commission* Vols. (Washington, D.C. 1911), 3: 4-5; and the *Annual Report of the Commissioner-General of Immigration to the Secretary of Labor, fiscal year ended June 30, 1918* (Washington, D.C. 1919), p. 140.

3. See the *Reports of the Immigration Commission*, 6: 35, 8; 199, 16; 588; and Peter Roberts, *The New Immigration* (New York, 1914), p. 156.

4. For a fuller description of this phenomenon, see my "Building Slovak Communities in America", in *The Other Catholics*, ed. Keith Dyrud, Michael Novak, and Rudolph Vecoli (New York, 1978).

5. Oscar Handlin, *The Uprooted: The Epic Story of the Great Migration that Made the American People* (New York, 1951), pp. 170-71, 176; and *Národný hlásnik* (Martin, Slovakia), August 31, 1872, pp. 242-44; Ignác Gessay, "Spolsky pred organisáciami" (Lodges before Organizations), *Národný Kalendár, 1911* (Pittsburgh), pp. 67, 74; and P. V. Rovnianek, *Zápisky za ziva pochovaného* (Notes of One Buried Alive) (Pittsburgh, 1924), p. 147.

6. Alzbeta Gácsová, *Boje slovenského ludu proti feudálenmu útaku a vykoristovaniu* (Struggles of the Slovak People Against Feudal Oppression and Exploitation) (Bratislava, 1960), p. 64; *Národni hlásnik*, March 31, 1874, pp. 62-63; *Národnie noviny* (Martin), February 8, 1881, p. 1; Gessay, "Spolky," pp. 68-74.

7. "Sbierkia dejín slovenských spolkov v Bethlehem, Pa." (A Collection of Histories of Slovak Fraternals in Bethlehem, Pa.), in *Dejiny Bethlehemských Slovákov v Spojených Státoch Severnej Ameriky* (A Hisotry of Bethlehem Slovaks in the United States of North America), ed. Milan P. Pauliny (Bethlehem, 1921), pp. 33-49.

8. "Membership Roll and Dues Book of the Society of Sts. Cyril and Methodius, South Bethlehem, Pa., 1891-1904," and "Membership Roll and Dues Book, Sacred Heart of Jesus Society in South Bethlehem, Pa., 1891-1904." Since these ledger books had no formal titles, I made them up on the basis of their contents. They are both in the care of George Anthony of Bethlehem. See also "Prehlad dejín 74 c. spolku Narodenia Panny Márie" (Survey History of Branch 74, Nativity of the Blessed Virgin Mary Lodge), and "Prehlad dejín spolku Nanebevzatia Panny Márie" (Survey History of the Society of the Assumption of the Blessed Virgin Mary), in Pauliny, ed., *Dejiny*, pp. 35-41.

9. "Membership Roll of St. George's Lodge, Branch 350 of the National Slovak Society in South Bethlehem, Pa., 1900-1913" (in Slovak), in the care of Cyril Krajci of Bethlehem. See also "Prehlad dejín 135, odboru 'Ziveny' Márie Magdaleny" (Survey History of branch 135, Mary Magdalen, of 'Zivena'), in Pauliny ed., *Dejiny* p. 45.
10. Rovnianek, *Zápisky za ziva*, pp. 126-27; Ján Pankuch, *Dejiny Clevelandských a Lakewoodských Slovakov* (A History of Cleveland and Lakewood Slovaks), (Cleveland, 1930), pp. 9, 11, 32; *Amerikánsko-Slovenské Noviny* (Pittsburgh), July 4, 1896, p. 1; Gusto Kosik, "Prve desatrocie nasej Jednoty" (The First Decade of Our Union), in *Sborník Rimsko a Grecko Katolíckej Telocvicnej Jednoty Sokol, 1916* (Passaic), pp. 35-51.
11. "Sbierka dejín"; "Spolok Svatej trojice, cislo 45, E.S.Z.J" (Minutes of the Society of the Holy Trinity, branch 45 of the Evangelical Slovak Ladies' Union), July 4, 1909, in the care of Rev. John Daniel of Bethlehem; Andrej Baláz, "Krátke dejiny c. 158 S.E.J. v Bethlehem, Pa." (Short History of Branch 158 of the Slovak Evangelical Union in Bethlehem), *Slovenský Hlásnik* (Pittsburgh), February 2, 1936, p. 3.
12. Joseph J. Karabin, "The 50th Anniversary of Lodge 93, Bethlehem, Pennsylvania," in *Golden Jubilee, Slovak Gymnastic* Union Sokol Assembly 93, 1905-1955 (Bethlehem, 1955); "Zapisnica Sboru 93-ého Telocvicnéj Slovenskej Jednoty Sokol v So. Bethlehem, Pa." (Minutes of Branch 93 of the Slovak Gymnastic Union Sokol in South Bethlehem), 1915-50, in the care of John Husovsky, Jr. of Bethlehem and "Zapisnica Sboru 78 K. Sokoloch South Bethlehem, Pa." (Minutes of branch 78 of the Catholic Sokols in South Bethlehem) 1911-38, in the care of William Gazdacka, Jr.
13. "Prehlad dejín spolku 156. c. Ssv. Cyrilla a Methoda I. Kat, Slov. Jednoty" (Survey History of the Sts. Cyril and Methodius Society, Branch 156 of the First Catholic Slovak Union), in Pauliny, Ed., *Dejiny*, p. 33; "Protokol Spolku Sv. Apostoloch Cirila a Methoda South Bethlehem, Pa." (Minutes of the Sts. Cyril and Methodius Society of South Bethlehem, Pa.), June 1, November 2, 1902, in the care of George Anthony.
14. "Protokol Spolku. . . South Bethlehem, Pa.," September 7, October 6, 1902, April 7, 1929; "Zapisnica Sboru 93-ého," October 6, 1935; interview with Elizabeth (Slafkoský) Lipovský, Bethlehem, July 27, 1976.
15. *Slovák v Amerike* (New York), November 5, 1894, p. 7; "Protokol Spolku . . . South Bethlehem, Pa." June 1, 1902 to March 2, 1919; interview with Elizabeth Lipovský.
16. "Zapisnica Sboru 78," March 17, 1912, December 19, 1920; *Jednota* (Middletown, Pa.), October 3, 1923.
17. *Jednota*, October 3, 1928, p. 1 February 27, 1929, p. 1; "Protokol Spolku. . . South Bethlehem, Pa.," December 1, 1935; *Bethlehem Globe-Times*, November 8, 1939, p. 1.
18. Rev. George S. Dargay, *Historical Sketch of the Church of St. Cyril of Minneapolis, Minnesota, 1891-1941* (Minneapolis, 1941), p. 2; Ján J. Bartos, "Prehlad dejín osady Ssv. Cyrilla a Methoda v Bethlehem, Pa." (Survey History of the Parish of Sts. Cyril and Methodius in Bethlehem, Pa.), in Pauliny, ed., *Dejiny* pp. 81-82.
19. "Holy Trinity Lutheran Society and Parish, Minutes," 1892-98, Cleveland (in Slovak), on file at the Center for Immigration Studies, University of Minnesota; "Zapisna Kniha pre cirkev Sv. Jána Krstitela v So. Bethlehem, Pa." (Minute Book of the Church of St. John the Baptist in South Bethlehem, Pa.), August 6, 1911 to December 26, 1913, in the care of Rev. John Daniel.
20. "Prehlad dejín 429. c. Spolku Ssv. Petra a Pavla" (Survey History of Branch 429, Society of Sts. Peter and Paul), in Pauling, ed., *Dejiny*, p. 45; Joann Ledney, "Kratkyi ocerk Greko-Kaftoliceskej Russkej Cerkvy i Parafiji Svj. Verch. App. Petra i Pavla vo South Bethlehem, Pa." (Short History of the Greek Catholic Russian Church

and Parish of Sts. Peter and Paul in South Bethlehem, Pa.), in *Pamätnik 20. Konvencie Prvej Katolickej Slovenskej Jednoty, 18-23 septembra, 1922, v Meste Bethlehem, Pa.* (Jubilee Book of the 20th Convention of the First Catholic Slovak Union, September 18-23 1922, in Bethlehem Pa.), (Bethlehem, 1922), pp. 38-39; "Kalvínska Cirkev v Lakewood Ohio" (The Calvinist Church in Lakewood, Ohio), in *Kalendár pre Slovenských Klavíňov na rok 1927* (Pittsburgh, 1927), pp. 131-39.

21. Ibid., June 1, August 3, October 5, November 2, 1902, April 5, 1903, June 26, 1904, May 7, June 4, 1905, July 1, August 5, 1906, May 15, 1909.

22. Ms. "Protokol Spolku . . . South Bethlehem, Pa." March 2, August 3, 1924; "Zapisnica Sboru 93-ého," July 3, 1923.

23. "Protokol Spolku . . . South Bethlehem Pa.," March 6, November 6, 1921, October 8, 1922, November 25, 1923, May 4, 1930, June 6, 1931, May 1, 1932, May 6, 1934; "Zapisnica Sboru 93-ého," December 5, 1920, July 3, 1921, March 4, 1934, June 6, November 7, 1937, February 2, 1938; "Zapisnica Sboru 78," April 17, 1921, January 2, February 17, July 21, 1929, December 20, 1936, December 19, 1937. By 1976 the two local First Catholic Slovak Union Lodges had a combined membership of only 300 while the Catholic Sokols boasted 1,500 and the National Sokols 800 members. Cf. interviews with Joseph Karabin, June 17, 1976, and George Anthony, July 20, 1976.

24. "Prehlad dejín 350. odboru Sv. Juraja Nár. Slov. Spolku" (Survey History of Branch 350, St. George's Lodge of the National Slovak Society), in Pauliny, ed., *Dejiny*, pp. 41-43, and "Prehlad dejín 135. odboru 'Ziveny'," p. 45. Interviews with Gustáv Stefánik, July 21, 1976, and with Cyril Krajci, September 11, 1976. For the story of the World War I liberation movement see my "The Role of American Slovaks in the Creation of Czecho-Slovakia, 1914-1918", *Slovak Studies*, (Rome) 8 (1968).

25. Interviews with William Gazdacka, May 21, 1976; with Anna Jasso and Agnes (Jasso) Thomas, September 10, 1976; and with Elizabeth (Slafkoský) Lipovský, July 27, 1976. All four of these persons interviewed hold local lodge offices, and all four inherited them from their parents.

26. Ibid. See also such publications as *Golden Jubilee Wreath 32 Slovak Catholic Sokol* (Bethlehem, 1961), and *75 years, Branch 89, the First Catholic Slovak Ladies Association* (Bethlehem, 1975), for examples of women's activities.

Note: I have reproduced the titles of fraternal-benefit societies exactly as I found them in the minutes. I have not corrected their frequent grammar and spelling errors.

7. FINNISH-AMERICAN COOPERATIVISM

1. Hans R. Wasastjerna, ed., *History of the Finns in Minnesota* (Duluth, 1957), p. 477. For another account, see *Duluth Evening Herald,* January 22, 1908, p. 1.

2. Arnold Alanen, "The Development and Distribution of Finnish Consumers' Cooperatives in Michigan, Minnesota and Wisconsin, 1903-1973," in Michael G. Karni, Douglas Ollila, Jr., and Matti Kaups, *The Finnish Experience in the Western Great Lakes Region: New Perspectives* (Vammala, 1975), p. 107.

3. Ibid., p. 110; Thorsten Odhe, *Finland, A Nation of Cooperators* (London, 1931), pp. 28-29.

4. Alanen, *"Finnish Consumers' Cooperatives,"* p. 112.

5. *Työmies* quoted in Wasastjerna, *Finns in Minnesota,* p. 337.

6. *Pöytäkirja, Amerikan Suomalaisten Sosialistiostastojen Edustajakokousesta, Hibbinissa, Minn. Elokuun 1-7p. 1906* (Hancock, 1907), p. 76.

7. *Eveleth News,* August 28, 1907; Roland S. Vaile, ed., *Consumers' Cooperatives in the North Central States* (Minneapolis, 1941), pp. 271-82, 352; untitled manuscript, WPA Writers' Project Finnish Collection, Minnesota Historical Society.

8. *Pelto ja Koti* is on file at the Immigration History Research Center, St. Paul, University of Minnesota.

9. *Pelto ja Koti,* August 1, 1917, pp. 273-74.

10. *Pelto ja Koti,* September 1, 1917, pp. 281, 285, 304-06; see also Erick Kendall, *And Into the Future . . . A Brief Story of CCW'S 25 Years of Building Toward A Better Tomorrow* (Superior, 1941), pp. 5-9.
11. *Pöytäkirja, Co-operative Central Exchangen Vuosikokousesta* (Superior, 1919), pp. 4, 8, 9.
12. V. S. Alanne, "Through the Critical Years With the Central Exchange," *Northern States Cooperative League Yearbook, 1928* (Minneapolis, 1928), pp. 129-37.
13. William Kosiak, "The Two Harbors Cooperative Association: The Development and Influence of a Successful Consumers' Cooperative," Unpublished manuscript. University of Minnesota, 1973, pp. 11-12.
14. *CCE Vuosikirja, 1926,* Minneapolis, pp. 1, 53.
15. *NSCL Yearbook, 1928,* p. 168; *CCE Vuosikirja, 1928,* pp. 61, 76.
16. For a history of CLUSA, see Clarke A. Chambers, "The Cooperative League of the United States of America, 1916-1961: A Study of Social Theory and Social Action," *Agricultural History* 36 (April 1962); 59-81.
17. V. S. Alanne, *Fundamentals of Consumer Cooperation* (Superior, 1941), pp. 23-30.
18. George Halonen, "The 'Neutrality' of the Rochdale Pioneers," *NSCL* Yearbook, *1926,* p. 81. For similar sentiments by Halonen, see *Cooperative Pyramid Builder,* April 1927, p. 116, and November 1927, pp. 345-46.
19. Eskel Ronn, "Boy—Page Mr. Wolf!" *NSCL Yearbook, 1926,* p. 79; see also Ronn's "Pink Pills for Pale People," *NSCL 1925;* and "For We're All Good Fellows," *NSCL Yearbook, 1928.*
20. Alanne, *Fundamentals,* pp. 52, 98. He defines what he calls "Right Wing," "Left Wing," and "Cooperatist" philosophies of cooperations. He, of course, subscribed to the cooperatist philosophy.
21. Allane, "Some Vital Problems of Consumers' Cooperation," *NSCL Yearbook, 1928,* pp. 26-28.
22. *Cooperative Pyramid Builder,* January 1927, pp. 4-5.
23. See his *Fundamentals* cited above, and *The Cooperative Employee in Food and General Merchandise Stores* (Superior, 1944).
24. *NSCL Yearbook 1926,* p. 56.
25. For a description of the troupe's activities, see "A Curtain Call for the Gala Day Troupe," *NSCL Yearbook, 1927,* pp. 130-32. For the complete script of the production, see *Cooperative Pyramid Builder,* September-October, 1927, pp. 289-95.
26. Scripts for these plays can be found in *Cooperative Pyramid Builder,* January 1928, pp. 17-20, and September 1929; pp. 265-70.
27. For details on the "third period" and "the right danger," see Theodore Draper, *American Communism and Soviet Russia* (New York, 1960), pp. 300-14; and S. F. Cohen, *Bukharin and the Bolshevik Revolution: A Political Biography* (New York, 1973), pp. 291-94.
28. Unless specific citations occur in the text, the details of the 1929-30 controversy were reconstructed from the following sources: A. J. Hayes, "The Internal Struggle," *Cooperative Pyramid Builder,* April 1930, pp. 76-79; "What's It all About?" *Cooperative Pyramid Builder,* January 1931; *CCE'n Vuosikirja, 1931,* pp. 11-86; *Keskusosuuskunnan Tiedonantaja,* December 9, 16, 23, 31, 1929; *Työväden Osuustoimintalehti,* January through April 1930; *Työmies,* October 31, 1929-April 1930; William Marttila, *Osuustoiminta ja sen Merkitys Luokkataistelussa* (Superior, 1930); George Halonen, *Taistelu Osuustoimintarintamalla* (Superior, 1932); Walter Harju Collection, Immigration History Research Center, University of Minnesota, folders 11, 18; *Keskusosuuskunnan Toimeenpaneva Komitean Pöytäkirja,* July 1929 through April 1930; and *Keskusosuuskunnan Johtokunnan Pöytäkirja,* July 1929, through April 1930.
29. See *Taistelu Oikeistovaaraa Vastaan: Kominternin Opetuksia Amerikan Suomalaiselle Työväelle* (Superior, 1930).
30. *Cooperative League Yearbook, 1932* (New York, 1932), pp. 31-32.

31. Interview, Erick Kendall, Midland Cooperatives, Inc., Minneapolis, Minnesota, February 15, 1971; interview, Jack Heino, Midland Cooperatives, Inc., February 15, 1971.
32. *The Cooperative Builder,* August 31, 1940.
33. *Eveleth News,* January 12, February 16, 23, 1933; *Heikkila Memorial Journal* (San Francisco, 1960?), p. 8.

8. COLLECTIVE ECONOMIC ACTIVITY

1. Perry L. Weed, *The White Ethnic Movement and Ethnic Politics* (New York: Praeger, 1973), pp. 3-13.
2. Michael Novak, *The Rise of the Unmeltable Ethnics* (New York: Macmilian, 1972); and Weed, *White Ethnic Movement,* p. 3.
3. Harry A. Lansberger, "Labor Movements, Social Movements and Social Mobility," ed. Robert Dubin, *Handbook of Work, Organization, and Society,* (Chicago: Rand McNally, 1976), pp. 839-76; Brinley Thomas, *Migration and Economic Growth: A Study of Great Britain and the Atlantic Economy,* 2nd ed. (Cambridge: Cambridge University Press, 1973), esp. pp. 330-47; and Brinley Thomas, "Migration and International Investment," in *Economics of International Migration* ed. Brinley Thomas, (London: Macmillan & Co., 1958), pp. 3-16.
4. U.S. *Reports of the Commissioner of Immigration, 1907-1920* (Washington, D.C.; Government Printing Office, 1907-20); U.S. *Reports of the U.S. Immigration Commission, 1907-1910,* (Washington, D.C.; Government Printing Office 1910-14); and U.S. *Historical Statistics of the United States: Colonial Times to 1970* (Washington, D.C.; Government Printing Office, 1975), p. 1152.
5. Philip Taylor, *The Distant Magnet: European Emigration to the U.S.A.* (New York: Harper & Row, 1971), p. 326; George J. Prpic, *The Croatian Immigrants in America* (New York: Philosophical Library, 1971), p. 519; Emily Greene Balch, *Our Slavic Fellow Citizens* (New York: Charities Publications Committee, 1910), p. 619; Joseph J. Roucek, "Yugoslavs in America," in *Yugoslavia* ed. Robert J. Kerner, (Berkeley: University of California Press, 1948), pp. 136-47; Dinko A. Tomasić, "Americans from Yugoslavia," unpublished manuscript, Immigration History Research Center, University of Minnesota, p. 325; Johann Chmelar, "The Austrian Emigration, 1900-1914," C. Thomas Childers, *Perspectives in American History* 7 (1973); 275-380; J. Puskás, "Emigration from Hungary to the United States Before 1914," *Studia Historica Academicae Scientarum Hungaricae* 113 (1975); and Ivan Cizmić, "O iseljavanju iz Hrvatske u razdoblu 1880-1914," *Historijski Zbornik* 27-28 (1974-75); 27-47.
6. For a comprehensive history of the Slovenes' community and organizational growth, see Joze Zavertnik, ed., *Ameriski Slovenci* (Chicago: Slovenska Narodna Podporna Jednota, 1925), p. 632.
7. Richard de Raismer Kip, *Fraternal Life Insurance in America* (Philadelphia: College Offset Press, 1953), p. 187; Walter Basye, *History and Operation of Fraternal Insurance* (Rochester: The Fraternal Monitor, 1919), p. 224; Solomon S. Huebner, *The Economics of Life Insurance* (New York: D. Appleton & Co., 1927), esp. pp. 24-25; Yaroslav J. Chyz and Read Lewis, "Agencies Organized by Nationality Groups in the United States," *Annals of the American Academy of Political and Social Science* 262 (March 1949); 148-58; J. Owen Stalson, *Marketing Life Insurance: Its History in America* (Cambridge: Harvard University Press, 1942), esp. pp. 818-25.
8. Margaret E. Galey, "Ethnicity, Fraternalism, Social and Mental Health," *Ethnicity* 4, no. 1 (March 1977); 31.
9. Jozo Tomasevich, "Foreign Economic Relations, 1918-1941," pp. 169-214, in Kerner, ed. *Yugoslavia;* and idem, *Peasants, Politics, and Economic Changes in Yugoslavia* (Stanford: Stanford University Press, 1955), p. 743; Prpic, *Croatian Immigrants in America;* U.S. *Reports of the U.S. Immigration Commission 1907-*

1910: Volume 37, Immigrant Homes and Aid Societies, Immigrant Banks (Washington, D.C.: Government Printing Office, 1911), pp. 125-350; Balch, *Our Slavic Fellow Citizens;* and U.S., *Banking and Monetary Statistics* (Washington, D.C.: Government Printing Office, 1943), p. 979.

10. Figures are compiled from B. Angjelinović and I. Mladineo, eds., *Jugoslavenski Almanak* (New York: 1931); and Tomasić, "Americans From Yugoslavia," pp. 188-90.

11. The data on Slovene Catholic schools are taken from *Official Catholic Yearbook 1928* (New York: P. J. Kennedy & Sons, 1928), pp. 419, 421, 592, 732-33.

12. Ivan Molek, "petdesetletnica slovenskega casnikarstva v Ameriki," *Ameriski druzinski koledar* 26 (1941); 28-36; Fred A Vider, "Nekaj o bratskih podpornih ustanovah," *Ameriski druzinski koledar* 36 (1950); 42-44; Frank Zaitz, "Iz nase zgodovine," *Ameriski druzinski koledar* 36 (1950); 78-160; J. M. Trunk, *Amerika in Amerikanci* (Celovec: Tiskarna druzba sv. Mohorje, 1912); Bozidar Purić, *Nasi iseljenici* (Beograd: S. V. Cvijanović, 1929); Joze Premrov, *Izseljenska citanka* (Ljubljana: Mladinska zalozba, 1941); Eleanor Ledbetter, *The Jugoslavs of Cleveland* (Cleveland: Mayor's Advisory Council, 1918); and Ivan Cizmić, *Jugoslavenski iseljenicki pokret u SAD i stvaranje jugoslavenske drzave 1918* (Zagreb: Institut za hrvatsku povijest, 1974).

9. THE EXPANSION OF THE PUBLIC SECTOR

1. Thomas C. Cochran, *The Inner Revolution* (New York: Harper & Row, 1964), p. 33.

2. Stephen Marcus, *Engels, Manchester and the Working Class* (New York: Vintage Press, 1975), p. 10.

3. Terry N. Clark, "The Irish Ethic and the Spirit of Patronage," *Ethnicity* 2 (1975): 305-59.

4. Edward Levine, *The Irish and Irish Politicians* (Notre Dame, Ind.: University of Notre Dame Press, 1966).

5. Edward P. Hutchinson, *Immigrants and Their Children* (New York: John Wiley and Sons, 1956), pp. 83, 103, 126.

6. Discrimination against Irish Catholics is widely documented in Ray Allen Billington, *The Protestant Crusade* (Chicago: University of Chicago Press, 1964); Dennis Clark, "A Pattern of Urban Growth: Residential Development and Urban Growth in Philadelphia," *Records of the American Catholic Historical Society* 82 (September 1971); 159-70.

7. Sam Bass Warner, "Innovation and Industrialization in Philadelphia, 1800-1850," in pp. 65-68, *The Historian and the City,* ed. Handlin and Burchard. Edwin T. Freedley, *Philadelphia and Its Manufactures* (Philadelphia: Edward Young, 1859), pp. 15-43.

8. Board of Commissioners Minutes, Richmond District, 1852-1854, R.G. 219.1, Archives of the City of Philadelphia, City Hall, Philadelphia.

9. Deed Book Th 100 (1853), p. 549, Archives of the City of Philadelphia, City Hall, Philadelphia.

10. Carl Wittke, *The Irish in America* (Baton Rouge; Louisiana State University Press, 1956), p. 231; *The Evening Bulletin* (Philadelphia), September 14, 1856.

11. H. Morton Bodfish, ed., *History of Building and Loan in the United States* (Chicago: U.S. Building and Loan League, 1931), pp. 32-79.

12. A biographical note on Bernard Rafferty with titles of some of the Irish Building and Loan Associations is contained in John H. Campbell, *History of the Friendly Sons of St. Patrick* (Philadelphia: The Hibernian Society, 1892), p. 57.

13. For Thomas Costigan, see Wittke, *The Irish in America,* p. 228. For Francis McManus and William Nead, see Campbell, *History of the Friendly Sons,* pp. 486-89.

14. J. St. George Joyce, ed., *The Story of Philadelphia* (Philadelphia: City of Philadelphia, 1919), pp. 436-37.

15. See advertisement in Daniel H. Mahony, *Historical Sketches of Catholic Churches and Institutions in Philadelphia* (Philadelphia: D. H. Mahony, 1895), p. xxxviii.
16. Campbell, *History of the Friendly Sons*, p. 449; and Wittke, *The Irish in America*, p. 231.
17. Seymour Mandelbaum, *Boss Tweed's New York* (New York: John Wiley and Sons, 1965), p. 58.
18. Edward C. Kirkland, *Industry Comes of Age* (Chicago: Quadrangle Books, 1961), p. 238.
19. Asa Briggs, *Victorian Cities* (New York: Harper & Row, 1970), pp. 16-17.
20. Milton Barron, "Intermediacy: Conceptualization of Irish Status in America," *Social Forces* 27, no. 3 (March 1949); 256-63.
21. Joyce, ed., *The Story of Philadelphia*, p. 474.
22. Newspaper coverage of McNichol at the time was extensive. See *Philadelphia North American,* January 2, 9, 1908; *Public Ledger* (Philadelphia) January 3, 1908; *Philadelphia Record,* January 6, 1908; *Inquirer* (Philadelphia), April 12, 1908; *Evening Bulletin* (Philadelphia), April 15, 1908; and Edward Morgan, *City of Firsts* (Philadelphia: City of Philadelphia, 1919), p. 291.
23. Interview with James Duffin, grandson of David J. Duffin, Philadelphia, June 11, 1970.
24. *Evening Bulletin* (Philadelphia), October 29, 1934.
25. James Reichley, *The Art of Reform* (New York: The Fund for the Republic, 1959), p. 6.
26. *Evening Bulletin* (Philadelphia), May 29, 1963; Thomas O'Malley, "John McShain: Builder," *Columbia* (February 1955).
27. Reichley, *The Art of Reform*, pp. 9, 20.
28. *Evening Bulletin* (Philadelphia), September 21, 1935. Spring Garden Institute was a vocational and technical school.
29. E. Digby Baltzell in his book *The Protestant Establishment: Aristocracy and Caste in America* (New York: Random House, 1946), p. 122 passim, has written of the educational and social class barriers that insulated the Philadelphia old family socialites and the exclusionary practices that worked against men like the Irish contractors. See also Nathaniel Burt, *The Perennial Philadelphians* (Boston: Little, Brown and Company, 1963).
30. John G. Cawelti, *Apostles of the Self-Made Man* (Chicago: University of Chicago Press, 1965), p. 178.
31. New York's Irish in the 1870s are described in Mandelbaum, *Boss Tweed's New York,* pp. 87-104. Wittke, *The Irish in America,* pp. 23-31, 228-40, gives examples in other cities. James Walsh, ed. *The San Francisco Irish: 1850-1976* (San Francisco: The Irish Literary and Historical Society, 1978), gives California examples.
32. Clark, "The Irish Ethic."
33. Ibid. p. 305.
34. Some attention devoted to this topic by Edward J. Logue is contained in his essay "The Impact of Political and Social Forces on Design in America," pp. 236-56 in *Who Designs America,* ed. L. R. Holland (New York: Doubleday, 1966).

10. JEWISH ENTERPRISE IN TRANSITION

1. Ivan Light, *Ethnic Enterprise in America* (Berkeley: University of California Press, 1972).
2. Edna Bonacich, "A Theory of Middleman Minorities," *American Sociological Review* 38 (October 1973); 583-94.
3. Cyril S. Belshaw, "The Cultural Milieu of the Entrepreneur: A Critical Essay," *Explorations in Enterpreneurial History* 7 (1955); 146-63, as cited in Ivan Light, "Asian Enterprise in America," Chapter two of this volume.
4. Bonacich, "Middleman Minorities."

5. Andrew Greely, *Ethnicity in the United States* (New York: John Wiley and Sons, 1974).
6. Irving Howe, *World of Our Fathers* (New York: Simon and Schuster, 1976), p. 608.
7. Mark R. Levy and Michael S. Kramer, *The Ethnic Factor: How America's Minorities Decide Elections* (New York: Simon and Schuster, 1973), p. 96.
8. Edward C. Banfield, *The Unheavenly City Revisited* (Boston: Little, Brown, 1974).
9. Howe, *World of Our Fathers*.
10. Moses Rischin, *The Promised City: New York's Jews 1870-1914* (New York; Harper and Row, 1962), p. 89.
11. Howe, *World of Our Fathers*.
12. Oscar Handlin, *Boston's Immigrants* (New York: Atheneum, 1970); Rischin, *Promised City;* David Rogers, *110 Livingston Street* (New York McGraw-Hill, 1968).
13. Howe, *World of Our Fathers*, pp. 141-43.
14. Ibid., p. 50.
15. Ann Cook, Marilyn Gittell, and Herb Mack, eds., *City Life: Views of Urban America, 1865-1900* (New York: Praeger, 1973), p. 130.
16. Ibid., p. 144.
17. Ibid., p. 221.
18. Robert A. Caro, *The Power Broker* (New York: Random House, 1975), chap. 1.
19. Howe, *World of Our Fathers*, p. 47.
20. Rischin, *Promised City,* p. 105.
21. Ibid.
22. Howe, *World of Our Fathers*.
23. Ibid.
24. Edgar Litt, *Ethnic Politics in America* (Glencoe, Illinois: Scott, Foresman, 1970); Harry A. Bailey, Jr. and Ellis Katz, ed., *Ethnic Group Politics* (Columbus, Ohio: Charles E. Merrell, 1969); Angus Campbell, et al., *The American Voter* (New York: John Wiley, 1964).
25. Howe, *World of Our Fathers*, p. 614.
26. Maurice R. Berube and Marilyn Gittell, eds. *Confrontation at Ocean Hill-Brownsville,* (New York: Praeger, 1969).

INDEX

Alonen, Severi, 152
Alanne, V.S., 158

Banfield, Edward, 192
Barth, Frederik, 35
Barzynski, Jan, 118
Barzynski, Vincent, 117, 119, 121
Bedacht, Max, 155
Bensman, Joseph, 59
Benson, Allan, 148
Black Americans: business development, 5, 35
Black capitalism, 44
Bonacich, Edna, 36, 52, 59, 191
Book of Mormon, 90, 104
Briggs, Asa, 182
Burgess, Ernest, 8

Calhoun, Patrick, 187
Carlson, Jack, 109
Carniolan-Slovene Catholic Union, 170
Central Cooperative Exchange, 148-151, 154-158
Central Cooperative Messenger, 157
Central Cooperative Wholesale, 158
Chinese Americans: business development, 35, 38, 42, 46-51
Chmielinska, Stefania, 123
City Wide Development Corporation, 27
Clark, Dennis, 24
Clark, Terry, 187
Collectivism and economic development, 6, 9, 29, 36-67, 83, 110, 192
Commager, Henry, 90
Communism, 150-151, 155, 157

Communist Party of America, 120, 155, 159
Communitarian socialism, 92
Community Development Block Grants, 27
Community Development corporations, 25-29
Conwell, Russell, 86
Cooley, Oscar, 158
Cooperativism, 152, 156
Cooperative League of the United States of America, 151
Cooperative League Yearbook, 151
Cooperative Pyramid Builder, 154, 156
Contractor-boss, 178
Copper strike, 147, 155
Costigan, Thomas, 181, 186
Croatian Americans: collective business enterprise, 162, 167, 169-171; fraternalism among, 168; immigration, 163-164; real estate interests, 173; social welfare institutions, 174; socio-economic status, 165-166
Cultural theory of entrepreneurship, 33, 191

Davies, J. Kenneth, 109
Democratic Party, 182
Dickens, Charles, 98
Dillingham Report, 162
Disadvantage theory of entrepreneurship, 33, 191
Dugan, Thomas, 180
Duffin, David, 183
Dyniewicz, Wladyslaw, 117

INDEX / 233

Eastern European Americans: immigration, 162; socio-economic status, 14-17
Ely, Richard, 105
Exchange, (see Central Cooperative Exchange)
Farley, Janes, 184
Farmers' and Workers' Cooperative and Unity Alliance, 159
Federal Trade Commission, 148
Finnish Americans: collective business development, 21; immigration, 145; radicalism, 145, 157; socialism, 146-147, 152
Finnish Communist Party, 157
Finnish Socialist Federation, 147
Finnish Workers' Federation, 152, 159
First Catholic Slovak Ladies Union, 134
First Catholic Slovak Union, 133-134
Fitzgerald, "Honey Fitz," 186
Flanders, Robert, 95
Fong, 59
Foster, William, 155
Franklin Cooperative Creamery, 153
French Catholic Americans: socio-economic status, 14-17
Fundek, Stefan, 133, 138

Galey, Margaret, 168
Gardner, Hamilton, 93
General Strike of 1905, 145
German Catholic Americans: socio-economic status, 11-17
Gordon, David, 8
Gordon, Francis, 123
Greek Americans: business development, 22, 60-62; clan and family structure, 63-64, 72, 78-79; immigration, 61; serial sponsorship of relatives, 72
Greeley, Andrew, 11, 21

Hall, Gus, 159
Halonen, George, 151-152, 154-157
Handlin, Oscar, 132
Hebrew Emigrant Aid Society, 196
Hebrew Immigrant Society, 196

Individualism and economic development, 7, 9, 36-37, 59, 83, 91
International Ladies Garment Workers' Union, 198
Invasion and succession, 8
Irish Catholic Americans: immigration, 179; neighborhoods, 178; socio-economic status, 10-17

Irish Protestant Americans: socio-economic status, 11-17
Italian Americans: socio-economic status 10-17

Japanese Americans: collectivism and business development, 35, 38, 42, 48-51
Jerzmanowski, Erasmus, 120
Jewish Americans: collectivism and business development, 192, 195; immigration, 194; poverty, 193-194; self-help, 193, 196-198; socio-economic status, 11-17, 192; synagogues, 197

Karni, Michael, 23
Kaye, Jeffrey, 106, 107
Kelly, Florence, 6
Kelly, Grace, 183
Kelly, James, 183
Kelly, John, 183, 185-186
Ken, 59
Kennedy, Gerard, 42-43
Kennedy, John F., 184, 186
Kim, H., 44
Kiolbassa, Peter, 117
Kirkland, George, 148
Korean Americans: collectivism and business development, 38-39, 45-51, 53-57; immigration, 38-43
Kramer, Michael, 192
Krolik, Thomas, 125
Kurikka, Matti, 146
Kye, 42-44

Lafferty, Edward, 181, 186
Lanto, Ivan, 154
Lenin, V., 152
Leone, Mark, 111
Levy, Mark, 192
Light, Ivan, 22, 35, 59-60, 63, 73, 76, 83, 191
Lindsay, John, 213
Lovell-Troy, Lawrence, 22
Lyman, Stanford, 55

Magee, Michael, 181, 186
Maloney, Martin, 181
Mandelbaum, Seymour, 181
Marginal productivity, 7
Maris, Peter, 34
Marxism, 29, 120, 170
Mayer, Dominic, 119
McClelland, David, 37

McCloskey, Matthew, 184-186
McManus, Francis, 181
McManus, Patrick, 181, 186
McNichol, James, 182-183, 186
McShain, John, 184-186
Mesabi Range, 145
Mesabi Strike, 154
Middleman minorities, 36
Mills, C. Wright, 7, 58
Minor, Robert, 155
Morgan, Neil, 106
Mormon Americans: business enterprise, 23; capitalism, 102, 106, 108; conservatism, 107; early industrial development, 99; polygamy, 89, 103-104; separatism, 89, 102; socialism, 91, 101, 111; socio-economic status, 106-110; theology, 89

Na U Club, 43
National Fraternal Congress, 167-168
Nauvoo, 95
Neady, William, 181
Neighborhood Housing Services, 26
Neuman, Anna, 123
Northern States Cooperative League, 151, 153
Novak, Michael, 160
Nummivnurii, Juhn, 148

O'Dea, Thomas, 94, 110
Oh, Kwan-Chi, 42

Park, Robert, 8
Perpetual immigration fund, 97
Peters, John, 137
Pilsudski, Joseph, 120
Pitass, John, 119
Polish Americans: fraternals, 23, 117, 124; immigration, 115-116; nationalism, 113; peasantry, 114-115; socialism, 120; socio-economic status, 11-17; real estate interests, 127
Polonia, 116, 118
Polish Roman Catholic Union of America, 117-118
Polish National Alliance, 117, 119, 120-123, 126, 128-129
Polish Women's Alliance, 123, 128
Puro, Henry, 157

Rafferty, Bernard, 180
Red Star Chorus, 154
Reichley, James, 184
Reilly, James, 181

Renkiewicz, Frank, 23
Rigdon, Sidney, 91
Right Relationship League, 146
Republican Party, 182
Rischin, Moses, 197
Rochdale principles, 151
Ronn, Eskel, 151-152, 156-157
Roosevelt, Franklin Delano, 184
Rosentraub, Mark, 24
Rotating credit associations, 35, 42
Russian Revolution, 150
Ruyak, George, 137
Ryan, William, 8

Schumacher, E.F., 175
Schumpeter, Joseph, 85
Scrip, 100
Second Socialist International, 170
Self-help institutions, 5, 6, 29
Serbian Americans: collective economic development, 162, 169-171; fraternalism, 168; immigration, 163-164; real estate interests, 173; social welfare institutions, 174; socio-economic status, 165-166
Slovak Americans: fraternals, 23, 181, 133-135; immigration, 130-131; lodges, 132-133; sokols, 134-135, 138
Slovene Americans: collective economic development, 162, 167, 169-171; education, 174; fraternals, 168; immigration, 163-164; social democracy, 175; social welfare institutions, 147; socio-economic status, 165-166; real estate interests, 173
Slovene National Benefit Society, 170
Slovene Progressive Benefit Society, 170
Small Business Administration, 45
Smith, Joseph, 90, 95
Smith, Timothy, 130
Smoot, Reed, 107
Smulski, John, 123
Socialism, 151, 153, 155
Socialist Party of America, 148
Sojourning, 55
Somerset, Anthony, 34
Somolinska, Teofila, 123
St. Stanislaus Kosta Society, 119
Stipanovich, Joseph, 24
Stolarik, M. Mark, 23
Stull, Valiant, 45
Swietochowski, Aleksander, 115

Taebel, Delbert, 24
Tagert, James, 180
Taylor, George, 186
Tenhunen, Matti, 151
Terry, L. Clay, 45
Thomas, Brinley, 179
Tithing, 99-100
Työmies, 147, 152, 154, 156-157, 159

Union Sarah Economic Development Corporation, 27
Urban Development Corporation, 26-27

Vidich, Arthur, 59

Vogt, Evan, 111

War on Poverty, 25
Warbasse, James, 151
Waterbury, John, 37
Weber, Max, 7, 36-37, 67, 85
Weed, Perry, 160
White, O. Kendall, 23
Workers' Party, 152, 155

Young, Brigham, 95, 98, 101

Zion's Cooperative Mercantile, 101

CONTRIBUTORS

DENNIS CLARK is Executive Director at the Samuel S. Fels Fund, Philadelphia. He has published extensively in the areas of ethnic studies, intergroup relations, and urban history. His many works on the American Irish have become established reference points in the field of ethnic studies.

SCOTT CUMMINGS is Associate Professor of Urban Studies and Director of the Urban and Regional Affairs Division, Institute of Urban Studies, The University of Texas at Arlington. His research interests include race and ethnic relations, community and neighborhood development, urban education, and comparative economic systems. He has published numerous articles in the areas of intergroup relations, ethnic politics, and urban education. He received his Ph.D. in Sociology from the University of Connecticut.

MICHAEL KARNI is Assistant Director of the Iron Range Interpretive Center, Chisholm, Minnesota. He has published several articles and books dealing with the Finnish-American experience. Dr. Karni received his Ph.D. in American Studies from the University of Minnesota and is the recipient of a Fulbright Fellowship to teach American literature at Turku University and Abo Academy, Turku, Finland, 1979. He collected and compiled the Finnish holdings at the Immigration History Research Center, The University of Minnesota.

LAWRENCE A. LOVELL-TROY is Assistant Professor of Sociology, Indiana University-Purdue University at Fort Wayne. He received his Ph.D. in Sociology from the University of Connecticut. His research interests include minority enterprise, social stratification, sexism and patriarchy.

236 / CONTRIBUTORS

IVAN LIGHT is Professor of Sociology at the University of California at Los Angeles. Professor Light's book, *Ethnic Enterprise in America,* has become a classic in the field of minority economic development. He has published extensively in the area of minority enterprise and ethnic studies.

FRANK RENKIEWICZ is Professor of History at the College of Saint Teresa, Winona, Minnesota. He is also editor of *Polish American Studies* Dr. Renkiewicz has published several articles explaining the Polish-American experience and documenting the details of Polish immigration. Dr. Renkiewicz also helped to develop the Polish-American collection and coordinated the Polish Microfilm Project at the Immigration Research Center, University of Minnesota.

MARK ROSENTRAUB is Assistant Professor of Urban Studies, Institute of Urban Studies, The University of Texas at Arlington. Dr. Rosentraub has published extensively in the areas of public finance, coastal zone management, and evaluation research. He is currently conducting research in the areas of race and public education and the distribution of mortgage lending money in urban areas.

JOSEPH STIPANOVICH is Director of the Minnesota Iron Range Historical-Cultural Survey, a project jointly sponsored by the State of Minnesota and the Minnesota Historical Society. He received his Ph.D. in U.S. Social History at the University of Minnesota. His primary interests in research are the phenomena of migration, industrialization, and urbanization in the American context of growth and development.

M. MARK STOLARIK is a specialist in American and ethnic studies. He has published one book and numerous articles on these topics and formerly taught ethnic studies at Cleveland State University. After a year as Head of the Slavic and East European Programme at the National Museum of Man in Canada, he was appointed Executive Director of the Balch Institute for Ethnic Studies in Philadelphia.

DELBERT TAEBEL is Professor of Urban Studies at the Institute of Urban Studies, The University of Texas at Arlington. He has published extensively in the area of urban politics. Having recently completed a book dealing with the politics of urban transportation, he is presently exploring the factors influencing minority representation in local and state political bodies. He received his Ph.D. in Political Science from The University of Texas at Austin.

O. KENDALL WHITE, JR. is Associate Professor of Sociology at Washington and Lee University. A student of organized religion, Professor White has published numerous articles dealing with Mormon life and culture, the sociology of religion, and the social organization of religious institutions. In addition to his interests in the sociology of religion, he has published in the area of formal organization and urban politics.